Praise for *Talking to t[...]*

"One tough journey, luminously remembered."
—*Kirkus Reviews*

"*Talking to the Ground* seduced me from the first page. Having Douglas Preston and his wife and daughter as guides on horseback for 400 miles through Navajo country is like traveling across unknown territory with Lewis and Clark to the Pacific."
—Dee Brown, author of *Bury My Heart at Wounded Knee*

"Entertaining, contemplative, evocative, and haunting. Forget the blue highways. Saddle up and ride the trails into America's native past with Preston and you will be richer and wiser for it."
—Rodney Barker, author of *The Hiroshima Maidens: A Story of Courage, Compassion, and Survival* and *The Broken Circle: A True Story of Murder and Magic in Indian Country*

"A fascinating and powerful journey, weaving together the ancient threads of profound prophecy and the integrity of Douglas Preston on his earth walk."
—Lynn V. Andrews, author of the Medicine Woman series

"Mr. Preston has written another entrancing adventure story on the Southwest, which held this reader's attention page after page."
—Evon Z. Vogt, professor of social anthropology, emeritus, Harvard University

"This is a bold, eloquent book, marking a singularly important literary achievement."
—Paul G. Zolbrod, author of *Diné Bahane':
The Navajo Creation Story*

"A family in the making canters on horseback into the heart of Navajo desert country. . . . Doug Preston carries the reader along with Indian stories and landscape, Anglo insights, and humor."
—Kenneth Lincoln, coauthor of *The Good Red Road: Passages into Native America* and author of *Indi'n Humor: Bicultural Play in Native America*

"In *Talking to the Ground*, Douglas Preston leads us on horseback across the sacred land of the Navajo, in some of the remotest parts of New Mexico and Arizona. Preston is accompanied by his fiancée and her 9-year-old daughter; this book is as much about the creation of their new family as about the land and legends of the Navajo creation story."

—*Smithsonian Magazine*

Douglas Preston

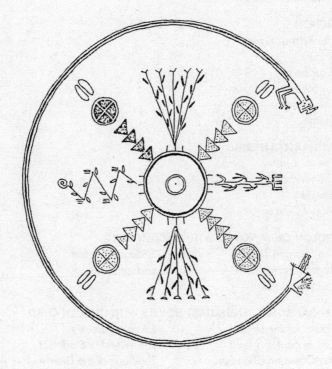

Talking to the Ground

One Family's
Journey on
Horseback
Across the
Sacred Land
of the Navajo

Simon & Schuster Paperbacks
New York • London
Toronto • Sydney
New Delhi

Simon & Schuster Paperbacks
An Imprint of Simon & Schuster, Inc.
1230 Avenue of the Americas
New York, NY 10020

This Simon & Schuster trade paperback edition June 2019

SIMON & SCHUSTER PAPERBACKS and colophon are
registered trademarks of Simon & Schuster, Inc.

For information about special discounts for bulk purchases,
please contact Simon & Schuster Special Sales at 1-866-506-1949 or
business@simonandschuster.com.

The Simon & Schuster Speakers Bureau can bring authors
to your live event. For more information or to book an event,
contact the Simon & Schuster Speakers Bureau at 1-866-248-3049 or
visit our website at www.simonspeakers.com.

Designed by Levavi & Levavi
Photos by Christine Preston
Maps and drawings by Douglas Preston

Manufactured in the United States of America

1   3   5   7   9   10   8   6   4   2

The Library of Congress has cataloged the hardcover edition as follows:
Preston, Douglas J.
Talking to the ground : one family's journey on horseback across
the sacred land of the Navajo / Douglas Preston.
p.   cm.
Includes bibliographical references.
1. Navajo Indian Reservation. 2. Packhorse camping—Navajo Indian
Reservation. 3. Preston, Douglas J. 4. Navajo Indians. I. Title.
E99.N3P74 1995
979.1'3004972—dc20   94-46362
CIP

ISBN 978-0-684-80391-3
ISBN 978-1-9821-1219-6 (pbk)

For Christine

Contents

Chapter 1

ANASAZI HAND
—MONUMENT VALLEY

 Durango, Colorado
April 1990

I'll never forget the first time I saw Christine. I was at a posh gallery opening, watching an art video in which a man moved a piece of black plywood around a white prison cell, when I glimpsed her across the room. I thought she was the loveliest woman I had ever seen. She was talking to some fellow, and when she laughed at a joke of his I decided he must be a humbug and went over to rescue her. It turned out she was from Boston like me; our parents lived only four miles apart and our families had friends in common. I was marveling at my luck when a little girl with red hair and freckles came skidding over and grabbed her arm, and I knew instantly that this was her daughter.

"This is Selene," said Christine proudly.

"Oh yeah hi," said Selene without glancing at me, already heading off again.

There was an awkward silence.

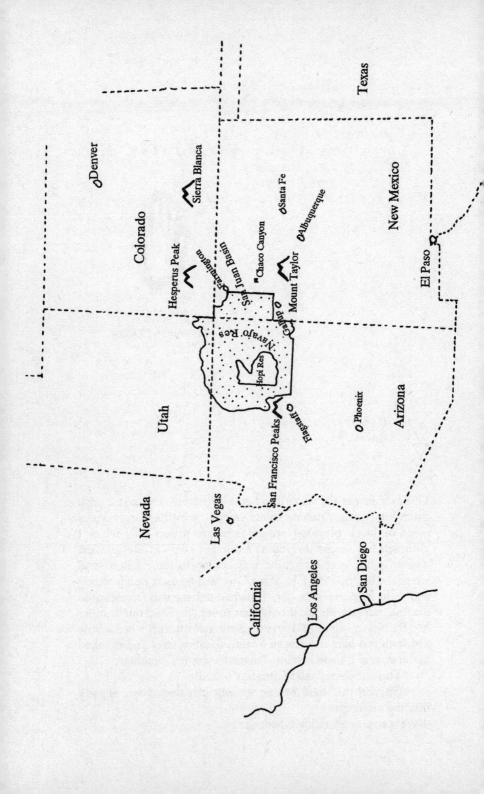

"Your daughter?" I asked vaguely. Christine seemed awfully young to have a daughter that age.

"Yes, isn't she beautiful?"

"Oh, yes. Definitely."

The conversation drifted.

"Are you married?" I finally asked.

"Oh no," she said. "Never."

A reading began. A woman in tight jogging shorts began reciting poetry about limbs, digits, and orifices. The audience fell into rapt silence. I excused myself and retired outside with a fresh drink, breathing the April night. The stars flickered in the cold sky and a new moon rose over the elms, like a bright fingernail clipped from a goddess. An unmarried woman with a daughter? I was sensible enough to avoid that.

Soon Christine appeared in the doorway with the same humbug. Why was he following her around? I went over.

"You like the poetry?" I asked, striving for neutrality in tone. One had to be careful in a small town like Durango; the poet was well known locally.

She made a face. All her freckles jammed together and her blue eyes crossed and her tongue stuck out and a sound, uncannily like retching, came from her throat. I had to laugh: it was so eloquent. I couldn't stop myself. "So, do you want to go horseback riding with me sometime?"

▽ ▽ ▽

Two days later, Christine arrived for her ride. It was a warm April afternoon. I lived alone in the hills behind Durango, Colorado, with two horses and a yellow dog. The snow was gone, and the piñon woods behind my house were speckled with wild geraniums and senecio. The dead horse at the cattle pond had disappeared over the winter, the bones dragged off into the woods by the coyotes. Behind the ridge, another spring building boom had begun again, and in the mornings I could hear the grinding of bulldozers opening the earth.

Christine was wearing high-top red sneakers. Her short brown hair stuck out from under a baseball cap and the Colorado sun had browned the freckles on her nose and cheeks.

I was wearing a brand-new black cowboy hat and I thought it looked particularly authentic. I wanted to show her how well this Boston Yankee turned cowboy could ride. I brought her down to the corral, and she watched while I worked on the horses. I brushed out their coats, picked their hooves, and saddled them up, murmuring soothing words, hoping they would behave.

I finished with Wilbur the Appaloosa, and went to bridle Redbone. Redbone was my favorite horse, of no recognizable breed, a perfect mutt, but nevertheless intelligent, full of heart, and possessed of an exquisite sense of mischief. Sensing the importance of the occasion, he clamped his jaws together and would not take the bit, shaking his head and throwing it back when I tried to slip it into his mouth.

This does not look good, I thought, while grabbing his ear and trying to pull his head down, my black hat being knocked off in the process.

"Do you need any help?" Christine asked.

"Oh no," I said. "This'll only take a second."

This had been a recurring problem with Redbone and he knew better, so I did what any respectable cowboy would do: I uttered a terrible oath and vigorously applied the side of my boot to his ribs. After that he couldn't open his mouth fast enough, but when I looked over at Christine, I saw the face of someone horrified to be having a first date with a horse-beater.

"This horse is a troublemaker," I said feebly. "He needs a firm hand."

"Oh," said Christine, backing away slightly.

"He knows perfectly well what he's supposed to do. He's just trying to make a fool out of me," I said.

"Of course," said Christine.

We rode across the piñon hills behind the house and down into a deep valley called the Arroyo de los Chamisos. The arroyo has since been cut up with roads and developed, but back then it was still unspoiled, a bed of sand wandering between grassy embankments and tall ponderosas. The last of the snow was melting in the hills and a trickle of water threaded down the bottom. Under the warm sun the pines released a resinous scent.

We rode down the arroyo, splashing through the water, and skirted the old tank. A leg bone and hoof, with a rusted shoe attached, lay in the cheat grass. The horses could still smell death in the air and passed with a wary eye.

A mile down the wash, in a hidden meadow, we stopped. While the horses cropped the new grass, we sat under a big pine and talked about trivial things. With the nervousness of a teenager I finally kissed Christine. My mind was elsewhere when it came time to remount our horses, and Redbone (always mindful of an opportunity) spun sideways just as I swung into the saddle. I went right over the top and fell to the ground on the other side. Then the brute promptly stepped on my hand, and it swelled up like a cantaloupe. I tried to hide it but Christine noticed and made a terrible fuss.

"Oh no," she cried, "every bone in your hand must be broken! You've got to see a doctor!"

I was mortified.

▽ ▽ ▽

Despite the inauspicious beginning, we began seeing each other. Once, early on, I asked about Selene's father, and Christine replied that Selene was the product of immaculate conception. When I pressed the subject she replied, tartly, "He's in prison." It wasn't until later that I managed to drag the full story from her.

Christine spent her junior year of college in Paris, at the Sorbonne, and met him on a trip to Dublin. He was charming and sincere, as only an Irishman can be. He was a revolutionary and he talked, in soaring phrases, about freedom for Ireland and the equality of women. Christine was captivated. He followed her back to France and then to Boston.

There shortly followed the technical failure of a birth control device. They decided to make a go of it.

The trouble began around this time. He tried to force her to drop out of college. He complained that marriage was a bourgeois institution that enslaved women. He began to drink. She graduated college five months pregnant, with a degree in French literature.

He pressured her to go on welfare and Medicaid so he wouldn't have to pay for the birth, and made her apply for food stamps so he wouldn't have to buy food. His financial matters, he said, were none of her business. He spent all day in the cigarette and variety shop that he owned, selling stolen merchandise, and stayed out much of the night in the Boston bars, drinking and weeping about freedom for Ireland.

Selene rarely saw her father. For her first few birthdays, Christine had no money to buy presents, so she took home some toys from his shop, but he brought them back a week later and sold them. "She won't notice they're missing," he said. He was violent and abusive. He used to come home at night so drunk he would brush his teeth with the baby's Desitin.

One evening, Christine was watching the evening news. Suddenly there he was, with a dazed expression on his face, being shoved into a paddy wagon by men in brown suits. The FBI had videotaped him buying a planeload of automatic weapons, grenade launchers, and a redeye missile, destined for Northern Ireland.

It was the last she ever saw of him outside a prison cell.

The FBI had seized ten thousand dollars he had secretly saved while Christine and Selene were on welfare and food stamps. The trial was quick and he was convicted and sentenced to nine years in prison, to be followed by deportation to his native country. Christine, for her daughter's sake, tried to stay in touch with him, sending him letters about Selene's progress, but he was angry at her and returned them unopened. At the same time he wrote letters to Selene, chastising her for not writing him herself, as he was apparently unaware of the fact that a normal four- or five-year-old girl cannot read or write. The letters soon slowed to a trickle as he lost interest in his daughter, and those that did come had a hectoring, self-justifying tone, and were full of strange pronouncements and dark allusions. They upset Selene terribly. Christine began to realize that he was not only abusive, but potentially dangerous. She secretly left Boston, being careful to cover her tracks, and moved to Durango.

And where was he now?

He was about to be released from prison and deported. Christine had learned that he was looking for them. He wanted to take Selene away to Ireland. Christine heard indirectly, from one of his brothers, that he had been threatening to have Selene kidnapped and taken out of the country, beyond the reach of American law.

And that, Christine explained to me, was how things stood.

I had heard all this late one night, in the living room of her house. The only light came from a fire, dying on the grate. When she finished, silence filled the room. The city was peaceful, and the fragrant smell of piñon hung in the air. There was the distant sound of a barking dog. Selene was sleeping quietly in the back bedroom, hugging a large stuffed tiger. Everything, in the face of this story, suddenly seemed unreal, as if the evil of the world were seeping into the very air we were breathing.

Christine laughed nervously at the silence. "Aren't I just a terrible embarrassment? Aren't I *difficult?*" Then she added, shakily, "So what do you think?"

I didn't tell her what I thought. My thoughts were terrible. This was not at all a picture of the strong, independent woman that I had gotten to know. My life in the house on the hill, with two horses and a yellow dog, was orderly and calm. I had no enemies to speak of. I had always been careful to avoid unpleasant entanglements and hysterical love affairs.

I had many reasons for avoiding a commitment: my income from writing was too unstable, my house was too small, I hadn't met the right person. Most important, I felt that marriage was a dangerous business. Many of my friends who had married in their twenties were already going through divorces of extreme viciousness. Their children would be scarred for life and they financially ruined. I reflected that these people had started fresh with all the advantages: good careers, money, friends, supportive families. They had not started with an IRA terrorist-kidnapper lurking in the background. My life, in short, was exactly the way I wanted it. I couldn't possibly take on a relationship with Christine. What would happen, I thought, if I fell in *love* with this woman?

I broke it off as soon as I could. I didn't tell her why; in a parking lot behind the bank one sunny winter morning I said I was sorry, that it wasn't working out, goodbye, and got in my car and left, while she stood in the cold sun, crying and hurling insults and pieces of ice.

Within twenty-four hours I had the greatest shock of my life: I discovered that I was already in love with her. It was something I had never felt before, so overwhelming that I could not even function without her. I also realized, to my utter consternation, that I loved her daughter as if she were my own child.

▽ ▽ ▽

Selene looked like an eight-year-old version of her mother, glorious red hair, an archipelago of freckles across her face, eyes the blue color of faraway hills, a dimple on her left cheek.

I loved Selene because, despite everything, she was so utterly happy. She couldn't help it: she was one of those children who loved being alive. Her life was not easy. They were very poor. They had to turn off the heat in wintertime, switching it back on only to keep the pipes from freezing. Christine worked seventy hours a week as a baker, getting up at five o'clock every morning. Selene was lonely and she missed Boston. And yet, every night she sang herself to sleep, and I could always tell when she was awake by the joyful song bursting from her room. Gershwin, Cole Porter, Louis Armstrong, Rodgers and Hammerstein, she knew them all. She did cartwheels and handstands and squealed with delight when I ran around with her clinging to my back like a monkey.

When Selene and Christine moved in, I built a tiny room for her by walling off part of our bedroom. In the mornings, Selene would crawl out of bed in the dark and get into our bed, and squirm and burrow and giggle until she had firmly wedged herself between me and Christine. If I touched Christine or kissed her good morning Selene would cry out, "Hey! No touching!"

Every night when I came in to say goodnight she demanded a story. Her favorites were the stories of bad things I had done as a child. "Tell me about the time you put the dead skunk on the Ginns' doorstep and set it on fire!" she would cry out, or: "Tell me about when you shot a bottle rocket at the police car!" Whenever I tried to leave she clung to me like an octopus, wheedling and begging another story, demanding hugs and kisses at the same time. I found her irresistible.

She was a brilliant and unusual child. She thought television was boring. Instead she read books, devouring them at the rate of ten to twenty a week. She was intensely curious about the world but tried to feign indifference.

"So Selene," I said, "do you know what's beyond the edge of the universe?"

"No and I don't care."

And then a day later she said, "There *is* no edge to the universe, so there, Mr. Know-it-all."

At eight she could calculate whole-number square roots, cube roots, and fourth roots in her head. If she got bored with the dinner table conversation, she sometimes demanded: "Give me a problem!"

"What is the cube root of 216?" I asked.

She crawled under the dining room table. We could hear her giggling for five minutes.

"Six?" her muffled voice came up tentatively from underneath.

When we got up we found that, in addition to figuring out the problem, she had tied all our shoelaces to the chair legs.

There was, however, an undercurrent of tension in my relationship with Selene. Ours was not a simple relationship; it had an unfortunate complexity. For the truth was, Selene was not sure if she even liked me. As far back as she could remember she had had her mother to herself. My intrusion into this satisfactory state of affairs was unwelcome.

Even at eight Selene knew her feelings were irrational and she tried to control them, but they erupted often. She was sometimes sullen and rude, and made it a point of principle to refuse to do anything I asked.

Once I made the mistake of pressing her a little too hard. She finally erupted, "You're *not* my dad and you have *no* right to make me do *anything*."

▽ ▽ ▽

In October, under a fat cottonwood in the playground of Selene's school, Christine asked me to marry her. I hemmed and hawed and we had a rather heated discussion. When she pressed me I brought up the fact that I had to think about it since I would, after all, be taking on a threat from a convicted IRA terrorist-gunrunner who was at that very moment plotting to kidnap her daughter.

She accused me of cowardice. "If you *really* loved us," she said, "you would take on any danger for me and Selene. You would want to protect us instead of running away."

She finally told me that I'd better hurry up and decide, because if I thought she was going to wait, then I was a bigger fool than I looked. I'd never find another woman like her nor could I expect to have a daughter as wonderfully brought up as Selene, or as lively and pretty and intelligent, and therefore the decision should be obvious to anyone with common sense. Under the rustling yellow light of the cottonwood and the autumnal aroma of piñon smoke, she said, "If you miss this opportunity, you'll regret it for the rest of your life."

I eventually had to agree. I knew from the outset that I didn't have a choice, and that I loved her and Selene (despite the fact that Selene didn't love me). We set the wedding date for July.

Selene tried to be happy about the impending marriage, but

she was moody. She was particularly upset when she learned we were thinking of going on a honeymoon without her. "You can't *wait* to get rid of me," she cried.

One day that winter we found ourselves on a long drive to Salt Lake City.

As usual, Selene called for a story. "Tell me about the time you blew up the golf course!" she squealed.

Christine turned to her. "You know, Selene, soon Doug and I are going to be married."

"Yeah, I *know*," she said.

"Maybe you might start thinking about calling him something other than 'Doug.' "

There was a sudden, unbearable silence.

"Like what," Selene said flatly.

"He *is* going to be your dad, you know," Christine said.

There was another long silence. The wheels hummed on the road. I felt my face burning. I liked Christine's directness but this was going a little too far.

"No," Selene said.

"What do you mean, 'no'?" Christine asked. "Why not?"

"Because I don't *want* to," she said firmly.

"It's okay," I said hastily. "Selene can call me whatever she wants."

"Will you think about it?" Christine asked, looking intently at her daughter.

Selene was silent, staring out the window at the barren Utah desert, covered with windblown snow. I felt my heart sink; I felt unaccountably hurt, although she'd been calling me "Doug" now for over a year and I knew perfectly well she wasn't going to change.

Later, I asked Christine never to bring the subject up with Selene again.

"I just wanted to put the idea in her head," she said. "Now it's up to you."

"Up to me what?"

"To win her over."

Chapter 2

ATTACKING UTE, UTE RAID
PANEL
—CANYON DEL MUERTO

American Museum of
Natural History
New York City
March 1983

The journey that forms the heart of this book had its origin ten years ago, long before I met Christine. I used to work at the American Museum of Natural History in New York City. One day, while I was researching an article for the museum's magazine, I found myself in the rare book room. It was a once-elegant tower office that had been converted into a small fortress, the fireplace blocked and the windows barred, the door steel-plated and equipped with an alarm. It stored the museum's most valuable books, several of which were worth over a million dollars. I was sitting at a baize desk, going through some rare anthropological monographs. The place was cool and dim. Through the old oaken doors I could hear the faint cries of children in the dinosaur hall beyond, as well as the noises from the streets of New York City filtering in through the blocked windows.

The stack emitted an acid smell of decaying paper, and the pages were as brittle as mica. These monographs were very rare, and they contained transcriptions and transliterations of creation myths from various cultures around the world. The librarian had required me to don a pair of white gloves before I was allowed to handle them, and I had to agree to be locked into the room.

I shuffled through them, reading about the creation of the Earth and the naming of the landscape; I read tales of floods, earthquakes, and a distant era when animals spoke like people. Most of these myths had been collected in the late 1800s, before the great tidal wave of the present century changed our world forever. They came from hundreds of obscure tribes, from Siberia to Tierra del Fuego, subsequently swept into eternal oblivion.

I had found it an unexpectedly disturbing experience to read the origin myths of these peoples, most of whom had undergone complete physical and ethnic extinction. Nothing exemplifies the inner spirit of a people more than its creation myths. "Myth," Joseph Campbell wrote, "is the secret opening through which the inexhaustible energies of the cosmos pour into human cultural manifestation." Locked up in the rare book room, I read again and again, in lines of soaring beauty, of the creation of a great and enduring people; I read how the sun, moon, and stars had been placed in the heavens to delight and warm them; I read how their gods had showered them with kindness and beneficence, as proof that they were a people favored above all others. At times I found myself almost weeping at the irony of it: for their gods had left them, their fellow human beings had destroyed them, and the world had forgotten them.

The anthropologists who collected these myths knew well the grim future that awaited the tribes they studied, and they worked feverishly to save what they could, from their dirty spoons to their creation myths. The physical remains of that desperate salvage effort are stored in dozens of vaults in the museum's attic, while the spiritual remains are sealed in buckram and buried in the depths of the library. Today, all that remains of humanity's rich spiritual past is a stack of abandoned and decaying books, locked in a small room in a museum in an alien city, tended by strangers.

On that particular day, I had checked out a monograph by one of these early anthropologists, a man named Washington

Matthews, entitled *Navajo Legends*. It was the first attempt to record the Navajo creation story. The book was nearly a hundred years old and, according to a date stamped on a library slip, it had not been opened since 1943; when I spread the covers on the table there was an ominous cracking as the binding gave up its ghost.

I browsed through the old book from the back forward. The first thing I came across was a long poem buried in an appendix, which was Matthews's translation of the first 100 lines of the Night Chant, a Navajo healing ceremony for mental illness. It was an invocation to the mythic Thunderbird who dwells in the mountains with the gods. I have shortened it here.

In the house made of the dawn,
In the house made of the evening twilight,
In the house made of the dark cloud,
In the house made of pollen,
In the house made of grasshoppers,
Where the dark mist curtains the doorway,
The path to which is on the rainbow,
Where the zigzag lightning stands high on top,
Oh, male divinity!
With your moccasins of dark cloud, come to us.
With your mind enveloped in dark cloud, come to us.
With the dark thunder above you, come to us soaring.
With the darkness on the earth, come to us.
With these I wish the foam floating on the flowing water over
*   the roots of the great corn.*
My body restore for me.
My mind restore for me.
Happily I recover.
Happily abundant dark clouds I desire.
Happily abundant passing showers I desire.
Happily may fair white corn, to the ends of the earth, come
*   with you.*
In beauty I walk.
It is finished in beauty.

I was stunned. There was something about the poem, combined with the quietness of the room, the crumbling volume, and the faint clamor of New York City filtering in through the shaded windows, that moved me. It was a prayer, a magical incantation meant to do nothing less than invoke the presence of a living god. And I suddenly felt, for a suspended moment, that there was another presence in the room.

The word "poetry" was not, in fact, a good description of this chant-poem-song-prayer. Like the other creation stories I had been reading, it was a use of language more powerful than anything we have in Western literature; these were words that pierced the veil of the material world, that summoned the gods themselves. I continued reading *Navajo Legends*, this time starting at the beginning.

This was my first encounter with the magnificent *Diné Bahane'*, the Creation of the People, the Navajo account of the origin of the universe, the building and naming of the landscape, and the spiritual evolution of human beings.

The story opens in a small dark world sunken beneath the surface of the Earth. In the beginning there was darkness. Darkness joined with darkness in sexual union, and the darkness lying on top brightened into a white light that arose in the east: the first dawn. As a result of this union, a vast, boundless entity known as *Nílch'i*, Wind, was created. Wind is the life force itself: it suffuses all of nature and it gives thought, speech, and movement to all living things. The wind in me and the wind in you, the wind in the antelope and the sagebrush, the wind in the mountains and rivers and in the moon and stars, is all one living, breathing entity.

After that first union, little fragments of life came drifting out of the sky, the *Nílch'i Dine'é*, the Peoples of the Wind. And then, in this First World:

> White arose in the east, and they regarded it as day there, they say; blue rose in the south, and still it was day to them, and they moved around; yellow rose in the west and showed that evening had come; then dark arose in the north, and they lay down and slept.

And thus was the first day.

I read the passage again. Dawn comes, and then day. And the people move around. Then sunset, then night, and the people sleep. This creation was timeless and even passive; it evoked only a primeval diurnal rhythm.

At that moment I began to think about our own creation story: Genesis.

In the beginning God created the heaven and the earth.

And the earth was without form, and void; and darkness was upon the face of the deep. And the Spirit of God moved upon the face of the waters.

And God said, Let there be light: and there was light.

And God saw the light, that it was good: and God divided the light from the darkness.

And God called the light Day, and the darkness he called Night.

And the evening and the morning were the first day.

How different are these two descriptions of the First Day.

People are defined by their creation myths. Even though few of us still believe Genesis literally, it continues to animate us as a people. It tells us who we are, what we are, and how we are to act. The story is full of action, movement, and command. It proceeds with vigor; events follow thick and fast in specific time periods. God creates by fiat the Earth and the heavens, the plants and trees, the sun, moon, and stars, the moving creatures and whales, cattle and every creeping thing. He creates man and woman in his likeness, and he commands them to multiply and have dominion over the Earth; and he sends rain and creates a beautiful garden eastward in Eden for them to live in. When we disobey his edicts, without a second thought he casts us out to wander the Earth and earn our keep by the sweat of our brow. All this happens in the first few pages of Genesis.

Sitting in the rare book room at the museum, as I mulled over these thoughts, I could still feel this other presence in the room, this rustling of wings and roll of distant thunder, this spirit from the house made of dawn. At the same time I could hear the murmuring city around me, filtering through the covered windows. They were small sounds, the vendor's shout on the street, the sound of an insistent car horn, the drone of a jet, the traffic on West 77th Street. And I thought, here *is* the sound of our creation, the sound of Genesis: this muttering of a great city grown on the shores of America, a city built by strangers from across the sea. It is a city, within a country, positive of its rightness. We are a people of action and command, domineering, not usually given to contemplation or doubt. We do not feel ourselves part of nature; we are separate from it and have commanded its obeisance. This is what we have produced: New York City, a place of cement and steel whose weight is deforming the bedrock of the earth itself, a city fed by great pipes bringing water from distant hills, fed by asphalt arteries of automobiles, fed by underground cables of copper and glass, fed by immense wealth stored in Boolean logic within databanks. What is our Genesis, I thought, if not the very root of our conquest and domination of the world?

Thinking these thoughts, it suddenly seemed that the sound filtering in through the blocked windows was strange, a malevolent rapid whispering, a crackling of bones, a thudding of flesh. I was almost afraid of what I would see, had I torn the coverings off and looked out upon the city.

The feeling passed quickly. It was as if I'd glanced, for a brief second, from another world back into my own.

▽ ▽ ▽

A human culture is a framework that allows a group of people to comprehend the world. That framework is normally built from myth and ritual, what Claude Lévi-Strauss called the "myths [that] operate in men's minds without their being aware of the fact." Indeed, the word "myth" is oxymoronic. A myth must be believed in order to exist and to impart its truths; when it becomes "myth" it ceases to be *myth*. With the terrible destruction of so many of the world's fragile cultures, belief itself has been crushed out of the world. We are becoming a single, global culture. For the first time, however, it is not a framework based on spiritual beliefs, but one constructed of the values of technology and material progress.

My grandmother, who was born a week before the turn of the century, saw her first electric light at five; the first automobile in her town at seven; saw the bomb dropped at forty-five; saw men walk on the moon at sixty-nine; saw the population of the world increase 500 percent; saw an ecological reordering of the planet's surface unlike anything in the previous forty million centuries of Earth history. She is still alive, bedridden, bewildered, living in a world that is utterly different from the world she was born into. When you and I finally lie bedridden and confused, it will be in a world equally strange and different. Our grandchildren may yet find our myths, and our dirty spoons, locked up in an alien attic. As Chief Seattle said to the men who had taken his tribe's homelands: "your time of decay may be distant, but it will surely come, for even the White Man . . . cannot be exempt from the common destiny."

It was these thoughts, and many more, that led us to take the journey recorded in this book.

Chapter 3

FIGURE OF NAVAJO
HUMPBACKED GOD, WHO
CARRIES ALL THE SEEDS OF THE
WORLD IN HIS BACK.
—CANYON LARGO

Durango, Colorado
January 1992

Not long after Christine and I became engaged, we were brows-ing in a bookstore, and I picked up a book called *Diné Bahane':*
The Navajo Creation Story, by Paul Zolbrod. It was a new transla-tion of the Navajo creation story, based on Washington Mat-thews's original text. As I started reading it, I immediately recalled that day in the rare book room of the American Museum of Natural History nearly ten years before.

It was more than a new translation. Zolbrod understood that this epic creation story, the *Diné Bahane'*—which means the Creation of the People—was still believed by the Navajo people. As a result, he was able to collect many unknown portions of the story, as well as restore passages that Matthews had left out for reasons of Victorian propriety.

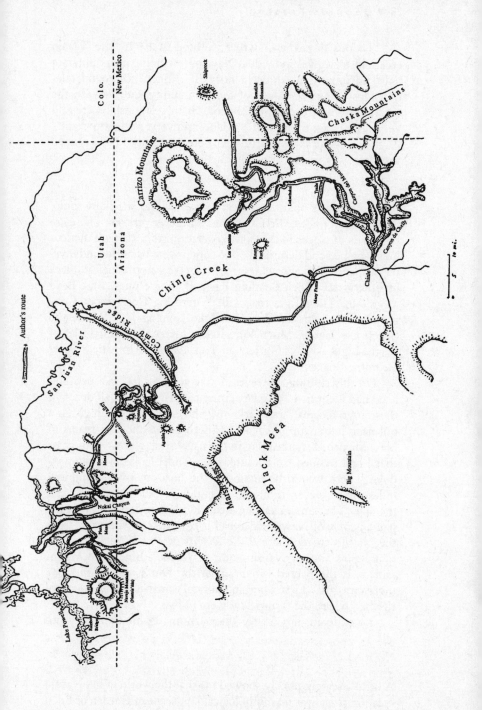

"To this day, then," wrote Zolbrod in 1984, "the Navajo creation story gives individual Navajos (including many illiterate ones) an important ethnic identity. It defines meaningful relationships among members of the community and between the community and the entire cosmos. Such relationships are still very real among traditional Navajos, and very, very important."

It struck me as wonderful that a creation story I had assumed was dead was, in fact, very much alive.

▽ ▽ ▽

I read Zolbrod's book with great interest. I was struck by something I hadn't noticed reading the Matthews version. There are hundreds of places in the Navajo creation story that are meticulously named and described. The names were beautiful and mysterious, and I had always assumed they were mythological: Place of Emergence, Rock Bending Back, Boiling Dunes, Blue Bead Mountain, Their Eyes that Kill, Where Big God's Blood Congealed, Stars Strung Out, Antelope Coming Up, Where the Sheep Lie Down, Much Fur, Reeds under the Rim, Head of Earth, Light Always Glitters on Top, Among Aromatic Sumac, Grinding Snakes.

On this reading, however, I was given pause, because Zolbrod had identified and given American names to a half dozen of these mythological landmarks. My house is perched high on a hill near Durango, and it looks south across the vast plains of New Mexico. I was reading in my usual spot, a great Taos chair that I had rescued from a junk shop, and I looked out the window. There was a mountain on the horizon, over a hundred miles away, eleven thousand feet high, a blue smudge against the sky. The American maps call it Mount Taylor. The Hispanic people of New Mexico call it San Mateo. And now, from the Navajo creation story, the *Diné Bahane'*, I learned that this mountain's ancient Navajo name is *Tsoodzil*, Blue Bead Mountain. It is the Sacred Mountain of the South, one of the four mountains that First Man and First Woman built to delineate the area where the future *Diné* were to live.

I wondered: if a few of these landmarks are real, why not all?

▽ ▽ ▽

A little research quickly showed me that the world of the Navajo creation story was no mythological landscape, a Garden of Eden where the rivers Pison and Gihon flow. It was a real place of stone and sand, earth, river and sky. It was right here, in America. The Four Corners area of the United States was, literally, a dense and intricate atlas of creation, with almost every rock, hill, and river marked by some mythological event.

The place where human beings emerged into the world actually exists; so does the hill where Changing Woman was born, and the flat rock where she conceived twin sons by the Sun and Water. On top of Huerfano Peak, the Sacred Mountain of the Center, one can actually see the crumbling remains of a hogan believed to be that of First Man and First Woman. The spring where Monster Slayer ambushed the chief of the enemy gods still bubbles south of Grants, New Mexico. Near it one can see the congealed mass of the dying god's blood, which is the great lava flow of El Malpaís. To the north, the alien god's head, decapitated by Monster Slayer, lies on the landscape as Cabezón Peak. The heat of their battle scorched a nearby mountainside, turning it white.

I spent several months mapping the Navajo creation story. No one had done it completely before, but many sources existed: Zolbrod's book, the Matthews text, other anthropological texts. I pored through legal documents from land claims cases, in which Navajo medicine men and singers had testified to the sacredness of various landmarks slated for development. I read monographs, Navajo language dictionaries, ethnographies, and the writings of missionaries. I learned some Navajo, mostly words relating to or describing the landscape. I discovered that many of the crude, transliterated names recorded by the USGS surveyors in Indian country originated in some sacred event that had occurred at the beginning of time. I bought dozens of USGS topographical maps and pored over them, carefully mapping the journeys of the gods, the epic battles, and the wanderings of the First People across the landscape during the creation era.

▽ ▽ ▽

It was Christine who saw the possibilities in this creation map. I spread the map out for her one afternoon on the kitchen table.

She was fascinated. "We ought to go to some of these places," she said. "This could be your next trip."

Since coming west, each year I had taken a long and difficult horseback journey across many hundreds of miles of the southwestern deserts, traveling with nothing that could not be packed on the back of a horse. Once in a while I needed to escape the wearying complexity of the twentieth century, to resharpen a sense of what was really important in life and what was just background noise. The first time I crossed the Navajo reservation was in 1989, when I was retracing 1,000 miles of Coronado's 1540–42 search for the legendary Seven Cities of Gold. That trip resulted in the book *Cities of Gold*, published in 1992.

Retracing Coronado's route took me across the southeastern corner of the *Diné Bikeyah*, the Land of the People. I had glimpsed something while riding through: something mysterious, elusive, even magical, something in the wisp of smoke curling out of a hogan, something in the faces of the Navajos I saw herding sheep on horseback, something in the ragged cornfield that grew unirrigated in the middle of a desert, something in the whispered voice of an ancient shepherd, telling about the fateful coming of the *Bilagáana*, the white people. The Navajos I spoke to remembered the tales passed down of Coronado's coming, the glint of sun on armor, the blond hair of one of his captains. The people were frightened and hid. After Coronado passed, the Navajos blocked off a spring the Spaniards had stopped at, in a futile attempt to discourage their return.

After the Coronado trip I made several more journeys that took me into the *Diné Bikeyah*. I retraced two hundred miles of the ancient roads of the Anasazi going to and from Chaco Canyon, trying to understand something about that vanished civilization. Another time I followed an ancient Navajo trade route, abandoned for 150 years, from Santa Fe to San Mateo, New Mexico.

Christine had been telling me she wanted to go on one of these trips, but I had always put her off. Now she wanted to explore the vast Navajo reservation, which straddled the Southwest's harshest deserts.

"Most of these creation places are incredibly remote," I said. "It would require horses to get there." The Navajo reservation is huge, covering some 25,000 square miles, an area as large as Vermont, New Hampshire, Massachusetts, Connecticut, and Rhode Island combined.

She looked at me. "We've got two. We could get some more."

I chuckled and folded up the map. "Oh no," I said, "you have absolutely no conception of how rugged and dangerous that desert country is. And besides, these places are sacred. It wouldn't be right to intrude on them."

"You don't have to *intrude* on them," she said. "These are hills, mountains, and rock formations that are visible for miles around. We could just ride past them. Admire them from a respectful distance."

"That's true."

"You said you wanted to do another long ride," Christine said. "Let's borrow some mules and pack our food and really get out there. Maybe take as long as a month."

"You have no *conception* of how dangerous and difficult a trip like that would be," I said. "We could easily be hurt or even die."

"It can't be *that* dangerous," Christine said.

"You would hate it," I said. "Every day is a challenge. The heat, the lack of water, the loneliness, the physical danger. It's not something a woman would enjoy."

There are words one wishes one could retract.

She jumped up. "What do you think I am, just some wimpy broad? Do you think that just because you're a man you're tougher than I am?" Her freckles were starting to consolidate into one angry patch and she advanced on me with a set look on her face.

I backed down. She was, of course, capable of making the trip. She was capable of anything.

Then Christine added: "Selene will come too."

This was the limit. "Take a nine-year-old kid from Boston out into those deserts," I cried, "who's never been on a horse in her life?"

There was a look on Christine's face that I could not immediately interpret. There was a drawn-out silence.

"Yes," she said. "That's exactly it."

"It's *impossible*," I said. "It's too dangerous."

"It's dangerous driving into town," she said. "The whole world is a dangerous place. Some things are worth the danger, as you yourself have discovered."

I was silent.

"I think," she said quietly, "this could be a very important journey for her, and for us."

"What do you mean?"

"It would give her a chance to get to know you." Then she added, "Look around you, look at the kids in Selene's class.

They're good kids but they're growing up in a barren society. They don't know much beyond the values of television. With a trip like this, among the Navajos, we could give Selene a sense that there's more to the world than the mall."

"There must be other ways to do this," I said.

"I don't think so. There'd be nothing but our horses and ourselves against this vast landscape. We'd be dependent on each other for our very lives. That's something no modern American family ever experiences."

I was silent, but the idea was starting to appeal to me, on many different levels. It would be something of profound worth that we could give to each other, as a family starting its journey in a difficult world—a world whose values we did not fully accept. It would be a way for us to step outside the prison of our culture and, perhaps, find a new way of looking at the world. It would be an intriguing way to begin a family. Still, it was a crazy, ridiculous, absurd, and dangerous idea.

"Let me see that map," Christine said.

She pulled it over and examined it for a moment.

"What's this?" she asked, tracing her finger along a yellow line I had drawn.

"That was the path of a Navajo deity called Monster Slayer, who rid the Earth of the alien gods who were destroying humanity."

"That's it!" she said, sweeping her hand across the map. "Let's retrace it."

"That's four or five hundred miles right there, across the worst desert in the whole Southwest. You have no idea—"

"Wonderful! It will be our honeymoon. *With* Selene."

▽ ▽ ▽

Christine introduced the idea to Selene that evening, at dinner. She was less than enthusiastic.

"What!" she cried. "You expect *me* to ride four hundred miles across the desert? Forget it. No *way*." She set her fork down with a clatter and planted her elbows on the table.

"You'll love it," Christine said. "It'll be the adventure of a lifetime."

"You want me to sleep in a tent for a whole *month?* What are we going to eat? I've never *heard* anything so horrible. Like, where am I supposed to go to the bathroom?"

When she heard the answer to that she burst into tears. "I

am *not* going to *pee* in the *sand,*" she wailed. "And I *hate* beans! *I'm not going* and that's *final.*" Her face got very red and the tears leaked out of her scrunched-up eyes.

"Doug will buy you your very own horse," Christine said.

"I don't *want* a dirty old horse," she cried.

When her mother impressed on her that she had to come along, that she had absolutely no choice, she said, "Look, I'm not going to do this for *nothing*. I mean, *God*, I'll have to be *paid* or something."

"Don't say 'God' like that," Christine said.

"Well," she said, "what about the way Doug talks when he gets around his horses? All that swearing? He says a lot worse things than *God*."

Christine gave me a dark look. I meekly promised I would try my best to clean up my language around my horses.

Selene finally accepted the inevitable, especially after I bribed her with a portable Nintendo Gameboy to take on the trip, which was the thing she wanted most in the world. I bought her and Christine horses and saddles, and we rode in the National Forest behind our house, through snowstorms and up and down mountains. In the month before the trip I taught Christine how to saddle, how to throw a diamond hitch, how to tie breakaway knots, how to trail a packhorse, how to stake out, hobble, and sideline a horse, how to balance a set of panniers and cinch up a sawbuck packsaddle, how to inject drugs and doctor wounds in a horse, and then we were off on a 400-mile ride across the harshest deserts in the Southwest, deserts that would unnerve and even kill a seasoned cowboy.

If we survived—or more to the point, if our *relationship* survived—we planned to be married in July.

Chapter **4**

Navajo Mountain
Rainbow City
April 27, 1992

Naatsis'áán! Naatsis'áán!
Black Wind, splendid Chief!
From the tips of your fingers a rainbow put out.
Thrust out a rainbow from your brow,
A rainbow from the palm of your hand—
By which let me walk . . .
Wrapped in your cloud garments let me walk.
Earth Woman, send the rain,
The rain, kind and gentle—
That all may be happiness before me,
That all may be happiness behind me,
That all may be happiness round about me . . .
   Now all is happiness, now all is happiness.

—PRAYER TO *NAATSIS'ÁÁN*, NAVAJO MOUNTAIN[1]

Christine and I began planning our journey in detail on sixty U.S. Geological Survey maps of Utah, Arizona, and New Mexico. We spread them out, one by one, on the living room floor, plotting our route.

The terrain varied tremendously. Some maps were virtually empty, a white piece of paper costing $2.50, representing fifty square miles of America where government surveyors found almost nothing: no roads, no water, no trees, bushes, or hills. Others were dark with topographical density, a fractal riddle of lines, a landscape of unimaginable complexity. We examined about five hundred square feet of maps, inch by inch, drawing the mythical route of the Navajo god Monster Slayer with an uncertain yellow line. As Monster Slayer traveled, he battled the alien gods that had taken over the Earth and were destroying all life. He left their bodies strewn about the plains and mountains, where they slowly turned to stone. The landscapes we would see, thus, were nothing less than the ancient battlegrounds for control of the Earth.

The names on the maps were evocative and hinted at something more than mere geography: places like Rain God Mesa, Many Ghosts Hill, Porras Dikes, House of Hands Cave, the Ear of the Wind, Wild Horse Trap Mesa, Old Man Sorrel Horse Spring. These were among the last areas mapped by the USGS in the lower forty-eight states. Surveyors penetrated the land by jeep, stopping at hogans and standing in the thirsty sun, listening to the alien vowels of Navajos who spoke no English. They did their sighting along pointed fingers, squinting at the landforms, laboring to spell out the names in their notebooks. Many words they had not managed to translate; sprinkled on the map, like fragments of alien poetry, were names such as Toh Dah Hee Dat Conii, Ttoh Ts Ositah, Chaiyahi Rim, Todicheenie Bench, Tsekadebehgon. They reminded us that while this place was in America, it was not *of* America. It was the *Diné Bikeyah*, the Land of the People.

▽ ▽ ▽

We decided to begin our journey at Navajo Mountain. It lies just north of the Arizona-Utah border, a 10,000-foot dome of rock standing among red canyons. The Navajos call it *Naatsis'áán*: the Head of the Earth. This is where many Navajos believe Monster Slayer and his twin, Born for Water, were born. After killing the alien gods, Navajo Mountain is where the twin brothers returned, to be cleansed of the taint of death. It was here that they brought all the slain Navajos back to life in one of the first Navajo ceremonies ever performed.

For these reasons, Navajo Mountain seemed like an appropriate starting place for our journey.

From there, we planned to ride from Navajo Mountain eastward to Monument Valley, across a section of the Navajo reservation known as the Utah Strip. (It is sometimes called the Paiute Strip because some of the land was formerly the domain of the Southern Paiute Indians.) It is a harsh land, fissured by canyons and dotted with vast isolated mesas. Precipitation averages less than six inches per year, the lowest in the American Southwest. Sometimes all six of those inches will fall in a single day and sweep through the canyons as terrifying flash floods. The temperature ranges from over 100 degrees in the summer to 30 below in the winter. The wind blows incessantly. There are few springs and most are either salty or poisonous. The population density here is among the lowest of any inhabited place on Earth; about twenty families live between Navajo Mountain and Monument Valley, an area larger than the state of Rhode Island.

Due to the ruggedness of the terrain, there is only one east-west route in the entire Utah Strip. It is a very rough trail, many centuries old, winding in and out of canyons half a mile deep. It once had a name among the white traders in the area: they called it the Navajo Trail. The Navajos call it *Óoljéé'tó atiin:* the Moonlight Water Trail. Most of the trail was abandoned thirty years ago, when a dirt road from Shonto to Piute Mesa was built, and most of it had washed away and disappeared.

▽ ▽ ▽

We left Durango on the morning of April 27, 1992. We arose in the dark, the stars glittering hard in the sky. I had hired a local rancher, a man named Red, to take us and our horses to Navajo Mountain. He arrived in the dark in a big Cummins diesel pickup truck towing an eight-horse, slant-load trailer. We loaded up and set off. The sun rose as we hummed down the interstate, turning the tarmac a liquid orange.

We had brought along Acomita, our excellent guard and trail dog. She came from the ancient Indian pueblo of Acoma. While we drove she sat on top of the gear in the back, ears perked with excitement, sniffing the air. She was as glad to get away from civilization as we were.

Four hundred miles later we turned off the last paved road. The dirt road left the highway between Shonto and Kaibeto, in Arizona, and headed northward. It was the only road to Navajo Mountain and the tiny Navajo settlement of Rainbow City, where we would camp. For a few miles the road was bladed, ditched, and crowned, but it soon deteriorated into a tooth-chipping washboard, shaking bone and steel. Red braked heavily and we crept along at fifteen miles an hour, the trailer with our five horses rattling as we lurched through the ruts.

No sign marked the Utah border. Borders here were irrelevant; it was all the *Diné Bikeyah*.

▽ ▽ ▽

Red squinted ahead at the dirt road, a slash of shadow hiding his eyes. Christine was leaning back against the seat, dozing. Selene sat in the back, furiously battling monsters on her Nintendo Gameboy. We had been driving for about thirteen hours.

Red took off his hat and fitted it back on, and said, casually: "So what're you doing for feed for your horses?"

"We were hoping to find grass," I said. "But it doesn't look too promising."

His face was inscrutable in the shadow of his hat.

"Haven't seen a blade of grass in a hundred miles," he said, his voice flat.

"I've noticed that," I said.

There was a silence. "Well," he said, "a horse could chew on this stuff out here and live for about eight, nine days, I'd say, before starving to death. That's if he's loose, not hobbled, and not being ridden."

He was looking straight ahead.

"Right," I said. "Maybe the Navajos around here will have some feed."

"Where they growing it," he replied, not making it a question.

There was a long silence, filled by the throbbing of the engine. The gears whined into a downshift and the truck lurched.

"This is quite a place," he said, "to bring five horses, a lady, and a nine-year-old girl." He grunted a laugh, but I could see he was not joking.

"And a dog," Selene called out.

▽ ▽ ▽

The road narrowed and became a slew of ruts in soft sand. Here and there a pair of tire tracks veered off into the brush. The road finally became so tentative that we convinced ourselves we must be lost. We drove for an hour or more, not seeing any sign of human habitation. Then, in the distance, a ramshackle collection of barracks-like buildings came into view, enclosed by a barbed-wire fence. We stopped to ask directions. A ghostly blue cross painting on the side of a building indicated it was a Christian mission, and a no-trespassing sign, pierced by several large-caliber bullet holes, rattled on the gate.

I climbed through the fence and walked around, shouting into the wind, but there was nothing. The central building was empty, a bare blue room with a harsh bar of light across the floor. The good brothers had gone.

We continued on. The road carried us eastward of Navajo Mountain and along the edge of a canyon so deep I could not see the bottom, with a blue wall five miles away, and beyond that another canyon, and another blue wall, and yet another, as far as the eye could see.

We inched around a bend, and there, ahead of us, a riderless horse trotted along the road. It was a small, dun-colored mustang, his winter coat shedding in ugly strips. He was saddled and dragging one rein, the sweat pouring off his flanks. He heard us coming, flattened his ears, and broke into a lope.

"Uh-oh," Red said, "will you look at that."

It was a chilling sight. We all knew what it meant: his rider was probably lying in some remote canyon, miles from anywhere, maybe with a broken leg and no water.

"Maybe we should catch it," I said.

He shook his head. "He's probably heading back to his corral. The people back there need to see he lost his rider so they can send someone out to backtrack."

The horse quickened his lope and jumped off into the brush, kicking savagely backward at us.

"You couldn't ketch that son-of-a-bitch anyway," he said, with a snort.

We drove in silence.

"I think we're going in the right direction," I said.

The truck heaved across a washout.

"Next time," Red said, "I'll have to charge extra for the dirt road."

We were all coated with dust. The sun hung low and hot

over the brow of Navajo Mountain. We dipped down and crossed an arroyo. As we climbed and topped out I could see a settlement come into view, a row of bleak HUD houses, a few trailer homes, a scattering of mud-covered hogans. We had been driving for over two hours on the dirt road.

"Maybe this is it," I said.

"I *hope* so," said Selene.

We pulled up into the center of town, an expanse of hard-packed sand. A small cottonwood tree grew in the center, next to a water spigot. A hand-painted wooden sign, almost indecipherable, stood at the base of the tree. The sign was broken in half, and had been knocked over so that it touched the ground. It read:

RAIN
CI

"We're here," I cried out.

"*Finally*," Selene said grumpily, climbing out of the truck and dropping to the ground with a little puff of dust. Acomita leapt out of the back and raced off, nose to the ground, excited to be back in the desert.

Christine got out and stretched. "Look at this place," she said. "It's like we've reached the end of the earth."

I looked around at the endless scrub, rock, and sand. "I guess we can camp anywhere," I said.

We unloaded the horses and a few bales of hay and piled our four hundred pounds of gear in a secluded spot between a large rock and a crescent sand dune.

"How much do I owe you?" I asked Red.

He ducked into his truck, checked the mileage, and calculated some figures on the back of an envelope. "At a dollar fifteen a mile, that'll be four hundred and sixty dollars."

I wrote out a check. We were a hell of a long way from Durango.

He looked eastward into the blue canyons, and he murmured, "This is going to be some trip."

There was an awkward silence, and then he turned and grasped our hands warmly and with the sudden feeling of a man making a final farewell.

"If you need anything, or if anything happens, you give me a call, you hear? Any time of the day or night."

"If we can find a telephone booth," I said, attempting a joke.

He placed his old boot on the running board, grasped the handle, and swung himself into the truck. There was a diesel roar and the truck moved off in a cloud of dust. I watched the dust billow upward like a fire and sail out across the lonely desert. A dog barked and then everything was silent.

Christine came up and put her arm around my waist.

I looked at her smiling up at me, her short mahogany hair filled with dust, freckles all over her face, brand-new cowboy hat slung behind her head. I looked over at Selene, in her shiny boots, white hat, and orange bandanna, rummaging irritably in a pannier for one of her books. I looked eastward, down an old wagon road that went to the edge of the mesa. Beyond that lay more mesas, rising thousands of feet above the blue canyons, socked in by sheer rimrock, like islands in a sea. A chill went down my spine.

"What's the matter?" she asked. "You look a little pale."

"I just hope we're not making a terrible mistake," I said.

"Mistake?" Christine asked. "What kind of mistake?"

"The kind of mistake that's going to get us all killed in those canyons out there."

She grinned and tightened her arm on my waist. There was a long silence.

"*Nah,*" she said.

▽ ▽ ▽

The evening cooking fires were being lit and the fragrant smell of juniper smoke drifted past. A rich light filled the air, the peculiar terra-cotta light of evening found in Utah.

We heard high-pitched laughter. A cluster of Navajo kids had gathered around Selene, jostling and shouting. Selene had her saddlebags over her shoulder and was passing out fistfuls of hard candy. The kids were jamming the candies into their pockets and holding out their hands for more.

"I just gave you some!" Selene said to one persistent boy. He had a crew cut sticking out in all directions and was wearing a Teenage Mutant Ninja Turtles T-shirt.

"But it's for my *momma!*" the boy hollered, holding out both hands with the fingers spread, jumping up and down on one leg and then the other. "Please! For my *momma!*"

Soon they had departed, racing off through the sand. Selene held up her saddlebags, which had a sadly deflated look. "Look at how much candy they took," she said. "And besides, they were rude."

"Rude?" I asked.

"They wanted to know what was wrong with my face. They asked me what all the spots were on my nose. I told them they were freckles and then they asked why didn't I wash them off or get rid of them. It was like I had a *disease*."

"Oh Selene," said Christine. "They didn't mean any harm. They'd just never seen freckles before. I don't think Navajos get freckles."

"I *hate* these awful freckles," she said.

"I love freckles," I said. "Your mom's covered with them."

"Gross me out," said Selene.

▽ ▽ ▽

While Christine and Selene set up camp, I walked to the nearest house to see if we could put our horses in the empty corrals. A quiet lady answered my knock, dignified, with curled hair and a polyester jacket. In the gloom of the house, I could see a living room with shag carpeting, a Mediterranean-style couch, and a marbled mirror.

"Sure," she said, "you can use those corrals. They're community corrals. Anybody can use them." She spoke softly with a strong Navajo accent, a singing, whispery way of speaking. Navajo is a tonal language, like Chinese, and some Navajos almost sing their English.

I had been given the name of one person in Rainbow City, a Navajo man named Herman Ateene. I asked if she knew him.

She smiled. "I think I know him. He's my husband."

I marveled out loud at the coincidence. She nodded slightly, unimpressed; it was, after all, an extremely small town.

"Is he around?"

"No, he's giving a ceremony. He's a medicine man. Over there, near his sister's house, where the drum is beating."

I realized then that the fast tattoo rising and falling on the wind—what I had thought was a generator—was actually the very even beating of a drum.

"How long will it take?"

"Couple of hours."

She withdrew quietly into the dark interior of the house.

Back at the camp, Christine and Selene had organized everything. The tents were pitched in a hollow, sheltered by an old juniper tree, its ancient trunk screwed into the ground. Acomita sat like a jackal with erect ears and twitching nose, watching everything with great interest. The saddle blankets had been spread on the ground, our dinner unpacked, the Dutch oven and silverware laid out, and a pot of spaghetti was bubbling on a fire. Selene was curled up on a horsepad reading a book out loud, while Christine listened, occasionally stirring the pot with a stick.

It's a funny thing about mothers and fathers, she was reading. *Even when their own child is the most disgusting little blister you could ever imagine, they still think that he or she is wonderful . . .*

Selene erupted in giggles. " 'Disgusting little blister'!" she repeated. "Mommy, am I a disgusting little *blister?*"

"Of course not!" Christine said, smiling.

"What book is this?" I asked.

"It's *Matilda*," said Selene. "Listen!" and she continued reading, with expostulations of delight and laughter. I lay back, feeling contented. Two hours ago, this place had been a sand blowout behind a boulder, and now we had made it our home. I thought how quickly we humans can erect an edifice against the wilderness, how we can humanize and tame a landscape by our mere presence. This landscape that had seemed so viciously alien only a few moments ago was now becoming merely strange. Tomorrow, it might even be beautiful.

▽ ▽ ▽

The deserts of the *Diné Bikeyah* offer little to the overland traveler. We had to pack everything we needed for a month of existence.

Our most precious possessions were our five horses: three for riding and two for packing. The first lesson I had learned in long-distance desert travel was that the horses came first. To ignore the needs of our horses, even for a short time in this unkind environment, might be to find ourselves permanently on foot. Being on foot in a desert where sources of water were highly uncertain and often more than 20 miles apart would be more than inconvenient.

Christine's horse was named Chaco, a stout gelding the color of a mouse. Selene's horse was Blaze, a small sorrel gelding, lazy and ugly, and utterly without personality, but sure-footed and more or less bombproof. He was a good horse for a nine-year-old from Boston. I brought my horse Redbone, companion on nearly two thousand miles of desert journeys.

We had also brought two packhorses, which I was forced to buy in a hurry when a deal for some mules fell through. Brazos was the first, a big nasty thoroughbred, a brute, always pushing and shoving to get his way. He was a horse who had learned how to intimidate people, and he made an unlikely pack animal. About all I could say in his favor was that he was intelligent (at least for a thoroughbred) and sound. He was all I could get on my $650 budget. Our last horse, Roscoe, was black and shaggy, with a white blaze. He had a sly sideways look, peering at you through a straggly lock of mane, showing the whites of his eyes. Cowboys sometimes call this a "kicking face," which is why I was able to buy him cheap—a few dollars above the "killer price," what he would fetch if sold for dog food. He was of no recognizable breed and carried a head on his shoulders the size and shape of a coffin. I found his ugliness endearing. He was tough, big-boned, short-legged, medium-withered, with skin as hard as untanned cowhide: a perfect packhorse build. He was only six years old and would turn out to be a magnificent horse.

Acomita was our camp dog. She stood guard over the camp when we were gone. She patrolled at night and barked at anything strange. On command, she would herd range horses or cattle away from camp, but she never chased livestock, sheep, or chickens. She could sometimes find water when we could not. She was a most useful and intelligent animal.

We packed all our supplies on two ancient sawbuck packsaddles. We had sacks of dried food, beans, dried pasta, flour, rice, lentils, oatmeal, grits, dried fruits, nuts, powdered milk, sugar, coffee. We also carried horse supplies: hobbles, ropes, extra shoes, medicine, a cowbell. Selene had filled her saddlebags with two enormous sacks of candy, leaving just enough room for a book and a Polaroid camera. She kept her precious Gameboy in a waist pouch. We also had medicine, a water purification pump, books, batteries, a camera, film, notebooks, and paper.

We were self-sufficient except for two things: water and grass. These two essentials we would have to find in the desert. The problem was, when I looked into those canyons, I could not see the slightest trace of either.

▽ ▽ ▽

After dinner, Christine and I walked through the dark toward the sound of the drumming. The sister's house loomed out of the darkness, a flimsy HUD structure, cracked and scarred by the weather. In the darkness we could hear muffled chanting, a rhythmic pulse in the twilight. A child was playing in the dirt yard and she stood up and watched us approach. A woman came out of the house, smoothing her dress. She smiled and shook our hands. I said we were looking for Herman Ateene.

"Ceremony should be over anytime," she said, and went back inside.

We waited, and the twilight became night. There were no lights in the houses. The chanting continued under a vast dome of stars.

"We really have stepped into another world," Christine whispered, grasping my hand.

The chanting grew suddenly louder and then softer. Someone had left the hogan. The lights of a pickup truck switched on, shooting into the darkness. An engine started; voices speaking Navajo. There was the sound of laughter, and the slamming of Detroit steel. The lights edged out into the darkness and vanished down the road.

A shape emerged in front of us and paused.

"Herman Ateene?" I asked.

"Yes," he said, his face hidden.

I told him about our trip and asked him if he knew anyone who might like to ride the Moonlight Water Trail with us.

There was a long silence.

"Hold on a moment," he said, and vanished.

Soon a young man, really a boy, limped out of the darkness and shook our hands. It was a very soft handshake. His name was Frank Fatt.

"I live over there on Piute Mesa," he said. "The trail goes right by my house. I'll ride with you."

"What's the trail like?" I asked.

"It's an easy ride to Piute Mesa," he said. "Beyond that, to Monument Valley, it's not so good."

"How bad?" I asked. "Could our horses make it?"

"Depends on your horses. The black one, he'd make it."

"You've seen our horses?"

I think he must have grinned. "Everyone seen your horses."

Two other shapes emerged from the darkness, and there was much talk in Navajo.

"Yeah," Frank said, "I guess your horses'll make it."

"How far is it exactly to Monument Valley?"

"Three days."

"Three days? It looks longer." My maps indicated it must be at least 80 miles by the trail, and I had planned to take seven days.

"If you're going to camp at water," he said, "you *have* to do it in three days."

There was a silence.

"How much water is there between here and there?"

"There's water at four places, but three are salt. Lot of horses won't drink that water."

"Could we drink it?"

"Well, when you have to . . ." His voice trailed off.

"Is there any grass along the way?"

Frank shrugged in the darkness. "Not really."

There was a long silence.

"I'll see you in the morning," he said, and melted into the darkness.

$$\triangledown \quad \triangledown \quad \triangledown$$

In the middle of the night, I awoke to hear a sudden shaking of the tent, followed by silence. As I drifted back to sleep the tent shook again, harder this time.

"What the hell was that?" I said, sitting up. There was another brief silence and then a storm fell upon us. Within minutes the wind had risen to a howling pitch, and clouds of stinging sand were driving through the useless mosquito netting, penetrating everywhere. Christine buried herself in her bedroll, huddled like a ball, trying to keep the dust out.

The tent was sawing back and forth and I expected it to rupture at any moment. I tried to call out to Selene but no sooner was my mouth open than it was filled with choking grit.

We heard a thin cry rising over the howling wind, coming from the direction of Selene's tent.

Christine bolted upright. "Selene, is that you?"

The crying became a sobbing. "I hate this, I *hate* it," Selene cried above the wind. "Why did you force me to come on this stupid trip! I can't *breathe!*"

"I know," Christine shouted. "It'll be better in the morning."

"I'm scared. Let me sleep with you!"

"There's not enough room!"

A huge gust buffeted through camp, the sand drumming on the tent. "Help!" Selene yelled. "My tent is blowing away!"

"I'm sure it must feel that way," said Christine.

"I'm not *kidding!*" she hollered. There was a real panic in her voice.

I poked my head out the door with a flashlight, peering into the murk. I couldn't believe it: her tent really was blowing away, with her inside it. The wind had rolled it upside down.

"I'm coming!" I cried out.

I crawled into the maelstrom and tried to restake the tent, but the sand was too deep and soft to hold the stakes. I could feel bits of flying gravel lashing my back.

"It's blowing away again!" Selene cried as the wind roared through, tumbling her another half turn.

"Add some weight!" Christine shouted. "Put Acomita inside!"

Acomita was only too glad to get out of the storm. I rolled the tent back with Selene protesting loudly at being tumbled yet again and staked it down with long juniper sticks from our firewood pile. The wind was still strong enough to be pressing both tents nearly to the ground, but they held.

The wind died off sometime before dawn, the air settling into a deathlike stillness. I finally drifted into a restless, dream-plagued sleep.

▽ ▽ ▽

We emerged in the dawn light covered with dust, our eyes and lips rimmed with crust. The sand around our camp had been scoured by the wind, leaving a clean, ribbed surface. Navajo Mountain loomed behind us, pink in the light of morning, a tatter of snow still wedged into a high ravine on its face. I could feel the press of solar radiation on my cheek; it was going to be a hot day.

I fed the horses the last of our hay while Christine got breakfast. When I came back I found her examining a strange pattern of tracks around the camp. Between the time the wind stopped and dawn, dozens of some kind of creature had emerged, leaving a precise, almost machine-like pattern. Some of the tracks were nearly two inches wide.

"What could they be?" Christine asked.

"Kangaroo rats," I said confidently.

Christine looked dubious. "Rats? I wonder what in the world they find to eat out here."

"*Rats?*" said Selene. "There're *rats* out here? Geez!" She started tugging on her boots, looking very put out.

Frank appeared at the edge of camp. He was riding a blue roan Indian pony, unshod and ragged-looking. His saddle was three-quarter rigged, with bucking rolls and a high cantle, the tooling almost burnished off. In the daylight I could see him for the first time. He had a round, quiet face and was wearing a black shirt, battered cowboy hat, and a pair of old boots. There was a lonely, shy look in his eyes, and when he got off the horse he walked over slowly and painfully, troubled by an infirmity.

He was traveling light. An old Mexican serape was rolled and tied behind the cantle, and a small canvas sack of food dangled from the horn. That was it; no canteen, slicker, bedroll, or tent. I couldn't help comparing it to our quarter-ton pile of equipment and provisions.

We shared our breakfast and coffee with him. He squatted by the fire, cradling his cup.

"What're these tracks everywhere?" Christine asked, pointing at the rat tracks.

A small smile invaded Frank's inscrutable face.

"Scorpions," he said.

"What? All of them? *Scorpions?*"

Frank nodded. "They come out before dawn. Looking for food."

Christine looked at me. "Kangaroo rats!" Then she glanced over at Selene, sitting off by herself reading her book. "Perhaps," she mumbled, "we shouldn't mention the, ah, scorpions to her."

We packed up camp. When I tipped our tent up to shake out the sand, there I found clinging to the bottom not the nest of scorpions I had been expecting, but a fat, glossy black widow spider, knitting the air with her fangs. I decided not to say anything about that, either.

▽ ▽ ▽

When it was time to go, Frank swung up on his horse easily, and once in the saddle all signs of his infirmity vanished. He was a beautiful rider, with a light, balanced seat.

With much fussing and grumbling Selene climbed aboard her horse.

"Are we all set?" I asked cheerfully.

Selene scrunched up her brow with displeasure.

We reined our horses around to the east, toward the rising sun, and set off on the mythical trail of *Naayéé' neizghání*, the Slayer of the Alien Gods.

Chapter 5

ANASAZI FIGURE
—ANTELOPE POINT, CANYON
DE CHELLY

*North America
ca. 15,000 B.C. to A.D.
1492*

One ear of corn was yellow. The other ear was white. Each
ear was completely covered at the end with grains, just as
the sacred ears of corn are covered in our own world now.

Proceeding silently, the gods laid one buckskin on the
ground, careful that its head faced the west. Upon this skin
they placed the two ears of corn, being just as careful that
the tips of each pointed east. Over the corn they spread the
other buckskin, making sure that its head faced east.

Under the white ear they put the feather of a white
eagle.

And under the yellow ear they put the feather of a
yellow eagle . . .

Then from the east Nílch'i łigai the White Wind blew
between the buckskins. And while the wind thus blew, each
of the Holy People came and walked four times around the
objects they had placed so carefully on the ground.

*As they walked, the eagle feathers, whose tips protruded
slightly from between the two buckskins, moved slightly.*
Just slightly.
*So that only those who watched carefully were able to
notice.*
*And when the Holy People had finished walking, they
lifted the topmost buckskin.*
And lo! the ears of corn had disappeared.
In their place there lay a man and there lay a woman.

—THE CREATION OF FIRST MAN AND FIRST WOMAN, FROM
THE *DINÉ BAHANE'*[2]

Navaho or Navajo Indians: North American Indians
Whose language belongs to the Athabascan branch
Of the Nadene linguistic stock.
A migration from the North to the Southwest is
thought to have occurred
In the past
Because
Of an affiliation with
Northern Athabascan speakers;
The Navaho settled among the Pueblo and
Also
Assimilated with the Shoshone and the Yuma
Both physically and culturally.

—A *BILAGÁANA* POEM ABOUT THE HISTORY OF THE NAVAJO[3]

There are two histories of the Navajo people. One is the history
they give themselves—the *Diné Bahane'*, the Creation of the People. The other is the history we have given to them. Each, on its
own level, is true.

The history of the *Bilagáana* version of the truth begins in
September 1908, in the rolling short-grass prairie of northeastern
New Mexico, on a place called the Crowfoot Ranch. Here, in an
arroyo, a black cowboy named George McJunkin discovered a
great deposit of bones of a long-extinct animal. Mixed with the
bones were spearpoints made by early man.

Up to this point, the prevailing theory held that human beings had only come to the New World in the past few thousand
years. McJunkin's discovery of what became known as Folsom
Man pushed that date back at least one hundred centuries.

Human beings probably first entered the New World during one of the great ice ages, when sea levels dropped across the world. Asia became connected to America by the Bering Land Bridge. When that happened, a population leak developed from the Old World to the New. Bands of humans moved southward along a narrow ice-free corridor, hunting and fishing, eking out an existence along a thin margin of exposed land. They may have even ventured across the great ice itself.

They found themselves in a vast new land, an untouched paradise of woolly mammoths, mastodons, sloths, prehistoric horses, and bison. They expanded southward, forming new bands, following great herds of game, living and loving and multiplying and dying, arguing and fighting and stalking off to start families and tribes in new areas. Hunger was the prime motivation for spreading. But there were other forces at work. Like the feather of the dandelion seed that evolved to catch the wind, human beings had characteristics that ensured their widest possible distribution: their contentiousness in society; their love of travel; their joy in the landscape of emptiness; their curiosity about the unknown which is religious in its force.

Within a few thousand years, or perhaps as little as a few centuries, they had reached the other end of the earth and were stopped by the southern ice. Human beings occupied the New World from Tierra del Fuego to Baffin Bay.

Sometime after the first human wave crossed the Bering Land Bridge, the sea levels rose again or the ice advanced, and the population leak was cut off. These first people had the New World to themselves.

We know very little about these first people. Because they were hunter-gatherers living in temporary camps, the archeological record is vanishingly small. Our best clue lies in language. We believe they spoke a language from Eurasia which linguists call Proto-Amerind. Linguists have pieced together this extinct language inferentially from the hundreds of languages it eventually became. So ancient is Proto-Amerind that some linguists claim to have found its ghostly roots in most of the languages spoken in Eurasia, including English. The word "milk" in English, for example, comes from the Proto-Indo-European word *melg-. This ancient root, some believe, finds a cognate in the word *maliq'a in Proto-Amerind, meaning "to suck." This word became *malq'a* in the language of the Incas: *malqi* in the language of the Hualapai Indians of the Grand Canyon; and *mülk'* in the language of the Kwakiutl Indians of Canada. Such linguistic evidence tells us that in the deep past, the ancestors of Europeans, Asians, and American Indians all shared the same language. Genetic studies have also shown that all human beings are descended from a single woman, or at most a closely knit band. Once we were all, literally, brothers and sisters. What binds us is ancient and deep; what divides us is recent and trivial.

▽ ▽ ▽

In what would become New Mexico, Amerind people lived in small bands, following herds of prehistoric bison, gathering seeds and roots, camping at intermittent lakes. These early peoples followed a simple, nomadic way of life for thousands of years.

About 1500 B.C. corn first made its appearance in the Southwest, the seeds having been traded up from Mexico. Agriculture had been invented in Mesoamerica about 7000 B.C. At that time the ancestor of corn was a tropical grass called teosinte with a seed head smaller than wheat. In one of the first examples of genetic manipulation, the Indians of Mexico altered teosinte by choosing, over many centuries, the seeds from the largest seed heads to plant. Over a period of thirty to fifty centuries, the seed head evolved from a skinny, one-inch spike with about ten seeds to a fat, eight-inch spike with thousands of seeds.

Until recently everyone assumed that the "invention" of agriculture was a natural stage in the upward progress of humanity. It was one more step in humanity's control of nature. The assumption was that farming led to better nutrition, a more stable food supply, and more leisure time for such things as art, music, writing, religion, and science. In short, the argument went, the things that we cherish in our culture today were made possible by the invention of agriculture.

Anthropologists recently discovered, to their profound surprise, that agriculture did not appear to have been a step forward. By comparing farmers to hunter-gatherers, they found that farming peoples were more poorly nourished than hunter-gatherers; that farming required child labor whereas hunting and gathering did not; that farming required an average of four to six days a week of labor while hunting and gathering required only two; that hunter-gatherers had a more varied diet and were healthier than farmers. They discovered that farming in many cases produced a *less* reliable source of food than hunting and

gathering: agriculture left its population more, not less, susceptible to famine, because farming encouraged a dense, sedentary
population. If things went bad—if there was a localized drought
or a flood, for example—a small band of hunter-gatherers could
up and move to a better locale, but a large farming community
could not. Finally, the large concentration of genetically identical crops was more susceptible to pests.

By most quality-of-life measures, agriculture was a step
backward.

In light of this, it is perhaps not surprising that hunting-
gathering peoples tended to despise their agricultural neighbors.
One thinks of the Sioux, Comanche, and Apache and their attitudes toward Pueblo Indian farmers and white sod-busters. And
finally, agriculture seems to have been adopted by tribes only
under great duress—tribes that had ruined their environment or
had to contend with population pressures caused by an alien
invasion.

The story of the expulsion related in our own Bible strangely
corroborates this unwilling descent to agriculture. The Garden
of Eden was a hunter-gatherer paradise; when Adam and Eve
were expelled, one of God's punishments was to make them toil
in the earth for their food: "In the sweat of thy face shalt thou
eat bread, till thou return unto the ground." Agriculture was not
a gift: it was a punishment.

Once agriculture came to the Southwest, the Amerind peoples began building more permanent homes and making pottery
in addition to baskets. Around 1,300 years ago their culture
started to undergo a rapid florescence. The seasonal pit house
became a circular religious chamber cut into the ground, called
a kiva. Their pottery became finer, often painted and decorated.
Their dwellings became solid houses of stone mortared with
adobe. The concentration of population led to a loss of egalitari-
anism, the development of a priesthood, a stratified society, and
possibly a ruling class.

They became the Anasazi.

Small Anasazi settlements began coalescing into larger and
larger communities which farmed bigger and bigger areas. The
population became more and more centralized. Ceremony and
religion seem to have become of increasing importance—indeed,
of *utmost* importance. While we know very little about the Anasazi, we do know they were an intensely, fanatically religious
people. This is not surprising: there is, in fact, a strong correla-

tion between farming and the development of elaborate rituals to control nature.

Eventually the Anasazi appeared to have become one unified culture centered at Chaco Canyon, embracing more than fifty thousand square miles of the Southwest. The early Anasazi communities spoke different languages and possibly had different religious and social customs—as their descendants, the Pueblo Indians, do today. Around A.D. 900 many Anasazi groups started to cooperate, and they transformed themselves, for a while, into a single culture. Agriculture and trade allowed them an almost unprecedented population density, but also left them, as we now know, more susceptible to drought and environmental changes.

▽ ▽ ▽

Around A.D. 950 the Anasazi started building the Great Houses in Chaco Canyon. The nine Great Houses of Chaco necessitated the cutting of 215,000 trees more than ten inches in diameter, all of which had to be carried by hand from the nearest stands of ponderosa pine forty miles away. They constructed with lavish care, using beautifully coursed stonework and adobe mortar. Pueblo Bonito, the largest of the Great Houses, had 650 rooms and was four stories high. Each small room required about 100,000 pounds of shaped sandstone blocks. One archeologist wrote that Pueblo Bonito would not be equaled on this continent until 1882, when the Spanish Flats apartment building was erected at the corner of 59th Street and Seventh Avenue in New York City.

The Chacoans laid out sophisticated irrigation systems on the canyon floor. They built a network of roads for hundreds of miles from the Chaco hub and erected a great religious complex at a place called Pierre's Site, ten miles north of Chaco. They built solar and astronomical observatories. They built lighthouses and signaling stations across the Southwest, allowing for rapid communication across hundreds of miles.

But the greatest engineering feat of all—and the most profound expression of Anasazi religious beliefs—was the Chaco road system, in particular the Great North Road. The Anasazi roads radiate in arrow-straight lines from Chaco Canyon and other Chaco-era ruins in the Southwest. These were not "roads" by any normal definition of the term, since the Anasazi had neither the wheel nor any beast of burden and had no need for a thirty-foot-wide, graded and surfaced road system.

The builders of these mysterious roads went to great lengths to keep them straight, cutting and filling through hills and obstacles rather than bending around them. The North Road is so straight that it departs from true north by only a few hundred yards over its entire length. And yet the builders did not have the compass or the benefit of a North Star in a precise enough northerly position.

The Anasazi lined the Great North Road with lighthouses and signaling stations, where fires built at night could be seen for miles. They also built mysterious religious shrines and small structures of unknown function. Beautiful painted pots appeared to have been deliberately smashed on the road surface. When the road was finally abandoned in the thirteenth century, it appears to have been ritually "closed" by lining it with burning brush.

Some individuals at Chaco Canyon—probably a priesthood class—accumulated tremendous wealth. Only a small number of burials have been found at Chaco, but some of these were the richest Anasazi burials ever found, the graves stuffed with exquisite pots, textiles, and thousands of pieces of shaped and carved turquoise. By the eleventh and twelfth centuries, the culture centered at Chaco Canyon encompassed an area nearly one hundred thousand square miles in extent, crisscrossed with roads and dotted with Great Houses and religious complexes. Chaco Canyon, one group of archeologists wrote, "was at the heart of a vast regional system and a community of unprecedented complexity . . ."

There were many mysteries about Chaco. Why did the Anasazi build the Chaco complex in the middle of one of the harshest deserts in their realm, where the nearest trees were forty miles away? Why did they lay out fields and irrigation systems in a highly marginal area that receives only nine inches of rainfall a year? Why in an area where game would be unusually scarce? Why in an area of freakish temperature extremes, where summertime temperatures often exceed 100 degrees Fahrenheit and wintertime temperatures can be as low as minus 38 degrees? Why in a canyon which sometimes has no more than 100 frost-free days per year, when their staple food, corn, required at least 120 frost-free days to ripen? Most important, why did Chaco culture collapse? Why did they leave?

These were among the greatest questions in American archeology. We finally think we know some of the answers. The Navajos also have long had their own answers to these questions, answers connected with their creation story. We will look at these two versions later; the comparison will be most interesting.

▽ ▽ ▽

By the middle of the twelfth century the great Anasazi experiment centered on Chaco Canyon failed, and the San Juan Basin was gradually deserted by the Anasazi. Around that time a new people drifted into the San Juan Basin, settling into the canyons and on top of the mesas vacated by the Anasazi. They hunted, lived in brush huts, and gathered seeds and roots and plants.

These people were unrelated to the Anasazi. They came from a second great migration across the Bering Land Bridge, sometime between 11,000 years ago and perhaps 5,000 years ago. These new people were very different from the Amerind peoples, both physically and in language. They spoke Proto-Na-Dene, a language that appears to be related to Georgian, Chinese, Tibetan, and Basque. It is a much younger language than Proto-Amerind and of a lower-level classification.

The Na-Dene people moved across the Bering Land Bridge, but the continent they entered had changed dramatically since human beings first arrived. It was no longer a vacuum waiting to be filled. The old problem of population pressure and resource depletion now existed across the New World. The great herds of giant bison, the prehistoric mammoths and mastodons, the horses, the giant sloths and other animals had all disappeared since humans first arrived, many probably hunted to extinction.

The Na-Dene expansion was therefore slow and confined mostly to northern Canada and Alaska. There were two exceptions to this containment. More than a thousand years ago, two groups started moving south, one down the Northwest coast to northern California, and a second down the Rocky Mountains to the Southwest. These latter people were tall and lean, barrel-chested and high-cheekboned. They were nomadic hunter-gatherers, and they probably traveled down the eastern slope of the Rocky Mountains.

They called themselves the *Diné*, a word that can be loosely translated as the People, or more specifically the Earth Surface People. The *Diné* were an unusually resourceful and adaptable group.

When, precisely, they arrived in New Mexico is unknown. It may have been as early as A.D. 700, or as late as the fourteenth century. The best estimate is about A.D. 1100, the same date that *Diné* tradition places for the emergence into this world, the Fifth World of Creation. This date is about fifty years before the abandonment of Chaco Canyon.

In the Southwest, the migration slowed and the *Diné* split into many groups, like a river flowing into a broad delta. Some ended up in eastern New Mexico and the Llano Estacado of Texas; others went farther west and filled the basin-and-range country of southern Arizona and Sonora, Mexico. Those that went east and west would become the Eastern and Western Apaches.

One group of *Diné* drifted into what would become New Mexico and settled an area around Gobernador Canyon, in the north-central part of the state. As this branch of the *Diné* expanded, they moved westward into the sagebrush plano, dry washes, and mesas of the San Juan Basin—taking over the homeland vacated by the Anasazi.

When, exactly, the *Diné* moved into the Anasazi homelands is open to question. It may have occurred while the Anasazi were still there, with a brief contact made between the departing race and the incoming race; it may have occurred after they left. Either way, there is no evidence of strife or warfare between the *Diné* and the Anasazi. Archeologists believe the *Diné* simply took advantage of the departure of the Anasazi to move in and settle.

The *Diné* saw the fresh remains of the Anasazi Great Houses, their cliff dwellings, roads, irrigation systems, and dams. Many of the rooms had been left as if the people had simply walked away. They were full of beautiful painted pottery, grinding stones, mats and weavings, sandals and spear-points and quivers full of bows and arrows, jars and granaries still full of corn and beans. Even though the houses were very fine, and many were still roofed, the *Diné* did not care to live in them. They feared these places and left them just as they were.

The *Diné* wondered mightily and long about the immense ruins of the vanished strangers that dotted the land. These ruins, to a nomadic hunter-gatherer people living in brush huts, were inconceivably advanced. So powerful an effect did these ruins exert on the minds of the *Diné* that it transformed their entire view of the world, how it was created, and their place in it. The *Diné* incorporated what they knew of the Anasazi and their ruins into their story of creation and their myths and prophecies about the end of the world.

They called these vanished people the *Anaasází*, the Ancient Enemy, and their ruins the *Anaasází bighan*, the Home of the Ancient Enemy; they were dreaded places, *bááhádzid*, places of fear and reverence.

These *Diné* became the Navajo Indians. And when *Bilagáana* the White People came and built their great civilization around the Navajo, the medicine men and singers of the tribe began to see profound and frightening parallels between the once-powerful *Anaasází*, the Ancient Enemy of the Fourth World, and the *Bilagáana*, the American rulers of the Fifth World.

This is the background of the prophecy we would hear, in bits and pieces, during our long journey into the sacred land of the Navajos. It is a prophecy that explains the mysterious disappearance of the Anasazi and, in a stunning twist, links it to the ultimate fate of America.

Chapter 6

BASKETMAKER PICTOGRAPH
POSSIBLY SHOWING
SHAMANISTIC FIGURE WITH
POWER LINES EMANATING
FROM ITS HEAD.
—*PICTOGRAPH CAVE,
CANYON DE CHELLY*

*Piute Mesa
April 28, 1992*

We set off into the brittle Utah sun. Frank rode ahead, threading his way through a sea of sand dunes anchored by a scattering of scrub. We were followed by all the dogs of Rainbow City, who trotted along after us, their long pink tongues lolling out of their mouths.

Our horses were restless after their long day in the trailer. Redbone looked at the strange landscape with interest and slung his head impatiently. The air smelled of heated sand and the stalks of dry plants, and the sky arched above us like a hot pan. I could feel a quiver of anticipation along his flanks.

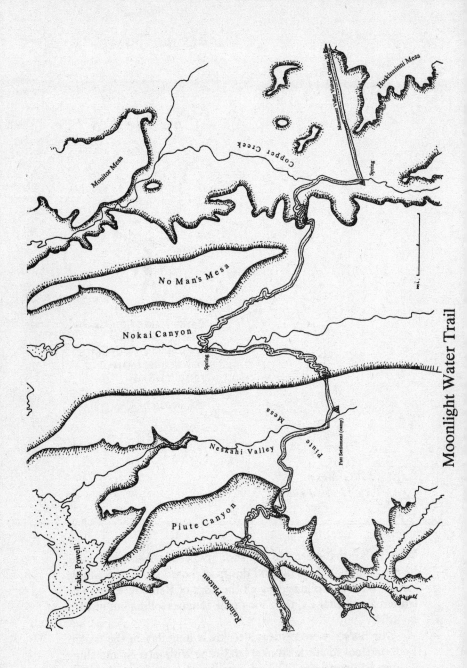

Moonlight Water Trail

I realized again how fortunate I was to have a horse like Redbone. I bought him for next to nothing from a dude ranch because he was temperamental and difficult, and even the wranglers had trouble riding him. He had no breeding and no papers, but he had a quality called *heart*—an irrepressible love of being alive. I could feel at that moment his joy in the landscape; I could see his ears perking at little sounds and his nostrils drinking in the smell of the morning. He had become, in a way, an extension of my own senses.

After a few miles of riding we passed an isolated hogan built snug against a bluff, with a corral and house trailer next to it.

"My uncle lives there," Frank said proudly. "He's a famous medicine man."

"What's his name?" I asked.

"Buck Navajo. A white man came and put him in a book."

I knew the book well, *Navajo Mountain and Rainbow Bridge Religion*. It came about as the result of an emergency among the Navajo people of the area. The waters impounded by the new Glen Canyon Dam were backing up Forbidding Canyon toward Rainbow Bridge, which lay in almost inaccessible country behind us. The bridge was deeply sacred to the Navajo people, having been the drumstick that Monster Slayer used in the first Enemy Way ceremony. The two inner forms of Rainbow Bridge were believed to generate rain. Seven Navajo medicine men and a medicine woman decided to share their knowledge with a white man named Karl Luckert to try to persuade the U.S. government to halt the rising water before it flooded under Rainbow Bridge. One of them was Buck Navajo. Luckert sent their testimony to bureaucrats in Salt Lake City, who had no idea what to do with it, and the $100 million dam stayed where it was. And now, people can drive their powerboats under Rainbow Bridge, drink beer and play music, and the Navajos no longer pray there. Since that time, there has been a severe drought in the area, which the Navajos have blamed on the desecration of Rainbow Bridge.

Frank squinted at the dust blowing along the dirt track leading to Buck Navajo's hogan.

"Not home," he said.

Another mile of riding brought us to the edge of Piute Canyon. It was over two thousand feet deep, stripped to the bone by erosion. The red sandstone cliffs plunged downward to talus slopes banded in indescribable hues of red, yellow, and green.

They reminded me of nothing more than the striped storms on the surface of Jupiter. From the rim I could see the waters of Lake Powell, shimmering at the mouth of the canyon fifteen miles away. To our far left lay the western side of the Rainbow Plateau, teased by erosion into fantastical shapes, domes, arches, and knuckles, a sandstone boneyard, and beyond that the Blue Mountains of Utah were lodged on the horizon like a fragment of broken sky.

There was a good trail winding down to the bottom of the canyon and back up the other side. We rested the horses at the bottom, where a creek ran, but the water was salty and the banks rimmed with alkali. Acomita went swimming, but the horses snorted disdainfully and turned away. The heat was intense.

We spent most of the afternoon wending our way up Piute Mesa. The mesa bore an uncanny resemblance to Manhattan Island in shape and size. It was twenty-six miles long, and varied from two to seven miles wide, with a blunt southern end and a tongue of land at the northern end. It was surrounded by cliffs, accessible at only four or five points along its perimeter. A total of nine families lived on its hundred square miles.

Piute Mesa was flat and hot. We rode through vast open areas covered with rattleweed that had burned up in the heat. We passed through groves of piñon and juniper trees and across dry waterpans laced with cracked silt, the horses' hooves crunching through the crust. The landscape had a peculiar half-silence; there were no birds, no sound of wind or rustling of grass, no distant noise from cars or planes. Yet, when we stopped our horses, I could still hear an underlying whisper, perhaps the white noise of the Earth itself.

"When was the last time it rained?" I asked Frank.

"Nothing since the snow melted," he said.

▽ ▽ ▽

Christine and I rode side by side, with Selene following but drifting behind. At one point I took Christine's hand and I heard Selene's shrill voice behind us.

"Hey! No holding hands! What about me!" She came trotting up, holding out her hand for Christine to take. We rode three abreast.

"How are you doing?" I asked Christine. We had spoken little on the long ride.

"All I know," she said, "is I want to get my butt *out* of this saddle."

"Me too!" said Selene. "But this horse is so slow and *lazy* that I'm afraid I'll never get there."

"You've got to show him you mean business," I said. "Give him a good nudge with your heels."

"I'm *trying!*" Selene cried out. "He just won't *go!*"

We were passing through some trees and I rode past a dead juniper and broke off a twig. "Try this," I said. "Just give him a tap on the butt when he doesn't respond to your heels."

We rode along, and Selene started to drift behind again. I heard a *whack* and suddenly the explosive sound of galloping hooves. She drew alongside and slowed her horse to a walk.

"Wow!" she said, laughing, her face red, her hat dangling behind her by its stampede straps. "That really *worked.*"

"Next time," I said, "just touch him ever so lightly with the stick. Just to remind him. Don't whack him for heaven's sake."

In the late afternoon, we emerged into another open area covered with red sand. On the far side stood three cottonwood trees, a cinderblock house, corrals, a mule, and two horses. A wisp of smoke curled out of the chimney. A battered pickup truck was parked in the sand nearby, and a rutted track wound its way to the south, where, over fifty miles away, it joined the closest paved road.

"We're here," Frank said.

"Yay!" cried Selene. "*Finally.*"

Frank pointed to what looked like a beehive of mud behind the house. "You want to stay in the hogan?"

"Yes!" Selene cried. "I love hogans!"

The hogan was the traditional Navajo home before the government started building HUD houses. Most Navajo families still maintain a hogan next to their house, necessary for religious ceremonies and weddings.

"You go ahead and put your horses in the corrals," Frank said, "and then you can come in and meet my family."

We rode our horses into an empty corral. Selene's horse Blaze, seeing a nice bed of soft sand and figuring his work for the day was over, decided to dump his hot scratchy burden and roll. The only problem was, his burden was Selene.

I heard a piercing scream and turned in time to see Blaze drop to his knees and flop heavily on his side. Selene jumped free at the last moment, landing in the sand unhurt. Her hat lay on the ground and her red hair was sticking out in various directions. She was furious.

"I *hate* you!" she screeched. "How *could* you, you stupid horse! I'm never getting on you again! You're slow and lazy and *stupid!*"

Christine rushed over and knelt in the sand, holding Selene in her arms, and they both broke down sobbing. I came over and put my arms around them, feeling as if a piece of ice had lodged in my gut. The accident brought home the extremity of our isolation. The nearest telephone was at least fifty miles away, and heaven only knew where the nearest hospital might be.

I helped them to their feet. Selene wiped her nose with her sleeve, threw a final dark look at Blaze and hissed, "I *hate* you."

Later Christine took my arm. "Selene was almost rolled on," she said. "She could have been killed." The tears began to course down her face again.

"Yes," I said.

"What on earth would we have done?" she whispered.

There was no real answer to the question, and I didn't offer any.

When we finally got our horses settled, Frank took us in to meet his family. It was a solemn and formal occasion; visitors to the Fatt house were extremely rare. We stepped through the doorway. There was the smell of coffee, dust, and old fabric. Slowly the dark interior emerged into view. A pail of drinking water, cool and still, sat on a countertop. Several people were gathered around the kitchen table, drinking Cokes and eating fry bread: Frank's brother and sister-in-law, Frank's mother and his uncle.

We said hello and shook hands all around. Frank then brought us into another room to meet his ninety-five-year-old grandmother. She was sitting on a bed, a small woman with a bent back. A shawl was draped around her shoulders and she wore a number of heavy turquoise rings. She looked up at us with curious black eyes that gleamed out of an impossibly wrinkled face.

Frank spoke to her in Navajo while she listened, motionless.

"This is my grandmother," Frank finally said, with great respect.

"*Yá'át'ééh,*" I said, shaking her hand formally and stepping back.

Christine greeted her and then Selene stepped forward. "*Yá'át'ééh,*" she said, holding the old woman's hand for a moment. The grandmother laid her other hand on Selene's and held it warmly, her face breaking into a rumpled smile. She said something softly in Navajo.

"She says you have a nice daughter," Frank said.

There was little grass on the mesa top; the Fatt horses were tough little mustangs that survived by living free, wandering far and wide looking for the odd clump of chamisa, winterfat, or Indian ricegrass. They showed up at the corrals once in a while to get a mouthful of oats.

I asked Frank where we might get some hay for our horses. He explained that the previous winter four feet of snow had fallen on Piute Mesa. The government had no way of contacting the people there to see if they were still alive, so they had flown over from time to time with helicopters, dropping hay and food. Frank thought that maybe one of his neighbors had saved a few bales from that airlift.

We got in the pickup truck and lurched and scraped over an absurd road to his nearest neighbor, an old woman who lived three miles to the south. She led us into a dark hogan, where three treasured bales of alfalfa were stacked in the gloom. It was the best government alfalfa, leafy, packed with crushed purple flowers.

The old woman reached down to one of the bales, screwed out a fistful, rubbed it in her palm, smelled it, and offered it to me. I inhaled the thick green fragrance of a newly mown field. A wave of homesickness swept over me.

I nodded. "Wonderful."

Frank conducted all negotiations in Navajo, as the woman spoke no English. I bought two bales at four dollars each, less than I would have paid in Durango, but with murmurs and apologies from Frank about his failure to obtain a better price.

When we had loaded the hay I took the woman's hand. "*Ahzsheh'eh,*" I said, attempting one of the most difficult phrases to pronounce in Navajo: "thank you."

She looked at me blankly, thinking I was speaking English, and then turned to Frank for a translation.

▽ ▽ ▽

Later that evening we sat outside the Fatts' house and watched the setting sun turn the sand the color of hot copper. Frank had a long discussion in Navajo with his uncle about the Moonlight Water Trail ahead. It was a discussion punctuated with much pointing, nodding, gesturing, and scowling. Then there was silence.

Finally Frank said, "The trail going down the canyon is bad."

"How so?" I asked.

Frank shrugged. "Have to unpack your horses and carry everything down."

"How far down?" I asked.

The uncle turned to Frank. "Don't just sit there. Take them out for a look!"

▽ ▽ ▽

The edge of Nokai Canyon was only a quarter mile away. The abyss came on us abruptly, a yawning blue space beyond the junipers. It was an ancient's vision of the edge of the world, looking as if the earth itself had been cleaved away. While we stood on the rim, a pair of crows rode an air current up past the edge, dipped, and glided back into the gloomy depths. From their vantage point one hundred feet from us, the earth was nearly half a mile below.

The Moonlight Water Trail tipped off the cliff and plunged down through a sheer wall of rock. I peered over the edge. A dry wash, sheeted with alkali, threaded among boulders along the bottom. I could see the crows a thousand feet below us, still spiraling lazily to the bottom. The silence was profound, broken only by the scratching of an insect somewhere in the dry rocks.

The canyon had no opposite rim, providing a breathtaking view that encompassed four states. I later calculated that we could see an area of more than twenty thousand square miles, a good portion of the *Diné Bikeyah*.

On our left, about five miles away, rose up a great tableland called No Mans Mesa, nine miles long, barricaded on all sides by merciless cliffs. Beyond that, the land dropped another thousand feet to a plain dotted with stone megaliths—the western edge of Monument Valley. The distorted perspective of the desert rendered these thousand-foot pillars of rock—some four miles broad—into mere stubs on the earth. They looked so close, so exquisitely chiseled in the evening light, that it almost seemed as if we could reach out and caress them. In the extreme distance, nearly 150 miles away, I could see the San Juan Mountains of Colorado, with a faint crestline of snow. To our north, beyond Lake Powell, the land turned into a wrinkled red blanket, a series of formations known by such evocative names as Waterpocket Fold, Nokai Dome, Red House Cliffs, and Whirlwind Draw.

It did not look like a landscape of this Earth. In these thousands of square miles there was no sign of human life: there was not a road, a footprint, a wisp of smoke, or even a gleam of light in the gathering darkness. It was a stony land, populated only by crows and insects.

The view reminded me powerfully of the First World as described in the Navajo creation story. It was a gloomy, reddish world. There were place names in the First World that seemed curiously apt: the House Made of the Red Mountain, the House of Red Rocks, A Big Amount of Water Coming Out, Among Aromatic Sumac.

Of this First World, the Navajo creation tells us that only insects lived there. The story reads:

> *Dark ants lived there. Red ants lived there. Dragonflies lived there. Yellow beetles lived there. Hard beetles lived there. Stone-carrier beetles lived there . . .*[4]

These were the People of the Wind, the insects that came drifting out of the sky after the union of darkness with darkness. And it seemed to me, looking off the rim of Piute Mesa, that this could still be their world, not ours.

The story of Monster Slayer takes place late in the creation, in the Fifth World, our world.[5] Before the birth of Monster Slayer, there were four previous worlds, each one inhabited in succession by the People of the Wind. It was events in these previous worlds that led to the Fifth World becoming out of balance, and overrun with alien gods. To understand Monster Slayer's quest, we must know what happened before.

The People of the Wind were part human and part insect. They crept into the ground as the cold of night settled across the land, and reappeared when the sun rose, milling about aimlessly, unintelligent and easily excited. They were unformed morally and physically. They had the power of speech, but they were disorderly and held meetings where they quarreled and shouted all night long, unable to make decisions. They were ugly and unclean. They had no morals and committed incest and adultery and practiced witchcraft.

The four chiefs of the First World objected to their disorderly behavior and rose up out of the four directions, commanding them to leave. When the People of the Wind were unable to agree on where to go, the four chiefs destroyed the First World with a great flood.

The People of the Wind flew upward and found a hole in the dome of the sky. They entered the Second World. But they had learned nothing and were expelled from the Second World, and again from the Third World. In each of these worlds, the insect people met a race of other beings who initially took them in and helped them. Each time the insect people abused their hospitality and were commanded to leave. The story is thought to be an allegory of the migration of the Navajos from their Alaskan home to the Southwest.

When the People of the Wind emerged into the Fourth World from a hole in the ground, they found themselves on a vast plain, barren and lifeless, encircled by four towering snow-covered peaks. They sent scouting parties in four directions to explore it. Two of the scouts saw nothing. One of them saw tracks in the sand that looked like those of a deer and a turkey. The scouts who came back from the north, however, found a strange race of people who lived in large stone houses and cut their hair straight in front. They grew things in the soil and knew how to irrigate. They were called the *Kiis'áanii*, the People Who Live in Upright Houses. The description of these people indicates that they were either the Anasazi or their immediate Pueblo Indian descendants.

The People of the Wind made friends with the Upright House People and settled down in the Fourth World. From them they received seeds and learned how to farm.[6] They tried not to misbehave and ruin this hospitable new world for themselves.

The four Talking Gods, however, were not satisfied with the People of the Wind; they were ugly and unintelligent. The gods wanted to transform them into something else. And so the four gods came together and undertook a great ceremony to create human life in the Fourth World.

The People of the Wind gathered to watch. The Talking Gods arranged themselves in a circle and laid a buckskin on the ground. On this skin they placed two ears of corn, a white ear and a yellow ear, each facing east. Under each ear they placed an eagle feather, and they covered them up with a second buckskin. They stood back. *Nłch'i*, the Wind, the invisible life force, entered between the buckskins. There was a faint movement. They waited a moment more, and then lifted the top buckskin. The Wind had transformed the yellow ear of corn into a woman, and the white ear into a man.

The creation story explains how this happened: "It was the wind that had given them life; the very wind that gives us our breath as we go about our daily affairs here in the world we ourselves live in.

"When this wind ceases to blow inside of us, we become speechless. Then we die.

"In the skin at the tips of our fingers we can see the trail of that life-giving wind.

"Look carefully at your own fingertips.

"There you will see where the wind blew when it created your most ancient ancestors out of two ears of corn, it is said."[7]

They were named *Ałtsé hastiin* and *Ałtsé asdzáá*, First Man and First Woman.

Chapter 7

BISON
—NEWSPAPER ROCK,
CANYON DE CHELLY

Nokai Canyon
Hoskinninni Mesa
April 29, 1992

Mountain Darkness, Darkness by which the body is renewed,
By means of Dark Cloud, by which the body is renewed.
The one who arises with Dark Cloud, Naatsis'áán!
Arise to protect me,
With lightning from the top of your head, arise to protect me!
I have survived! I have survived!
All of us have survived! All of us have survived!
I have survived for you! I have survived for you!
For many more years! For many more years!

—Part of a prayer to *Naatsis'áán* (Navajo Mountain),
thanking it for protection against Kit Carson and his
soldiers, who came to take the Navajos to Fort Sumner
in 1863[8]

Christine and I stood silently on the rim of Nokai Canyon watching the light die. I thought of that mythic time when Monster Slayer perhaps stood here, looking out over an Earth crawling with alien gods, an Earth out of balance.

Finally I roused myself. "I'd like to take a look at this trail," I said.

We scrambled down through the notch. The Moonlight Water Trail had been hacked into the cliff itself, descending so steeply that a staircase of logs had been laid down it. The trail was too narrow even for a mounted horse, let alone a packed horse.

We climbed back up and Frank and his uncle had another conference at the edge of the cliff, the uncle jabbing his fingers into the distance.

"My uncle says the trail gets worse farther on," Frank said.

"Worse than this?" I asked incredulously.

Frank nodded.

The uncle came over, bowlegged, grinning and rubbing his chest. "Long time ago, we go to Oljeto Trading Post this way." He gestured carelessly over the cliff. "Then we pack our stuff back. We not use this trail in thirty years. So it get pretty bad, but you do okay. Don't worry, you do okay!"

We returned to the Fatt settlement in silence.

▽ ▽ ▽

The hogan we were staying in sat behind the house. It was a style common only to this part of the reservation. The structure was made of adzed logs, stacked up in eight walls and then corbeled into a vaulted ceiling. The outside was completely plastered in dried mud, making it look like a big dome of earth pushing out of the ground. It had no windows. A stack of ripped mattresses lay against one wall, and there was the usual Navajo stove in the center, a fifty-five-gallon drum cut in half with a stovepipe running out through a hole in the roof. The interior was cool and smelled of old smoke, clay, and herbs.

We dug a firepit outside, not wanting to destroy the coolness of the hogan, and cooked dinner. The evening twilight was immensely quiet, broken only by an occasional bout of loud existential braying from the mule. The sand was soft and the horse blankets made a nice, if somewhat fragrant, dinner table.

The wind blew again that night. With every gust, I could

feel a gentle rain of dust sifting down through the roof timbers and settling on my face. I then dreamed about falling through space, horses, saddles, people, turning slowly in the rushing wind, falling down into the reddish gloom of a canyon.

▽ ▽ ▽

The next morning, we packed the horses and set off. We had not gone a hundred yards from the hogan when Roscoe, the horse I was riding, grunted and pitched me into the hot sky. I landed in a pile of soft sand, and when I sat up, I found Frank and his uncle looking at me with amusement; getting bucked off a horse is about the most embarrassing thing that can happen to a Navajo.

"So," Frank said, while I dusted myself off. "You gonna put that in your book, that you got bucked off?"

"Why," I said, "I'll say that when my horse started bucking I quickly and expertly dismounted."

Frank laughed. The uncle said, "You not even last your eight seconds."

I climbed back on the horse, feeling foolish. It had been my fault; in a moment of inattention I had allowed the lead rope to become wedged up under Roscoe's tail.

At the rim we tied up the horses and started to unpack them. Frank and I began carrying the four hundred pounds of gear down the narrow trail. Christine sent Selene ahead on foot, so she wouldn't be near any accident that might occur. We saw her little figure winding down the switchbacks. Far below us she stopped and sat down on a rock and started playing her Gameboy. Frank's uncle returned to the hogan.

"Go farther!" Christine shouted.

"What's wrong with here!" Selene cried. "I don't want to go any farther!"

"You're right underneath us, a horse might fall on you!" Christine said.

"Oh," said Selene, and continued down the trail until she had disappeared.

The unpacking and carrying down of the loads was extremely tedious. We found a wider place in the trail where we could repack the horses, and piled everything there. Frank and I then brought down the horses in relays, two at a time. Since there was no place to tie them on the trail, Christine held their lead ropes while we went to get the next set. We had gotten all but two horses down when we heard a shout from Christine. Brazos had decided to turn around and force his way back up. He started pushing his way past Redbone on the inside and shoved him toward the cliff, and Redbone heaved back, his feet scrabbling and teetering at the edge. Christine was frantically trying to hold the lead ropes.

"Help!" she shouted. "These horses are going to kill themselves! I can't hold them all!"

"Just let them go!" I cried while Frank and I scrambled down the trail. "Drop the ropes and get the hell away!"

Once free, all the horses decided that going back up was a capital idea. They crowded up the trail, trying to push past each other, biting and laying their ears back. Frank and I intercepted them and with much commotion got them turned around.

Then it came time to repack on the narrow trail. The trail was still too narrow to turn a horse sideways, so I found myself in the unpleasant position of packing the outside of the horse while balanced on the edge of the cliff. As I packed Brazos, the brute began prancing and I found myself being jerked about. I clung to the sawbuck of the packsaddle, thinking that if the horse shoved me off I could hang on. Or at the least, I thought grimly, I'd take the brute with me when I go.

We caught up with Selene a mile down the trail, sitting in the shade of an enormous split rock, singing softly to herself and playing her Gameboy.

"Are you all right?" Christine asked.

"Sure," she said. "What took so long?"

"Ugh," said Christine. "Those *awful* horses."

"That does it," I said. "As soon as we get home I'm sending Brazos to the knackers."

Selene looked at us curiously. "Wow," she said. "You guys are in a *bad* mood."

"Oh be quiet," said Christine.

▽ ▽ ▽

Once past the rimrock we picked our way down a nasty scree slope. The canyon was hot and lifeless. Orange rocks the size of houses, spalled from the upper walls of the canyon, lay tumbled about. The wash at the bottom was dry and white with salt, and curtains of alkali dust whirled upward with each gust of wind. No Mans Mesa rose ahead of us, an island of rock.

"Is there a way up?" I asked Frank.

"Yes," he said, "but it would kill your horses. Only the best horses can get up there."

"What's it like on top?" Selene asked.

"It's mostly sand dunes and some junipers. Some wild horses live up there, I don't really know how. There's a few seeps and some potholes that collect water."

Frank led us to a spring deep in Nokai Canyon. It was buried among boulders at a narrow slot in the canyon, and there was room for only one horse at a time. The water oozed out from under a rock, making a pool of mud. The horses refused to drink; the water was too alkaline.

"Horse got to be pretty thirsty to drink this water," Frank said.

"How far is the next water?"

"In the next canyon. We'll camp there tonight. It's salt, like this, but by then maybe they'll be ready to drink."

We followed a faint burro trail that wound out of Nokai Canyon and followed a benchland along the base of No Mans Mesa. Soon we could see five burros in the distance, watching us with erect ears. As we approached they wheeled about and ran off on stubby legs.

"We used to catch them burros," Frank said. "Break and sell them for fifty dollars."

"How on earth do you catch them?" Christine asked.

"With a tame burro and horses. There's a trick. Those burros run but they never leave their trails. So you know where they're going to go and you can set someone up ahead on a horse with a lasso."

"What's the tame burro for?"

"He calms them down, then acts as the lead when we take them back."

We continued to ride in the silent heat, the horses' hooves clopping on the slickrock. The boulders lying about were growing long blue shadows; it was getting late. Now and then a lizard shot away into the brush, like a bullet ricocheting off the ground. Soon, blue sky loomed up beyond a row of dead junipers, and we came to the edge of another cliff overlooking the far western edge of Monument Valley. Over a thousand feet below us a sand plain stretched eastward and disappeared around the darkening curve of the earth. The sandstone monoliths were closer now, rising straight and clean out of the plain, a skirt of talus around each base. They stood quietly in the late yellow light, the erosional stumps of a savage, fossilized desert of the Permian Age. They had a dignity born of utter indifference. I wondered how long they had been there, scoured by wind and fractured by ice, shrinking grain by grain, flake by flake, disintegrating into the sand that once formed them.

Frank pointed to the butte closest to us, a large mesa about five miles broad. It rose abruptly from the desert floor like a ruined palace.

"That's Hoskinninni Mesa," he said. "That mesa was named after my grandfather, *Hashkéniinii*."

"Wow," said Selene. "He must have been important."

"He was a great chief. When Kit Carson came to get the Navajos to take them to Fort Sumner, *Hashkéniinii* escaped with his people along this trail we're riding on. They hid behind Navajo Mountain, and the mountain protected them. The soldiers followed them to right down there, at the base of this cliff. But they turned around because it was too rough. They didn't dare go any farther. That was why my ancestors didn't go down there to Fort Sumner with the rest of the Navajos."

"What does the name *Hashkéniinii* mean?" I asked.

"That name means Passing Out Anger or Giving Out Anger."

"What does *that* mean?" Selene asked.

"He was good at getting everyone ready to go to war."

We dismounted and tied up our horses for a short rest.

"I'm hungry," Selene said. "And I'm thirsty but the water in my canteen is too *hot* to drink."

"Have some nuts," I said.

"Doug, you *know* I don't *like* nuts."

"Have some of your candy, then."

Selene extracted a fistful of candies from her saddlebags. "Anybody want some?"

We all took a candy. I usually disliked hard candy, but this time the sweetness filled my mouth and felt utterly delicious. We were all thirsty: you cannot seem to quench a thirst with hot water.

"I think you're a very brave girl," Christine said, hugging Selene.

"What's so brave?" Selene asked grumpily.

"Going on this trip," she said.

"You *made* me. That's not brave."

"Yes it is," I said. "You've been so cheerful, a great traveling companion."

"I just want to get this *over* with," Selene said crossly, "and get home and see my friends again."

Frank was walking here and there along the edge of the cliff, gingerly peering over and frowning.

"You see the trail?" I asked.

"It's around here somewhere," Frank said.

I finally worked up the courage to look over, but I could see no conceivable route down.

"Here it is," Frank called out.

It was a gully cut sideways into the cliff, pitched at a good thirty-degree angle. I suggested hopefully that Frank might be mistaken. We decided to climb a ways down it.

"This is definitely it," Frank insisted. "Not so good."

The trail was not as narrow as the Nokai Canyon trail, and we would not have to unpack our horses. It was, however, steeper and more dangerous, nothing but huge boulders and sliding cobbles lying on top of rotten, canted slickrock.

"Is this really the only way down?"

"Yes," he said.

"Surely there *must* be another route somewhere."

"Marsh Pass."

"How far is that?"

Frank poked his chin southward. "Forty, fifty miles."

We climbed back up.

"How does the trail look?" Christine asked.

"Ask me at the bottom," I said, feeling a certain queasiness in my stomach. There was no turning back: we had to get to water, and the water was down there, at the base of Hoskinninni Mesa.

There was a short silence.

"You want to rest longer?" Frank asked.

Christine jerked her lead-rope knot free and pulled her horse around.

"Hell no," she said. "Let's get this over with."

I thought, I'm marrying a woman who has far more courage than I do.

She looked at me. "Well? Are we going?"

"Sure," I said weakly. I remembered my pistol, foolishly

packed away in the bottom of one of the panniers. I hoped we wouldn't need it to put down a horse.

We had six horses and three people to lead them. The trail was too rugged to tie the horses together, so we each took the lead rope of one horse and drove a second horse in front. Again we sent Selene ahead with her Gameboy.

Right away, the horses balked at the lip of the cliff and we had to drag them down by their leads, one at a time, while whipping their rumps. Their flanks trembled, and they clattered among the rocks, dislodging boulders off the edge. The echoes of the bouncing rocks came up from below, and I could smell the gunpowdery scent of sandstone pulverized by horseshoe iron. What we were asking of the horses was at the very limits of their ability. I began to feel sick; there seemed to me an excellent chance we would hurt one of our horses. Even Frank's horse, who grew up in this country, was having serious trouble.

To make things worse, the sun was setting fast.

Here and there, small landslides had torn parts of the trail away. Christine and I rolled boulders around, trying to make crude stairs. In places the horses had to jump, landing on a ledge below without carrying themselves over. Nobody said a word. Acomita came creeping down the trail far behind us, tail clamped between her legs, whining with fear.

We inched our way down the cliff with maddening slowness, while the sun sank behind the rim. Selene stayed far ahead, occasionally holding a horse while we went back to get the others. She was quiet and calm, as if nothing out of the ordinary were going on.

It was soon six o'clock.

About halfway down we came to a place where an entire piece of the trail was gone, having slid down to the valley floor. Christine and I looked at each other.

"What do you think?" Christine said. "Is this it? Can we go on?"

"We have to go on," I said. "If we turn around now, we won't get back up to the top before dark. We'll be stuck here all night with no water and six frightened, wide-awake horses."

"In that case," she said, "I guess we better get to work."

We began moving stones around and prying pieces of rock out of the side of the slope, trying to make a series of footholds.

In fifteen minutes we had something that faintly resembled a narrow bridge across the gap.

Each horse then had to be forced across, with one person dragging him by the lead rope while another went behind, prodding, whipping, and cursing. The sweat rolled off their flanks and their bits were flecked with foam. I hated to treat horses like this, but only the most extreme measures would make them go. There was no alternative.

By seven-thirty, the shadow of the earth had risen in the east. The buttes on the plain below us blossomed crimson in the dying light and suddenly went dark. We continued on in the half-light, moving slowly and letting the horses pick their own way as much as possible. In another twenty minutes we struggled around one last switchback and saw the trail drop down and level out. We had reached the bottom.

We rested while I examined the horses' feet and legs. They had some superficial cuts from sharp rocks, but none of the horses had injured itself or thrown a shoe. It seemed a miracle. I went over and put my arms around Christine and Selene. Tears came into my eyes.

"I can't believe how brave you both are," I said.

Christine laughed. "Nothing," she said, "I mean *nothing* frightened me more than the look on your face at the top of the cliff." She gave me a kiss.

"Get *out* of here, Doug," said Selene, wriggling out of my embrace. "That wasn't so bad. That was *easy*. Piece of cake." She grubbed a piece of candy out of her jeans; there was a rustle of wrapper and she popped it in her mouth. "When's dinner?"

"We still got a ways to go," Frank said quietly.

The air filled with a mysterious twilight that came from nowhere and everywhere at once, like light trapped inside water. Hoskinninni Mesa, three miles away, had become invisible against the roseate sky. The wind suddenly brought a scent of cool earth.

"The water is down there," he said, pointing across the empty desert. "Maybe three miles."

We arrived in the dark. The water seeped out of an embankment, making a slick of alkali mud for a hundred yards down a dry wash. It had a sharp bitter smell of sulfur and copper. The horses became nearly uncontrollable at the sight of water, but they drank fussily, skimming the water with their muzzles, razzing air through their nostrils in frustration, prancing and pawing about in the muck.

We had just enough water in our canteens for dinner, with a small amount left over for drinking the next day. While preparing dinner I carelessly spilled two quarts of it, and we all looked on in stunned silence as the thirsty sand sucked it down.

"Where's the next water?" I asked Frank.

"There isn't any till Goulding's."

Goulding's Lodge and Trading Post was over twenty miles away.

After dinner, we sat around the dying fire. A single cricket chirruped for a while in the darkness, a cheerful voice holding out against the monumental silence of the night. Frank rolled himself in the serape, using his saddle as a pillow. We crawled into our sleeping bags and watched the galactic arm, a cloudy rubble of light, slowly rise over Hoskinninni Mesa.

Chapter 8

REVERSED SPIRAL
—FAJADA BUTTE, CHACO
CANYON

Nokai Canyon
Hoskinninni Mesa
April 30, 1992

Of it he is thinking, he is thinking.
Long ago of it he is thinking.
Of how Earth will come into being he is thinking.
Of how long life, how happiness will come into being he is
thinking.
Of how sky is to come into being he is thinking.
Of how darkness will come into being he is thinking.
Of how dawn will come into being he is thinking.
Of how evening twilight will come into being he is thinking.
Of how yellow corn will come into being he is thinking.
Of how pollen will come into being he is thinking.
Of dark moss dew he is thinking, of horses he is thinking.
Of how everything will increase without decreasing he is
thinking.

—FIRST MAN PONDERING THE CREATION OF THE EARTH[9]

First Man and First Woman were not human beings as we know
them today. They were the spiritual ancestors of human beings,
a people with both supernatural powers and human failings.

In the Fourth World, the First People received seeds and corn from the *Kiis'áanii*, the People Who Live in Upright Houses, and became a farming people themselves. For a while they lived well. More people were born and soon there was a village of First People on a shore of a river near the great eastern mountain, which they called Horizontal Black Belt. First Man taught the people the names of the other three mountains of the Fourth World: the mountain in the south was called Blue Bead; in the west, the mountain was named Light Always Glitters on Top; and in the north, Big Mountain Sheep.

▽ ▽ ▽

Life was good in the Fourth World. First Man became a great hunter and as a result First Woman grew very fat. One day First Man brought home a fine deer. His wife boiled it and they ate a hearty meal. Then she wiped her greasy hands, belched, and spoke loudly: "Thank you *shijóózh* my vagina," she said. "Thank you for that delicious dinner."

First Man was surprised and a little irritated to hear this. He asked her why she would say such a thing, when it was he who had hunted and killed the deer.

First Woman coolly replied, "In a manner of speaking it is *jóósh* the vagina who hunts," and she added, "You lazy men would do nothing around here were it not for *jóósh*. In truth, *jóósh* the vagina does all the work around here."[10]

First Man was furious. He "jumped across the fire," and in the morning gathered the men of the village together. They quarreled fiercely with the women and the sexes decided to separate. The men took all their tools and weapons, built a raft, and crossed the river to set up a new village on the other side. The women watched the men go, laughing and hurling taunts and insults.

▽ ▽ ▽

The story, despite its humor, tells a lesson of deadly seriousness. By splitting up in anger, First Man and First Woman disrupted a quality fundamental to the world. The Navajos call this quality *hózhó*. The word has no equivalent in English; it means a state of being that is balanced, beautiful, happy, and orderly. Applied to human beings, it is (as one translator defined it) a state of "continual good health, harmony, peace, beauty, good fortune, balance, and positive events in the lives of self and relatives."

The central idea in the Navajo creation story is the gradual attainment of *hózhó* by human beings and the Earth itself.

As our Judeo-Christian world is divided into good and evil, the Navajo world is divided into *hózhó* and disorder. The harmonious relationship between First Man and First Woman is central to this idea. It is a relationship patterned on the very male-female forces that created the universe. Their marriage, commanded by the gods, is the living manifestation of *hózhó*. When First Man and First Woman separate, they disrupt *hózhó* and throw the world out of balance. As a result, the entire world would feel the evil effects of their estrangement.

▽ ▽ ▽

For a while after the separation occurred, both men and women were in high spirits. That winter, the women had plenty of food. "They worked and they ate," the creation story tells us. "They sang songs and they told stories. Often they came down to the bank of the river where the men could hear them and see them. And there they taunted them.

"One of them would pull her sheath over her head and shake her bare body. Another would do likewise; then she would turn her back toward the men, and bend forward, and wiggle her buttocks.

" 'Hey you men,' called yet another meanwhile. 'Look over here! Look at that!'

" 'Don't you see what you're missing?' shouted still another. . . .

"They used their bodies to tempt the men until they were sure that the men longed for them as much as they longed for the men."[11]

A year went by. The women planted large fields, but they did not know how to make the tools to hoe and weed and harvest the crops. Their crops failed. Some of the women became overcome with loneliness and tried to swim the river and were swept away to their deaths. Others began to starve. The men likewise suffered.

By the end of the fourth year, both men and women became desperate and did many unnatural things. Disorder bred more disorder. They longed for each other so much that "members of both sexes indulged in the practice of masturbation." The women satisfied themselves with stones, peeled cactuses, horns, and bone, while the men used mud and the flesh of slain animals. They lived lives of sterility, and no children were born.

The men and women finally realized the seriousness of their mistake. They came to understand that life could not continue like this; that male could not exist without female and vice versa. Living without each other was unnatural and disorderly. The men and the women reunited.

But the damage had been done: *hózhó* had been disrupted, and terrible consequences would result. For the women were pregnant from self-abuse, and they carried within the seeds of destruction of the human race. [12]

▽ ▽ ▽

Soon, a great flood destroyed the Fourth World, and the people and animals fled up a tall reed, where they found another hole in the sky and emerged into the Fifth World, the present-day world. The *Kiis'áanii* came along as well, carrying with them the seeds of the corn.

The First People found themselves in an entirely new world. They had emerged high in the mountains, on an island in the middle of a lake. The Navajos call this place *Hajíínei*, Emergence Place. Today it is called Island Lake, a pristine glacial tarn in the La Plata Mountains west of Silverton, Colorado.

From their vantage point, the First People could see most of the entire Fifth World. It was not yet fully formed. There were no real mountains or strong geographical features. There were no stars, sun, or moon. The light was dim. It was not a place altogether hospitable to human beings.

But First Man and First Woman could see the possibilities of this world. They both thought long and deeply about how they could improve it, expand it, and make it beautiful. They thought how they could bring *hózhó* to the Fifth World.

They first decided to re-create the four sacred mountains of the Fourth World. Using soil taken from those four mountaintops, they rebuilt each mountain at the four cardinal points.

First they built the Sacred Mountain of the East, Horizontal Black Belt, or *Sisnaajini* in the Navajo language. Today this mountain is called Sierra Blanca in Colorado. In the south they created *Tsoodzil*, Blue Bead Mountain, which is Mount Taylor of New Mexico. As the Sacred Mountain of the West they made *Dook'o'oosłííd*, Light Always Glitters on Top, today the San Francisco Peaks of Arizona. And in the north they re-created *Dibé nitsaa*, Big Mountain Sheep, which is Hesperus Peak in Colorado.

These four mountains defined the world in which the future Navajo people were to live.

Then they decided to decorate the mountains and make them beautiful. They fastened Horizontal Black Belt to the sky with a bolt of lightning, and decorated it with a blanket of white shell, white lightning, white corn, dark thunderheads, and heavy rain. They threw a sheet of white dawn behind the mountain. And then they sang into the mountain two beings, a boy and a girl, who would enter the mountain and dwell there forever as its inner forms. The Sacred Mountain of the East became alive. They attached Blue Bead, the Sacred Mountain of the South, to the sky with a great flint knife, and decorated it with turquoise and dark mists and many different kinds of animals, and they adorned it with gray clouds and soft rain, and they threw blue sky across the mountain. They sang two gods into this mountain too, a male and a female, to dwell there forever as its inner forms. They fastened Light Always Glitters on Top, the Sacred Mountain of the West, to the sky with a sunbeam, and covered it with the yellow light of evening, and decorated it. Big Mountain Sheep, the Sacred Mountain of the North, they attached to the earth with a rainbow and covered it with the darkness of night. And they created other mountains and rivers, adorning them with life, and singing the inner forms into them.

First Woman then sang inner forms into the natural phenomena: the dawn, evening twilight, sky, darkness, fire, and water. She sang inner forms into other landmarks, hills, rock formations, springs, and rivers. And finally she sang the two inner forms into the Earth itself.

The Earth and everything in it became beautifully and vibrantly alive.

▽ ▽ ▽

From their hogan at the Emergence Place, First Man and First Woman looked about. The Earth now radiated beauty everywhere. So they set forth on a journey to the four sacred mountains and climbed each one, singing as they went. At each summit they looked at the inner beings of the mountain and saw that they were very beautiful. And from the summits they looked out over the *Diné Bikeyah*, the land in which the future

Navajo people would live, and they could see it was a world of unsurpassed beauty, breathtakingly lovely.

Their work was not yet finished. The light on the Earth was feeble, so First Man and First Woman created the sun. They shaped it from a disk of quartz crystal, and they inlaid deep blue turquoises around the rim. Beyond that they placed rays of red rain, then bars of zigzag lightning. They fashioned the moon out of rock-star mica, and they bordered it with white shell, and placed sheet lightning on its face, and they sprinkled it with water until it glistened. A young man was placed inside the sun, and an old man inside the moon.

The Earth and sky were still small. The First People prayed to the winds and were able to stretch the Earth and make it bigger. They raised the sky higher up and placed it upon the four sacred mountains and on several towering sky pillars set about the landscape.

First Man and First Woman thought the night sky was too dark when the moon had set. So they gathered up pieces of mica, spread them on a blanket, and began placing them in the sky in an orderly way. First Man placed a star in the north that wouldn't move, so that people could find their way. Then he placed seven more pieces of mica around that, which became the Little Dipper. He worked slowly and carefully.

While First Man worked, *Ma'ii* the Coyote, who had followed the First People up from the Fourth World, slunk around the edges of the camp watching him. Coyote became impatient at First Man's slowness, and he cried out: "Never mind doing it that way! Why must I wait this long for your work to be done?" And he flung the blanket skyward and blew, and the stars flew upward and stuck all over the sky in a haphazard fashion. Some of the stars fell back to earth and became a cluster of buttes, which are today called the Sonsela (Stars Strung Out) Buttes lying across the border of Arizona and New Mexico in the Chuska Mountains.

▽ ▽ ▽

The First People set off from the Place of Emergence and began a journey across this new and beautiful world. "But they carried within them," the creation story goes, "the seeds of the ugliness and disorder caused by the unnatural separation of the sexes." The women who had abused themselves were swelling from pregnancy and would soon give birth.

On the first day of travel the small band camped at a place called White Spot on the Earth, and during the night a young woman went into labor. The baby she had was a round, misshapen creature with no head. The First People were aghast and threw the baby into a dry gulch, expecting it to die.

The baby did not die. As the years passed, it remained in that blasted gully, crawling about, growing, patiently waiting for its time of revenge against the people who had abandoned it. It called itself *Déélgééd*, the Horned Destroyer.

The people traveled on, going westward to Navajo Mountain. On its slopes, at a place called Broad Flat Area Surrounds the Rock, a woman gave birth to a headless creature whose neck tapered to a crusty point. They threw it into a crack in a cliff and sealed it up with rocks, and quickly moved on.

It also did not die. It lived on in the darkness of the cliff, its hair growing into the cracks of the rocks. Its hatred grew apace, and it waited, its primitive brain filled with hatred for the People.

As the First People traveled across the land, more women gave birth to hideously deformed babies, which were abandoned among the rocks, canyons, and plains. Even the blood and afterbirth that spilled into the ground congealed and grew and became sentient, dreaming with infinite malevolence to a time of vengeance.

And so, as the First People traveled, they unwittingly spread *Naayéé'*, the alien destroyers, across the lovely new world they had created.

▽ ▽ ▽

As the years passed, the First People had children, and those children had children, and soon the Fifth World was teeming with human life. Meanwhile, the alien gods slowly matured and began moving about. They searched out the People and began killing and devouring them. Wherever they went, they ravaged the land, leaving it naked and lifeless. The People had no defense, and fled before them, moving deeper into the remote canyons of the *Diné Bikeyah*. Again and again, their hiding places were discovered and the alien gods rooted them out and slaughtered them.

In a dozen years, only six people remained alive. They found temporary refuge in the Gobernador-Largo canyon complex eastward of Huerfano Mountain in New Mexico. There they huddled in fear, planting their crops on the canyon bottom, keeping a watch out for the *Naayée'*. The Fifth World, which had once lain before them like a land of dreams, so beautiful and full of promise, had become a blasted place, crawling with alien gods working their plan of genocide. It was a world overwhelmed by disorder, a world without *hózhó*.

One dark morning during this time, First Man arose as was customary and began praying to the new day. As the sun climbed in the east, he noticed a curious cloud settling on a nearby hill, called *Ch'óol'í'í*, or Giant-Spruce Mountain, which is today an obscure hill in a remote part of New Mexico with the name Gobernador Knob. For four days he watched the cloud grow darker and lightning flicker about the peak. Torrents of rain fell, and once in a while great double rainbows glimmered around the hill, were extinguished, and reappeared. He became very curious: something extraordinary was happening on the mountaintop.

On the fourth day he ventured out of their hiding place and began walking toward Giant-Spruce Mountain, to see what was happening. As he went, he sang a song of protection against the alien destroyers roaming the landscape:

I am Aƚtsé hastiin the First Man,
Aƚtsé hastiin the First Man am I, maker of much of the Earth.
Aƚtsé hastiin the First Man am I, and I head for Ch'óol'í'í
  the Giant Spruce Mountain, following the dark, rainy
  cloud.
I follow the lightning and head for the place where it strikes.
I follow the rainbow and head for the place where it
  touches the Earth . . .
I follow the scent of rain and head for the place
  where the lines of rain are darkest . . .
Aƚtsé hastiin is who I am, and I am climbing Ch'óol'í'í
  in pursuit of long life and happiness
  for myself and my people . . .
Here I am where the rich, warm rain drenches me,
  in pursuit of long life and happiness
  for myself and my people . . .
Long life and good fortune I attain
  for my people and for myself . . .
All around me there is long life and good fortune.[13]

At the top of the hill, First Man was astonished to hear the crying of a baby. He looked around, and suddenly the clouds parted and a shaft of glittering sunlight illuminated a little baby girl lying on the ground. He picked her up and brought her back to their camp.

To this day no one knows where she came from. Some say she was the daughter of the Sky and the Earth, or perhaps the child of Darkness and Dawn. Still others say she was the offspring of the two inner forms of the Earth itself.

They called her Changing Woman.

Chapter 9

ANASAZI PETROGLYPH
—CHACO CANYON

 Monument Valley
April 30 to May 2,
1992

The next day, with the sun on our faces, we rode eastward past Hoskinninni Mesa and through the land of tall buttes. The horses plodded across the hot sand of the desert floor, heads down, sore and tired from the previous day. Twenty miles later, in the late afternoon, we approached Goulding's Lodge. Coming out of the empty desert, we struck a paved road, the main artery to the Monument Valley Visitor Center. The road was clogged with cars. It was strange to come across a gleaming traffic jam in such an isolated desert, and for a moment I wondered if it might be people fleeing a nuclear strike or some urban conflagration.

As we rode alongside the road, a van stopped and people bristling with cameras got out. *"Guck 'mal! Cowboys! Guck 'mal!"* one of them cried, pointing at us. I could hear a whispered staccato of clicks and whirs as a forest of lenses was pointed in our direction.

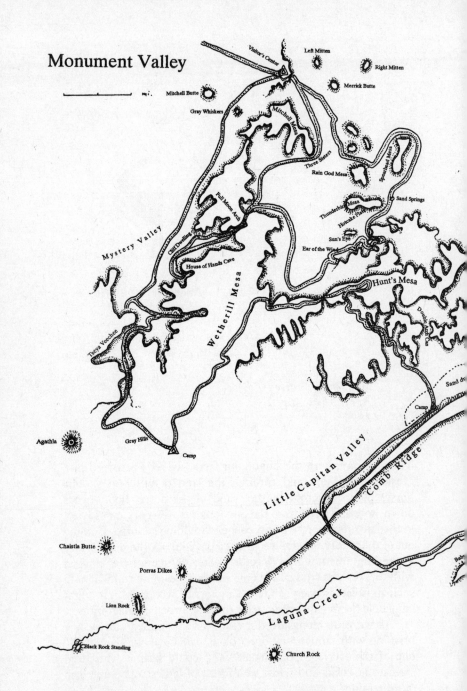

Monument Valley

Visitor's Center
Left Mitten
Right Mitten
Mitchell Butte
Merrick Butte
Gray Whiskers
Mitchell Mesa
Three Sisters
Rain God Mesa
Spearhead Mesa
Full Moon Arch
Sand Springs
Thunderbird Mesa
Hoteate Pinnacle
Mystery Valley
Cliff Dwelling
Sun's Eye
House of Hands Cave
Ear of the Wind
Hunt's Mesa
Wetherill Mesa
Tseya Venchee
Camp
Agathla
Gray Hills
Camp
Little Capitan Valley
Comb Ridge
Sand dun
Chaistla Butte
Porras Dikes
Baby
Lion Rock
Laguna Creek
Black Rock Standing
Church Rock

"What are they doing?" Selene asked.

"They're taking our picture, silly," said Christine. "I guess we're a tourist attraction."

Selene stuck out her tongue at them and made a vulgar noise.

"Don't do that!" said Christine.

"I don't like them taking our picture without even *asking* us! Geez!"

Frank gave a little half smile. "Now you know how we feel."

"They wouldn't do that in *their* country," Selene said, as yet another carload pulled off to take pictures.

"They never ask permission," said Frank. "They just stick a camera in your face and start shooting. It's like you're not even a person."

Selene, thus encouraged, razzed another vanload of tourists. We certainly looked authentic, riding across the desert trailing our tired packhorses, our clothes coated with dust, our cowboy hats battered and creased, our faces burned and lined with dirt. We were back in civilization, but no longer of it.

Six miles from the Visitor Center, both we and our horses gave out, and we stopped to camp. Frank and I sat down on a rock to work out his payment while the sun set behind Oljeto Mesa.

"You're not going to ride back tonight?" I asked.

Frank looked up. "Yeah."

"It must be fifty miles back to Piute Mesa, and it's nearly sunset."

Frank shrugged. "It's no big deal," he said. "Maybe I'll take two days."

I looked at his now empty food sack, his thin serape rolled behind the saddle, his lack of a canteen. We thought we were pretty tough, but for Frank it was a way of life.

"Let us give you some food and a canteen," I said.

He shook his head and we sat for a moment in silence. He seemed to have something on his mind. Finally he asked, "So where're you from?"

"Durango, Colorado."

"I mean, where originally?"

"Boston, Massachusetts."

Frank looked down. "Where is that, in Mexico?"

"It's in America, on the East Coast."

"So you're Anglos?" he asked in amazement. "*Bilagáana?*"

I was completely taken aback. "Yes, we are. Isn't it obvious?"

He was silent for a moment. "Well, I just never heard of white people doing the kind of thing you're doing. That's why I thought you might be Mexicans or something." He seemed embarrassed, and I suddenly realized that Frank, living on Piute Mesa, rarely saw white people and didn't really know what they were. Or perhaps, I thought, we were so sunburned and dusty that we no longer looked white.

We watched him take off down the road at a good lope, heading back over the Moonlight Water Trail to his mesa in the sky.

▽ ▽ ▽

The next day, we cut cross country toward the Monument Valley Visitor Center. As we approached, we saw a lone rider coming toward us at a fast gallop, his paint horse leaping the bushes and dodging through the sand hollows. He came straight at us and stopped at the last moment in a great spray of sand, a spectacular show of horsemanship.

He smiled shyly and touched his index finger to his hatbrim. "Hello," he said. "I'm Neswood Begay."

In order to ride through the Navajo Tribal Park section of Monument Valley, we were required to have a guide. Neswood would be our guide.

"That's some horse you've got," I said.

He was a beautiful medicine-hat paint, sturdy and spirited.

Neswood grinned and said nothing, but I could see in that expression everything I needed to know about his love of that horse. Its name was Warrior.

We arrived at a set of corrals on a windswept knoll at the edge of the escarpment, looking down on the Mitten Buttes. It lay about a quarter of a mile north of the Visitor Center. The place was owned by a man named Ed Black. He had sixty or seventy horses that he rented to tourists and movie productions.

As we unpacked our supplies, a windstorm swept in from the west, pushing an orange cliff of dust ahead of it. It landed on us like a bomb and enveloped everything in stinging sheets of sand. The horses hunkered down, backs hunched, butts turned to the wind. We sheltered in the lee of a horse trailer, waiting for the dust storm to pass. There was no possibility of setting up a tent or cooking dinner; indeed, it was almost impossible even to open our eyes. Of all the things that can happen to you in the wilderness—drenching rain, snow, bitter cold, parching heat, clouds of biting insects—without a doubt a dust storm is the worst. You simply cannot escape it.

A towering Navajo figure suddenly materialized out of the haze, striding toward us, dressed in black, long hair streaming out from under a cowboy hat, thin Fu Manchu mustache at the corners of his upper lip. He wore round John Lennon sunglasses and as he spoke he appeared to be looking over the tops of our heads. He was a striking presence, as solid and straight as a lodgepole pine. He was unfazed by the storm.

He enveloped my hand in his. "Ed Black," he said. "We been expecting you. You meet Neswood?"

I said we had.

"You can hobble your horses out there," he said, "behind the corrals. Take all the hay you want. We haul in water twice a day."

"How long will this storm last?" I asked.

"About six weeks," he said, and laughed.

Christine asked, "Can we sleep in one of these horse trailers?"

"Sure," he said. "My wranglers sleep in the stock trailer, but you could stay in the four-horse trailer. We haven't used it in a month, so the shit'll be pretty dried up by now. You can use the shovel and broom over there to clean it out."

"What a *great* idea!" Selene said, jumping up and down. "We get to sleep in a horse trailer! No more tent!" She was positively ecstatic, and she helped us enthusiastically, scraping out the dried manure and arranging the horsepads into a carpeting of sorts. I had to smile. A week ago she would have been horrified.

While we set up house, Neswood saddled up a dozen horses to take some Germans out for a sunset ride. They stood in a tight group, their clothes whipping about them, handkerchiefs wrapped around their faces, peering out with dark glasses. I could hear the thump of saddles on the horses' backs, the slap of latigo and clink of rigging. Meanwhile, Neswood's horse, Warrior, stood just beyond the corrals, loose, watching the proceedings with great interest.

When he was done, Neswood plucked his lariat off a post and swung up on one of the horses. He shook out the lasso, sliding the rope through the hondo with a zing, and trotted off after Warrior.

"What's he doing?" Christine said.

As soon as Warrior saw him coming, the horse galloped off. Neswood raced along behind him, whirling the lariat. They thundered away from the corrals and made a wide circle back around, leaving an arc of smoking dust. Just as they raced past the Germans Neswood flung the lasso, and it dropped neatly around the horse's neck.

"*Mein Gott!*" cried one of the Germans, as they surged backward en masse. They were suddenly abuzz, stirring with excitement.

"That was quite a show," I said to Christine.

"It certainly was," she said, grinning.

"I'm sure he could have just walked right up to that horse and bridled him without all that fuss."

"Ah! But that wouldn't have been any fun. He's giving these people what they came here to see."

When our horse-trailer home was cleaned out, we walked over to the Visitor Center, irresistibly drawn to the promises of civilization: fresh water, food, a sealed, air-conditioned environment. The building was a shabby affair, built in early seventies office-park style, perched on the edge of the escarpment. But the land had changed it, scorching and cracking the exterior, stripping the paint off the cinderblock, sandblasting the windows, transforming it into something that did not look entirely out of place. Inside it had a pleasant Navajo spareness.

Selene begged money from me and raced into the "Food Stop" while Christine and I sat on a sofa, watching the parade of humanity. I could hear Selene talking to the counter man, telling him about the horrible trip she had just made, amid the sounds of candy bars and sodas being stacked on the glass. She examined with great interest two dinosaur tracks propped up against the wall and explored the gift store, buying some postcards and a fake arrowhead.

The majority of the tourists were German, plump and rosy-cheeked, in hats and shorts. Their blue eyes, intensified almost to whiteness by the desert light, gazed about with a look of bewilderment. They had seen the John Ford films, and now they wanted to see the place. It was not what they expected.

We followed a group onto the observation deck. They braced themselves against the wind and placed optical devices to their eyes, the lenses reflecting the curved blue of an infinite horizon.

There was a small expostulation and a hat disappeared into the burnt siena sky, instantly swallowed by the endless space.

This was one of the most photographed views in the world, and yet the full reality of Monument Valley eludes the camera. Here there is no frame. You cannot escape it: you are surrounded with the white heat of its sky and the weight of its buttes; the dust is driven into your pores; and the dryness cracks your skin. The real Monument Valley, so familiar and yet so strange, reminds you that you are nothing, less even than the fire ants and coyote-dung beetles scuttling across the desert floor below. And yet, there is a mysterious pleasure in feeling your nothingness once in a while; it is to touch something profound.

▽ ▽ ▽

Back at the horse trailer, we fixed everything up in a most pleasing fashion. We covered the floor with horsepads, spread our bedrolls on top, and then arranged all our gear, journals, pens, and books. It was as cozy as a tiny cottage.

Selene burrowed into her sleeping bag in the far back and wired up her Gameboy. I heard a sudden electronic beat from out of the darkness. The beeps and squawks came thick and fast, punctuated with her muttered expostulations and squeals of triumph. She was getting better at killing the monsters. There was a particularly loud BEEP as some nasty creature was bopped on the head.

"All *right*," Selene said, punching her fist into the air. "Oh, I just *love* this horse trailer. I'm not going anywhere. You go on, and I'll stay right here and play my Gameboy *forever*."

▽ ▽ ▽

That evening the wind subsided. We built a fire outside the trailer to cook dinner. At sunset a Navajo man came walking out of the desert. He introduced himself as James Fatt, Frank's older brother. He was a tour guide in the valley. He was tall and narrow-hipped, with a bladelike face, a thin mustache, handsome and self-assured. He wore a baseball cap with long ponytail coming out. He shook our hands firmly—revealing himself as one who knew about the Anglo world—and I could feel the hard bones through his flesh.

"I heard about you guys," he said. "That was some ride you did, from Navajo Mountain."

I was still worried about Frank. "Do you think he made it back okay?" I asked.

"Sure," said James. "He grew up on horseback, riding around those canyons. He lives on a horse. See, he couldn't walk till he was eight."

"What happened?"

"When he was just a baby, someone fell on top of him and crushed his pelvis. So he just stays around there, doesn't go very far from Piute Mesa."

We talked for a while about our trip. I asked if he wanted to stay for dinner.

He eyed the pot with suspicion. "What is it?"

"Red beans and rice," I said. "It's good."

I could hear Selene make a derogatory noise from the back of the trailer.

"Sure, thanks," he said, a little doubtfully.

We piled the food onto tin plates.

He nodded. "What you're doing, this riding across the Navajo Nation, I never heard of any white people doing that before. Maybe you guys are the first."

As night gathered around the campfire, it was like the building around us of a house made of darkness.

"So why *are* you guys doing this?" he finally asked.

I explained how we were retracing Monster Slayer's route.

James laughed. "Well, you came to the right place. See all those buttes out there? A long time ago, this was once a big battleground. That all's what's left of the monsters that he killed.

"So," he started again, tentatively, "why are you so interested in this stuff?"

I tried to explain where our interest had originated, and why we were making the trip. I said that we felt that riding the route was the only way to fully appreciate the landscape, and that knowledge was often best won with a personal struggle. I told him we were interested in the Navajo creation story. He listened, nodding, and then there was a long silence while he stared into the fire.

"You see," he began slowly, "it starts with the Earth."

He raised his eyes and looked steadily at us.

"The space between the Earth and the Sky is like the space between a man and a woman making love. Moisture is created, water is created, like the mixing of fluids from the female and the male. Both create life. So the lovemaking between Father

Sky and Mother Earth created the green living surface of the Earth.

"That mountain, Navajo Mountain, behind where we live? We call it *Naatsis'áán*. *Naatsis'áán*. Which means, Head of Earth Laying Down on Its Side. That mountain's the *head* of the Earth herself."

He picked up a stick and poked it in the fire.

"Our land is just like a human being. It has feet, it has legs, it has a body and it has arms, and it's got a head. The head of our land is Navajo Mountain. And that's also *our* head, the head of the Navajo people. Because we *are* the land. And then Black Mesa is the body. And Balukai Mesa, that would be the legs, and then the feet. And then the mesa over there, I think it's called Escalante Mesa, that's the face of Navajoland.

"Navajo Mountain is the place where the Navajo people came alive. The Earth was overrun with monsters that were killing all human life. Monster Slayer and his twin, Born for Water, were given spiritual powers from their father the Sun to do away with these monsters. So what you see out there is what's left after one of those battles. Those two Mitten Buttes, those are the hands of a big monster, just sticking up, and Merrick Butte, that's the head. Turned to stone. The rest of the body is buried. And some of those other buttes are smaller monsters.

"After the twins won, they went back over to Navajo Mountain. Right back the way you came. That's the only trail. And they started drumming on the mountain, making that *beat*, the sound of the drumbeat. That was one of the first Navajo ceremonies ever performed, which is the Enemy Way ceremony, the *N'da*. See, that beating drum made the sound of a beating heart. As *our* heartbeat. The heartbeat of the Navajo people. And it brought back to life all the People killed by the monsters."

Selene turned off her Gameboy and crawled out of the back of the trailer, dragging her sleeping bag. She settled next to us by the fire.

"So when we look out here, at the land, what we see is our history. This land, it's our bible. Like you have your Bible, all black and white, written down, fresh and new. And we have our bible, old, worn, which is the land and the songs about the land. You can just put those two things together"—he raised his hands and folded them together—"and it's all the same. Because all belief comes from the same place. That is why I also consider myself a Christian."

The smoke rose in a gold cloud from the fire and went rolling into the darkness.

"But the land," James continued, "is no longer respected. The dam, over there, that really hurt us. My family used to go across the San Juan River. Now it's Lake Powell. The river is alive and sacred, and damming it up trapped all the blessings it carried. On the north side of the San Juan River, that was our hunting ground. Also a lot of herbs and medicine were found over there that were used for certain ceremonies. That was the closest area they used to go to get those plants. That was our land, they say. You can find old abandoned hogans over there. My grandpa used to have quite a bit of horses. In the wintertime he would take those horses over on that side of the river so they could have good pastures. When they got all fat and really nice-looking, he used to bring them back. Now we can't do that. Nobody asked us, they just *took* that land. Now we don't have enough land where our horses and cattle will get enough graze. As you look out here, this is all desert. You can't find very much water, most of the vegetation's only good for sheep, not horses or cattle. It doesn't rain anymore, like it used to."

He was silent. I shook a piece of wood out of the pile and shoved it on the fire. A whirl of sparks danced into the darkness.

"Did you grow up on Piute Mesa?" I asked.

"Yes. There's a place back there, where you rode, called *Neskahi. Neskahi* means 'fat.' Because that's where they used to fatten up the sheep for a ceremony. My grandpa lived there. He was so short and squatty, they called him *Neskahi'esh*, which means Short Man from Place of Many Fats. That's how our last name got to be Fatt. So we're all a family. We're all related as brothers and sisters and also cousins and uncles and aunts. Not like Yazzies!" James laughed. "Yazzie, or Begay,[14] that's a very common Navajo name. As you go all the way across to the other side of the Navajo reservation you will find a Yazzie or Begay everywhere."

He laughed again, and stirred the fire with a stick. A chill was starting to creep into the air. I threw a few more pieces of wood on, and the flames flared up, beating back the night.

"A long time ago," James said, "in the mid-1800s, Kit Carson came into this area and rounded up most of the People, and took them down on a long march, which we call the Long Walk, down to Fort Sumner, New Mexico, and kept them there as prisoners for four years. Our family, they didn't make that walk.

Because they hid in a place called *Nahometso*. *Nahometso* means A Place of Hiding. It is up there by *Naatsis'áán*. And they were there for about maybe two years. When the white man thought they had gotten all the Navajos from here, my family moved up on top to No Mans Mesa. That's where they lived until the other Navajos came back. But there's nothing living up there now, just some wild horses that gotten loose from my grandpa a long time ago. We used to bring the sheep up there in winter, when there was snow you could melt for water."

"What was it like growing up on Piute Mesa?" I asked.

"Piute Mesa! That's considered the most remote place on the reservation. We were pretty much raised the old way. No television, no bicycles, no toys, none of these Tonka trucks!" James leaned back and laughed.

"We used to herd sheep. We had about three hundred head of sheep at one time. That hogan you slept in, that was our original house. Before we moved to that spot, we used to just move from place to place, because of the number of sheep that we used to have and also cattle and horses. Now we just stay at one area. There's only nine families on Piute Mesa. Sometimes we get droughts, we don't get rain all year long. We just barely get enough snow, not even enough where it could melt into a pothole for a horse to drink out of. They used to have helicopters bringing us water. Then when the snow gets too deep they drop hay and food. They did that last winter. It was that dried-freezed food, which is *not* good." James chuckled.

"Before they built the well, the closest water that you could find was maybe fifteen miles or so from our place. The rain collected in there. We had to take the sheep over there one day then spend the night over there and come back the next day. We used to herd the horses on over there in a half day or so. There was also water down in Nokai Canyon. There's a natural spring down there. The water's pretty alkaline though."

"I think we watered our horses there," I said. "At the bottom in some boulders?"

"That's it. In the summertime when the water used to get real scarce we had to live down there. Just camped out, moved along with the herd. We'd get firewood from the wood that washed down from the top of the mesa. It was a hard life. Your parents don't have enough money to buy you clothes. They just sew together pieces of animal skins for your pants and shirts. You don't have enough food. Then again, this was the only life we knew of. It didn't bother us. When we went to boarding school, *that's* when we noticed there was another world, a place where they spoke English, where they had this thing they called *manners*. That's when we knew that there were things like toys and clothes! And that's when we felt *poor*."

"Boarding school?" Selene asked. "What was that like?"

"BIA took me away to boarding school when I was about eight years old. I had a bun. A special way that we tied our hair. It used to be that you weren't supposed to cut your hair, because it'll decrease rain. But as soon as I got into the boarding school they clipped it off. *Shhhhzzzz*. Shaved all my hair off."

"A bun?" Selene asked.

"Ah yes, the bun! You tie up your hair with a song and a prayer, and it brings rain. But since the Navajos have been cutting their hair, we've had these droughts. Everything's died.

"So after that, I wanted to see the world. The Anglo world. So I went to school to learn ironwork. Buildings, skyscrapers, high-rises, bridges. I worked as a connector for six years. Over in Page, and Phoenix, over around Tucson area a lot of copper plants down there. And also over in Chicago."

"Chicago?" I said, surprised.

James laughed. "*Chicago*. Now that's too fast for me. *Way* too fast. Too cold, too fast. Some of the people there are very disrespectful. So, I was working as an ironworker. And I fell thirty-five feet, landed on both of my feet and had a fractured pelvis. My pelvis was cracked and also both ankles were broken. So I kind of thought about it, if I should go back to ironwork. I came back here, figuring I wasn't going to be back to normal to work ironwork again. So I came back and I just stayed around here, over at Navajo Mountain area. Then I heard from my uncle, Tom Bennett, and also my aunt Martha, that I could come over here to Monument Valley and work for them as a tour guide. I've been working here for about four years now."

"Having seen the Anglo world, what did you think of it?"

James stared at the fire, quietly.

"There's a good side in everything, and there's a bad side in everything. I like the Anglo way of living. It's good to have a job, a good-paying job. It's good to be able to leave the reservation, to go anywhere, to any city. Because that way you're going to see the world, you're going to learn more about yourself, you're going to think for yourself. When I was here, I used to just speak Navajo only. I was very shy, very bashful to speak the English

language. But when I started working in other cities, I worked
with Anglos, Mexicans, blacks. The only way that I was going
to communicate with them was by talking English. So I started
to pick up the English language. To where I could sit down and
really be *able* to express what I felt to another person who is a
different color.

"But then again, there's the bad side. It was too fast for me.
If you're from here, really poor . . . if you see *money*, it can get
you into trouble. Start drinking, start going to places that before
you wouldn't even *think* of yourself as going. I used to get paid
about maybe nine hundred dollars a week. As an ironworker.
Right when I got my check, I would cash it to the bank. Go run
over, grab myself a drink, start pouring it down, pouring it
down. Pretty soon it got me. Pretty soon it got me into drugs,
cocaine and heroin and—"

He fell silent, his face hidden in shadow.

"Pretty soon that job was *nothing*," he said quietly. "All I
was working for was my habit. So that's the bad side.

"When I was in Chicago . . . See, my father died in 1983.
Alongside his grave, we put all the things he valued so much,
and then right on top of the grave we killed his horse. So that he
could have a stronger journey into the next world. His grave was
way back up there near *Naatsis'áán*. It was a beautiful place. And
when I was out in Chicago, I used to think about my father, and
the horse dying on his grave, *Naatsis'áán* in the background . . ."

He straightened up and looked at us. "It shook me up. It's
got to be *yourself* that says hey, stop, think about what you're
doing, why you're put on this Earth. You got a family, you got
loved ones. You got a place somewhere on this Earth.

"So when I broke my pelvis, I came back here. There's also
good and bad here too. When you can't get any job out here, it
drives you *nuts*. It's pretty hard to find a job around here. But
you're close to your family, closer to your land—you're *on* your
land. The land makes you free. When you're on your land,
you're safer. The world out there, the Anglo world, that's a
dangerous place."

We were silent. We had finished eating. Christine gathered
up the dishes and I fetched some water from the horse trough to
wash them.

"You think America is dangerous?" I asked.

There was a long pause.

"*America*," James said, expelling his breath in a long exhale.

"What is this country? I really don't know. I really don't know. *America*. I don't even know what the word 'America' means."

Selene suddenly spoke up. "America is named after Amerigo Vespucci."

"Who?" James said.

"He was a mapmaker," Selene said. "And he signed his name on the map, and everyone thought that his name was the name of the continent."

"Now I didn't know that," James said, laughing. "They didn't teach me that in the history class."

We all fell silent. Then James said, his voice low: "I overheard some stories, some older Navajos talking about the future and what will happen to the white man."

There was a hush.

"Is it a scary story?" Selene whispered.

James smiled. "Well, I guess it depends. It was the kind of story that's only passed on from the very old to the very old. To those who'll be wise enough not to misuse the knowledge. So you see, no one told me anything directly . . ."

There was another long pause.

"A long time ago, before the white men came, they said that a new people would soon come around, asking the Navajos questions about all the Anasazi ruins. And that happened. The white people came, and all these archeologists came around asking questions. Then the story goes like this, that someday the white people are going to disappear in the same way as the Anasazi, and leave their ruins behind. And nobody's going to know why or how. And then there's going to be new life that's going to form here, a new world. And they're going to be going around, asking the Navajos again, 'Ahh, look at this! Look at all these ruins! What do they mean?' "

"You mean the white man's ruins?" I asked.

"Yes, the white man's ruins. But I don't know, maybe it'll be our ruins too. Personally, I kind of think we're all in this together."

James suddenly began to laugh. "Anyway, they'll be saying, 'Look at all this *trash!* Where'd it all *come* from?' "

His laughter subsided and disappeared into the night. There was a short silence and he added, softly: "But nobody will know. Everyone will have forgotten how it all got there."

It was late and we all stared at the fire, mesmerized by the last flicker of flames from a knob of juniper wood. Nobody said anything for a while, and then James picked up a branch and vigorously stirred the smoldering coals. The flames hurtled up, banishing the darkness, the sparks crowding into the sky, and the spell was broken.

James rose to his feet and shook out a leg that had gone to sleep.

"Ah well," he said, "if only this old juniper tree could speak. I bet it's seen a lot of things over the centuries."

He grasped our hands and left.

▽ ▽ ▽

Later, lying in the darkness, Christine and I listened to the sounds of the wranglers getting the horses settled for the night. There was the snip of bales being cut, the thump of hay thrown into the corral, the stamp of hooves, the clink of wood being stacked. There was a low murmur of voices, speaking Navajo. I wondered: What was it that the Anasazi did to destroy themselves? And what is it that we will do?

We lay there, wrapped in our sleeping bags, holding each other's hands, buried in the magical night over Monument Valley, thinking about the ruins of the white man.

Chapter **10**

ANASAZI PETROGLYPH
—GALISTEO BASIN

Monument Valley
May 2, 1992

Rub your feet with pollen and rest them.
Rub your hands with pollen and rest them.
Rub your body with pollen and lie at rest.
Rub your head with pollen and put your mind at rest.
Then truly your feet become pollen.
  Your hands become pollen.
  Your body becomes pollen.
  Your head becomes pollen.
  Your spirit will then become pollen.
  Your voice will then become pollen.
  All of you is as pollen is.
  And what pollen is, that is what peace is.
The long trail ahead is now a beautiful trail.
Long life is ahead; happiness is ahead.

—THE PRAYER THAT SPIDER WOMAN TAUGHT THE TWINS TO
BRING PEACE TO THE EVIL CREATURES THEY MIGHT ENCOUNTER
ON THEIR JOURNEY TO THEIR FATHER[15]

The next day, Ed Black came over with a friend to find out more about the white people riding across Navajoland. They hung out nearby, with usual Navajo diffidence, beers in hand, until I walked past.

"Yo! Hey!" said Ed's friend, holding out his hand. I shook it.

"Beer?" he asked.

He wore dark mirrored sunglasses, white cowboy hat, with crew-cut hair. His Navajo accent was faint and I could tell by his manner and assertive body language that he had spent a great deal of time among the *Bilagáana*.

"Hey," he said, moving a little too close for comfort. "You know what? In the white man's war you call Vietnam, I saw my own brother blown away right in front of my eyes. There he was, and then it was like a big meat sound and he was everywhere, on my face, my pants, everywhere."

He stared at me, and I could see my own distorted face looking back at me from his mirrored eyes.

I mumbled something.

"That's right," he said. "And I'm glad to be alive and back here on the land. You really riding across the rez?"

Christine came by and he shook her hand too.

"We're really doing it," I said.

"From Navajo Mountain?"

"Yes."

"And where're you going next?"

"South to Chinle, Canyon de Chelly, Tsaile, and then across the Lukachukai Mountains to Shiprock. Where Monster Slayer went, while he was ridding the Earth of the alien gods."

"Monster Slayer, huh? That's a *long* ride. Yeah, and you're traveling just in time to see all the rattlesnakes. Right, Ed?"

"It's that time of year," Ed said.

He turned back. "You better be careful because there's rattlers all over the place."

I asked his name and he backed off, laughing, slugging his beer and opening another.

"No way, no way are you gonna have my name. Don't anybody tell him my name," he said, looking around.

"His name's Lewis Atcitty,"[16] Ed Black said.

"I told you not to tell him my name," snapped Lewis. "I fucking just *told* you. Anyway, about the rattlesnakes, what you do is, you get this snakeweed here, and tie it up into four bundles with yucca fibers, and hang it around your camp."

"And how long will it last?" Christine asked.

Lewis made a sly grin. "As long as you *believe* it. Like everything else in life, you got to believe it for it to work. Like witchcraft. You believe in it, witchcraft? Skinwalkers?"

I didn't answer; I was looking around, trying to figure out some graceful method of getting away from this man. He slipped a tin of Skoal out of his breast pocket, opened it, pinched out a wad, and fingered it into his cheek.

"Nice Navajo belt buckle you got on," he said to me, pointing. "And I bet you got no idea what it means."

"No, I don't," I said.

"How many points does it have?"

"Four," I said.

"Four! Four is the sacred number to the Navajo. Everything comes in four. See that? Those four points represent the four sacred directions. North, South, East, West. The four sacred mountains. And the four sacred colors: black, blue, white, and yellow. The four winds, Blue Wind, White Wind, Black Wind, and Yellow Wind. The four Talking Gods. Four."

He took off his hat. "See this hatband?"

He slid it off his hat and placed it in my hand. It was a braided leather band with beautiful beadwork at four places.

"Four again!" he said. "One for each direction. And each set of beads are in the peyote colors. Now when I made this, I put a blessing in each one of these sets of beads. And I've used up three of these blessings, but there's one left. The best one is left, and it's in this one, in the direction of the east."

"This is beautiful," I said, holding it back to him.

"Oh no," he said, "it's yours. Keep it."

I protested.

He held up his hands. "Really. It's for you, for your trip. And if you get in trouble, use up that fourth blessing. Believe me, you're gonna need it."

He grinned and cracked another beer.

I thought I should give him something in return. I had brought along a small sack of Morgan-head silver dollars, from the 1880s, given to me by my grandfather. I had decided at the last moment to take them along as gifts. I rummaged through my saddlebags and handed him one.

It created a sensation. He held it up, blew on it, rubbed it over his chest.

"Hey, no," he said. "No way. I can't accept this. Really,

man, forget it. No way." He suddenly looked very embarrassed and held it back to me.

"I insist," I said. "Keep it. I want to give it to you."

"No way." He tried to slide it back in my shirt pocket, but I stepped away. After a long protest he finally accepted it, cupping it in his hands and blowing or breathing on it again in a most peculiar way.

"This is fantastic," he said. "Ed, look at this. It's incredible. It's over a hundred years old. It was made right after the Long Walk."

Ed Black took the coin in one of his massive hands and inspected it solemnly.

There was a short silence.

"Michael Jackson's coming next week," said Ed.

The idea struck me as preposterous and I began to laugh. I looked around at the dust and the white-hot sky. "Michael Jackson isn't going to like it out here," I said.

"They always come with these big air-conditioned RVs," said Ed. "They'll have him outside for five minutes and then they'll put him back in and nobody'll see him again."

"What about this wind? How could they shoot anything in this dust storm?"

"Maybe they'll hire a Navajo medicine man to make the weather right," said Ed. "Like John Ford used to do."

"John Ford did that?" I asked.

"Sure. See all that stuff in the sand?" He pointed to a blowout twenty yards from us, where rotten pieces of wood, old tin cans, pieces of canvas, and other half-buried detritus poked up. "That was John Ford's camp. That's where he lived when he made those movies with John Wayne. And when they were filming he always hired a medicine man to make the weather right."

"Did it work?" I asked.

"Sure it worked."

"This landscape," I said, "it must be the most famous landscape in the world."

"All those buttes out there," Ed said, "those are what's left of the monsters killed by the warrior twins. Monster Slayer and Born for Water. You heard that story? My granddad is a medicine man. He knows all the stories. When I was a kid I used to help him with his ceremonies."

"What kind of medicine man?"

"He does the Beauty Way, the Evil Way, and, whaddya call it, that ceremony that you do to cure you when lightning strikes? I guess it must be called the Lightning Way. And the Air Way."

"Do you think he'll talk to me?" I asked.

Ed looked at me steadily, with an amused face. "No, no, he wouldn't talk to you."

"Oh," I said.

"So you want to hear the story?" Ed asked.

"Which story?"

"The story about Monster Slayer?"

"Yes, of course. We'd love to."

"It happened at *Tsé łigaii íí'áhí*, White Standing Rock. The First People were hiding in the canyons from the monsters. First Man saw that a strange cloud had covered a peak called *Ch'óol'í'í*. He went to check it out, and as he went he sang a song of protection to make himself invisible to the monsters. And right at the top, he heard this baby crying."

Lewis said, "The lightning crashed, the rain came down, and everything was black as night. He couldn't see shit up there. But he heard this sound, like a baby's cry."

"All of a sudden," said Ed, "the storm stopped, and the sunlight came streaming in, and there in front of him was this baby girl. Crying. So First Man picked her up and carried her back to their camp. Nobody knew where the baby had come from. They called her *Asdzáá Nádleehé*, which means Changing Woman. To us, she's like life itself, like the changing of the seasons, always growing older and then becoming young again. That's why we call her Changing Woman, because she grows older and then gets young again.

"In four days she grew up, and they had the first Walked into Beauty ceremony. That's what we still do when a girl becomes a woman. We call it *Kinaaldá*. After that, Changing Woman got lonely and she wandered around and lay down on a rock next to a waterfall. The Sun fell on her. And then she got up and washed herself in the waterfall.

"She got pregnant from that, and she had twin sons. They were Monster Slayer and Born for Water. They were from the Sun which had fallen on her while she slept, and from the water of the stream. They were born over there on Navajo Mountain."

Lewis Atcitty gestured toward the west. "It was right over there, where you started. There's a spring about halfway up. War God Spring."

Ed Black continued to tell the story. The twins, he said, grew up with their mother and the small band of First People. They lived in fear, concealing themselves in the canyons, moving about only at night. As the years passed, more and more humans were killed by the alien gods.

When the twins reached boyhood, they began asking questions about their unknown father. Who was he? Where was he? Changing Woman refused to tell, saying only that he was dangerous and might kill them.

As the twins approached manhood, they thought more and more about their mysterious father. They wanted to know who they were. So they decided to run away from home and find him. One morning, before dawn, they left home, without knowing where they were going. They ventured into the dangerous world, the world without *hózhó*, traveling eastward through deserts and canyons, pursued by the *Naayéé'*. Soon they came to a canyon and there they saw a hole in the ground, with a wisp of smoke coming out of the hole. They stopped and looked in. And they heard a voice saying, "Greetings! Come in, my sons!" They climbed down and found themselves in the underground house of Spider Woman.

"Spider Woman," Ed continued, "had a lot of supernatural powers. So she invited them to sit down and she said, 'What're you boys doing here? Don't you know there're monsters out there?'

"They said, 'We're looking for our father.'

"So Spider Woman said, 'I can tell you who he is. But you better forget all about going to see him, because the way to his house is long and dangerous, and even if you got there he'd kill you immediately.'

"But they begged her to tell them.

"So she sighed and said, 'Your father is the Sun himself.' "

"The Sun was a powerful guy," said Lewis Atcitty. "You don't mess with him. Our gods aren't like the Christian god. The Sun, see, he's not so nice, he doesn't really give a shit about us."

Ed propped his boot up on the trailer and continued the story. Spider Woman realized the twins were determined to go to their father, so she told them the way to his house. She warned that they would have to pass through treacherous landscapes that killed unwary travelers. There was a desert of shifting sands that would suddenly bury them; there was a swamp full of slashing reeds that would cut them. They had to go through a canyon that would suddenly collapse in on them, and cross a thicket of poisonous cactus that would stab them. There were four pillars of old, gray rock, which if they walked on the shady side of they would die of old age.

Spider Woman taught them a prayer, which when sung would bring peace to these restless landforms and wandering monsters. And she gave them supernatural charms, including an eagle feather, to help them defeat the alien gods.

"So," Ed said, "they walked and walked, and along the way they befriended all these animals and spirits who taught them the sacred names of the mountains, rivers, trees, and animals so that they might travel safely. When you speak these names, they give you protection. And they passed through the boiling dunes, and the cactus, and everything else, saying the prayer of peace she had taught them.

"They finally reached the Sun's house. It was in the East, and there were four doors. The first was guarded by lightning, and the second by cougars, and the third by snakes, and then bears. But using their supernatural powers they got past them. When they walked in, they saw the Sun's wife sitting down. She jumped up and said, 'Who are you?'

"They said, 'We've come to see our father.' "

"She was really pissed," said Lewis Atcitty, laughing and leaning back on the trailer. "She said, 'You? You're sons of his? You mean that son-of-a-bitch has been messing around with some other woman down there? I'm gonna kill that bastard!' "

Ed laughed. "Yeah. So she hid the two boys in a cloud and pretty soon the Sun came home. 'Who visited you?' he asked her. 'I saw someone come in here.'

" 'You're goddamn right you saw someone come in here,' she said. 'Your *sons* came in here.' And she whipped off the cloud covering and the two twins came flying out on the ground.

"And she really lit into him. She yelled, 'You liar! You told me you were just out there carrying the sun across the sky! Now I know what you've been up to.' "

Lewis just about doubled over with laughter. "That's right! And when the Sun heard that, he was *really* ripped. He grabbed them and said, 'You're no sons of mine, you pieces of *shit!*' and he threw them against the walls of his house."

"This was an incredible house," said Ed Black. "The four walls were covered with sharp flint knives, and he smashed them against each wall. But they didn't die, because they had the supernatural powers given to them by Spider Woman. So the Sun saw that and he said, 'Hey, maybe you *are* sons of mine.'

"He had other tests for them. He put them in a sweat lodge and tried to burn them with steam, and he gave them poisoned tobacco to smoke. But each time they survived. So the Sun finally said, 'You have to be my sons. No one else could have survived those things.' And he was really proud of them. So he asked them why they came and what they wanted.

"The twins told him about the monsters overrunning the land, and how they had killed most of the People. They asked the Sun for supernatural powers and weapons of war."

Ed opened a beer and shoved his hat back. "When the Sun heard this, he was pretty upset. Because the chief of the enemy gods, *Ye'iitsoh*, Big God, was also one of his sons. The Sun had been fooling around a lot. So he brought the twins to this room on the east side of his house. It was filled with incredible wealth, herds of beautiful horses, piles of buckskins and turquoise, sheep and goats.

" 'You can have all this instead of weapons,' he said.

"They refused. They saw a bow and arrow hanging on the wall, and so they asked for that instead."

The bow was made of thunder, Ed explained, and it shot arrows of lightning, and it was the Sun's most powerful weapon. The Sun with great reluctance gave it to them. Then the Sun retired and thought for a while, and returned with sadness in his face. He explained that because the chief enemy god was his wayward son, and, therefore, their half-brother, it was only right that he deliver the first killing blow.

"So he carried them way up to the center of the sky," Ed said. "But he had one final test for them. He wanted to know if they knew the sacred names of the landscape. He pointed to a mountain in the east, and he asked, 'What mountain is that?'

" '*Sisnaajiní*,' they said right away, because they had learned all the sacred names from the spirits on their journey to the Sun. I forget the American name for *Sisnaajiní*. It's way over that way, in Colorado. Anyway, he pointed to another mountain and asked them what it was. And they said it was *Dook'o'oosłííd*, the Mountain of the West. Those are the San Francisco Mountains over there, behind Black Mesa. And they said the mountain straight below them was *Tsoodził*, the Mountain of the South. That's Mount Taylor in New Mexico. And he asked them which was the Mountain of the North, and they said *Dibé nitsaa!* That's a mountain up in Colorado too. And then the Warrior Twins were able to name all the mountains and rivers. And those mountains right over there, on the horizon? The Blue Mountains? The Sun tried to trick the twins by secretly moving those mountains to where they are now. But they recognized them anyway. And they knew the sacred names of all the rivers, the San Juan, the Rio Grande, everything. So the Sun said, '*Ahhh!* You *got* to be my sons, because only I know where all those places are!' And he shot them to Earth on a lightning bolt, at a place called *Tó sido*, Hot Springs. And that's where the Big God came to drink. And when he came to drink, the Sun struck him a blow of lightning, and then the twins fought and killed him right there, and cut off his head, and brought back his scalp to show to Changing Woman.

"That was how Monster Slayer got his name. And his brother, Born for Water, got a war name too: *Naidigishi*, Cuts Up the Enemy.

"And then Monster Slayer went out looking for more monsters. Right here, that's an old battleground and a lot of those buttes out there are the bodies of monsters he killed and buried, which got washed out over time. And then when he was done they had an Enemy Way ceremony to cure him from the sickness of killing. And during that ceremony all the People came back to life.

"And so that's the story of the Warrior Twins and how they defeated the monsters."

Ed sat back and crossed his arms with a grin.

"You like that story?" Lewis Atcitty asked.

"It's an incredible story," I said.

"See," said Lewis, "you can't ride through here without knowing this stuff. Like, you heard about the Long Walk?"

"When the Navajos were taken to Fort Sumner?"

"Yeah, but not *all* of them went," said Lewis.

"My ancestors," said Ed slowly, "went back up in those canyons you came out of and got away. Kit Carson, the general, got as far as Hoskinninni Mesa and chickened out. There was a lot of people, though, who had to stay behind, the crippled and old. And even those old ladies and cripples fought Kit Carson. There was this one old woman who grabbed the leg of a soldier trying to come in her hogan, and cut it right off."

"Right on!" said Lewis, punching the air.

"Then there was another man named Bobcat Head, who was crazy and stayed behind. He went to sleep in the dust and woke up to find himself surrounded by soldiers. So he started jumping around, acting crazy, and throwing dust in the air and making faces, and the soldiers started laughing. And he threw more and more dust until a huge cloud hung there, and when the dust subsided he was gone."

Ed Black and Lewis Atcitty laughed uproariously.

"That motherfucker was *gone!*" Lewis said.

While we were talking, an old pickup truck hobbled up and coughed to a stop, and three teenagers got out. They opened the car hood and started tinkering around with the engine. All three were very drunk, and the drunkest staggered over and started talking to Ed in Navajo. Swaying, he turned to us and shook our hands, leaning into the handclasp, exhaling an alcoholic cloud.

"Yeah," said Lewis, "those soldiers came and took everyone to Fort Sumner. It was a war. Like all that shit going on over in Los Angeles."

"What's going on in Los Angeles?" I asked.

They both stopped and looked at me, incredulous.

"You don't know about those riots?" Ed asked. "Fifty people dead. They're burning the whole city."

I was stunned. "What? You've got to be joking."

Lewis laughed. "You guys've been out in the jungle too long."

"There's a big riot in Los Angeles," said Ed Black. "Whole blocks are burning down. Nobody knows what's going on."

"Did you say *fifty* people?"

"*More* than fifty. It's still going on. I was just hearing it on the radio when I drove down from Mexican Hat this morning. But it isn't just L.A., they're rioting all over, even up there in Canada."

"Why?"

"They're pissed because those cops who beat up that black guy got off. That Rodney King guy."

"They got a *movie* of those motherfuckers beating up that guy," said Lewis, "and *still* they got off. So, like, what else could they do?"

We talked about it for a while, and I questioned Ed very closely. He was vague on some of the details, but quite firm about the number dead. I asked more questions but in the end I did not quite believe it. I felt that it was likely they had gotten their facts wrong. There was no possibility that fifty people could die in a riot in Los Angeles. By the time news filtered out here, I thought, it must be considerably distorted.

Finally Ed said, flatly: "The Navajos believe that the Anglos are going to destroy themselves."[17]

Ed looked at me steadily with his eyes hidden by the John Lennon sunglasses. A moment passed and I said nothing. Then he said, "Maybe this is it."

There was a long silence that hung like a challenge in the hot desert air.

"But we also believe that the Navajo people will cease to exist too," Ed said, a little softer, "when the last Navajo who speaks the language dies. Then the Navajo people will cease to exist. Everything comes to an end, eventually."

Both of them were looking at Christine and me curiously, almost as if they were waiting for a reaction. I could not find anything to say. It was an awkward moment.

"You see," Ed said, "when the Navajo people die out, then the Earth itself's going to die. Without the ceremonies being performed to keep the Earth in balance, it'll go crazy, fall apart, destroy itself. Earthquakes, volcanoes, floods, hurricanes. It's already happening, with all the environmental destruction being caused by the white people. Look at this hole in the ozone layer. It's already happening. I think the white people will destroy themselves by wrecking the environment. Maybe it's already happened, only we don't know it yet."

"Do you think there's any hope?" I asked.

"Yeah," Ed Black said. "There is a way to stop this thing. The U.S. government should come to the reservation, hire all the medicine men, and conduct one big ceremony for the Earth. One big, powerful ceremony, all across the continent. Only that way will the hole in the ozone layer close up, and only then will the Earth heal itself. It'll be expensive, you know, because the medicine men will have to be paid a lot of money, but it'll be worth it. Look at all the money they're spending on these bombs."

I couldn't tell if he was kidding or not. He returned my look with an expressionless face behind his small, round sunglasses.

No, I realized, he was dead serious.

Lewis Atcitty spat a thin jet of tobacco juice into the dust. "You're damn right there, Ed. That would straighten things up. That's a good idea."

The drunken kid, who had been leaning on the flatbed with

half-closed eyes, suddenly spoke up. "Hey!" he said. "I'm not even gonna survive another year, so why should I give a fucking *shit*, let the *fucking* world go to *fucking* shit, blow the motherfucker *up!*" He leaned back in a great spluttering laugh, his eyes sliding around wildly behind his half-closed lids. Christine looked at me with horror in her face: the boy had not been joking.

"Aw *shit* fuck *shit*," the boy said, staggering to his feet and lurching off to the broken truck.

The sun was setting, and a long shadow fell across the buttes of Monument Valley. A nervous silence was filled by the sound of wind rattling the dry weeds.

"I gotta feed these horses," Ed said, sliding off the flatbed and jerking his hatbrim. Christine went back to the trailer.

Lewis and I stood in silence, looking out at the buttes, as the sun set behind our backs. The spell was broken by an eruption of savage barking from Acomita. I leapt up and found our dog bristling and yelping at a group of tourists who had unwisely parked next to the horse trailer. They were hastily climbing back into their cars. I scolded her and shut her inside the trailer. The tourists emerged cautiously. Lewis was laughing, and he motioned me back over.

"Hey, you got yourselves a pretty good little watchdog there," he said.

"Too good."

Lewis fingered a plug of tobacco into his cheek. "You see all those rock formations? Here, walk with me up there. Let me show you something."

I walked with him to the edge of the escarpment, and we gazed together down on the famous part of Monument Valley, the Mitten Buttes, Merrick Butte, and Sentinel Mesa.

"This is our land," he said, "this whole landscape is like a dream for us. This is what we dreamed, and then it happened like this, the land formed from a dream. It was dreamed and then it happened. You know what I mean?"

"I guess so," I said. "Well, not really."

"Hey, neither do I!" he said with a laugh. "No, really, this out here is a dream. An *Indian* dream, not a white man dream, and when you look out here you're looking at what was and still is a dream. Today it's partly real and partly a very old dream that's still going on. We Navajos are the land and the dream, and we're also the dreamer."

He fell silent. The half-light gathered in the air and the buttes lost their solidity and seemed to dissolve into the rose-colored air.

"When I was in 'Nam, I used to dream this whole place here. These buttes, just like you see them now, at sunset. They were more real in the dream than they are now. Because they are a dream, and so when you dream, you become them. And then I'd wake up in some fucking hooch in the jungle, and that was unreal, everything was totally unreal. You know what I'm talking about?"

"I'm not sure."

He gave me a penetrating look, and again I had to turn my eyes away from those distorting mirrors.

"You know," he said, "you think you can come here and spend a few weeks and understand the Navajo way, the *Indian* way, and then you're gonna write a book about it."

"I don't think that," I said, stung to the quick.

"Yes you do. Sure you do. That's the white man's way. But it takes a whole lifetime even to understand just a little tiny bit. And I don't know, being a white person, if maybe you can't really understand any of it."

"I know I'll only understand just a little bit," I said defensively.

"You say that, but you don't believe it. White people think they can learn everything right away, by reading it out of a book and asking questions at everyone. But it doesn't work that way, you got to *experience* and *live* it to learn it. Things take time. You can't get it all in a month. What you need to do is come out here, next year, the year after, keep coming back. Listen to people, spend time with them. Stop asking questions. You ask too many fucking questions. Because when you're ready to know, it'll be shown to you. Maybe by the end of this trip, you'll know just a little, tiny bit. And what you know'll be *good*. It'll be worth knowing. Yeah, but then maybe you won't want to write a book anymore, because it's impossible to write down those kinds of things. You can't explain them; you have to feel them. And people won't understand it anyway, because they didn't *experience* it."

Then he took off his hat again, and removed a long feather from the brim. He held it out to me. I took it.

"That's an eagle feather," he said. "That has a lot of power in it. Because it was plucked from a _live_ eagle. It'll give you and your family protection."

I looked at it. It was unremarkable-looking, dark gray-brown and flecked with white. I wasn't sure I believed him.

"How do you pluck a live eagle?" I asked.

Atcitty laughed out over the valley, not answering. Then he slid his hand into his pocket and withdrew the silver dollar, raised it up in front of his face, and flipped it. It landed in the dust and he quickly covered it with his boot.

"Heads or tails?"

"Heads."

"Heads," he said, reaching down. "You win."

"What did I win?" I asked.

"Nothing." He flicked his hand away and dropped the coin into his pocket with a grin. "Nah," he said, "you're okay, man. Don't worry too much about what I just said. You just do your thing. Forget what I just said. It's good that you're riding on horseback. That's something different, something most white people wouldn't do. Horses are sacred. That's the way to do it. Really, you might get something that way."

He paused, and said: "Like a sore butt!" And he tilted back his whole body and roared with laughter.

Chapter 11

ANASAZI PETROGLYPH
—MARSH PASS

 House of Hands Cave
May 3, 1992

The next day, Selene dragged us back to the Visitor Center to restock her supply of candy bars and soda. She had made friends with the man who worked behind the candy counter, Harold Simpson, and introduced us to him.

Harold was soft-spoken and articulate, a twenty-four-year-old college student with a gentle way of moving his hands while he talked. He was an albino Navajo, with white-blond hair and light blue eyes. He grew up in Monument Valley at a place called Three Sisters, and he spoke Swedish and German.

"You see all those signs in German out there?" he pointed outside to various tables set up to advertise tours in the valley. "I wrote all those signs. Somebody had to learn German because we get mostly Germans here."

Harold told us that he had recently returned from a trip to Scandinavia, where the Swedes ridiculed the idea that he was a pureblood Navajo from America.

"They'd say to me, 'If you're an Indian, say something in Indian.' So I'd say something in Navajo. And then they'd laugh and say, 'What kind of a language is that? You're just making that up! No language sounds like that. Look at you, you're whiter than we are.' " He laughed bitterly.

We talked for a while and I mentioned the stories Ed Black had been telling us about Monster Slayer.

"Do you believe in all that stuff?" Harold asked.

"Yes," I said, "I think there are deep truths in those stories."

"You do?" he said, incredulously. "Well, I don't. I think they're all myths. I mean, you don't *really* think people looking like insects came out of a hole in the ground somewhere? It doesn't make sense. Do you think it makes sense?"

"On a deep level it makes sense," I said.

"Well," Harold said, "I don't think it makes sense on any level. It's just a myth."

Later, we learned from Neswood that when Harold was a child, the tourists used to stop at Three Sisters and photograph the Navajo children at play. They didn't want Harold in the pictures because he looked white, so they would ask him to please move off to the side while they photographed.

▽ ▽ ▽

Later that morning, James Fatt invited Selene on a van tour of the valley. Christine and I went for a ride with Neswood. We rode down the trail to the valley bottom, following Neswood, and stopped near a lone juniper. Neswood turned around in the saddle. He was riding a horse called Blackfoot, a half-brother to Warrior. They could have been twins.

"So," he said, "your horses look like they're in pretty good shape."

"They've had a good rest," I said.

"You want to go a little faster?" he asked.

"Well, ah, sure," I said, "we could do a little trotting. Why not?"

Without another word Neswood wheeled his horse about and planted his heels in the flank. The hindquarters flexed in a shock of contracting muscle and the horse flew off like the wind. There was nothing to do but follow. We took off after him, tearing across the desert at thirty miles an hour, the horses leaping the sagebrush and chamisa, the wind roaring in our ears. I could feel a wild surge of excitement in Redbone as he let himself

go, running for the sheer love of it. In just two minutes we had
covered a mile of ground.

Neswood reined up in the bottom of a sandy wash and his
horse stopped almost instantly in a great spray of sand. Both our
horses blasted on by and we struggled to slow their flight and
turn them back around. We finally regrouped, the horses' flanks
heaving. Redbone trembled with excitement, prancing about,
wanting to run again.

"I like to run," Neswood said, smiling a kind of half smile.
"It gets kind of boring just walking all the time with the tourists."

I looked over at Christine. Her hair was blown back and her
face was red with exertion. A fleck of foam from the horse's bit
lay on her thigh.

"Are you having fun?" I asked.

"This is incredibly exciting," she said, breathing hard. "Galloping through this landscape is one of the most amazing experiences I've ever had."

"It isn't too fast for you?" I asked.

"Are you kidding? Nothing is too fast for me. Of course, if
it's too fast for *you*—" she laughed.

Neswood pointed to my bridle. "Let me see that," he said.
"Take it off."

I unbridled Redbone, keeping a firm grip on his halter.

Neswood held it up. "That's why you can't stop that horse.
He can hardly feel you pulling on that bit. You need a bit like
this. Try it."

He unbridled his horse and we traded. His was a bit with
long shanks and a deep port.

"Now we'll run and you can see the difference."

Before we knew it he was roaring across the plain, and we
were straining to keep up again. Redbone was the fastest horse I
had ever ridden, and he was much bigger than Blackfoot, but I
was still eating Neswood's dust.

"Stop him in the wash!" he shouted back at me.

We hit the wash and I hauled back on the reins. Redbone
threw his head up in surprise and stopped so suddenly that I
piled forward on the saddle horn and nearly went over.

"Works," said Neswood, "doesn't it."

"It certainly does," I said.

We had ridden into a narrow valley surrounded by complicated rock formations.

"Your horse is very fast," I said.

"No," Neswood said. "I had a palomino horse that was *fast*. He was the color of honey, the most beautiful horse on the reservation. He walked as fast as most horses trot."

"Do you still have him?"

"No," said Neswood. "He was stolen."

"Stolen?"

"In the winter we turn the horses loose, and they go wherever there's feed. So we have to find them in the spring and catch them. This horse, he was tough. In the spring, I had to use three or four mounts in a relay chasing him for three days straight before I could catch him. He could outrun a mounted horse, *any* mounted horse."

"Three days just to catch him?" I asked.

"He was a lot harder to catch than even a wild horse. When you're chasing a wild horse, he's really nervous, always tense, always looking behind at you. He's too nervous to eat or drink. So he wears out pretty fast, long before your own horse gives out. And he makes mistakes, letting himself be driven into a box canyon. But this horse, he wasn't nervous at all. He ran ahead and stopped and grazed and drank a little water, and ran ahead again. He stayed cool. When I tried to catch him in a water trap or box canyon he'd always peel off at the last minute. The only way to get him was a relay. Run him down till he couldn't move any more. It took three days straight, night and day, changing horses. That was a *horse*."

"So what happened?"

"One spring, I went looking for him, but he wasn't anywhere. I looked for weeks, smelling the air, because I thought maybe he might have died in a canyon somewhere. I found a lot of dead horses but not him. Then I went to a medicine man, a crystal-gazer. And he said that the horse was alive and well and making money for someone, but he couldn't tell me where."

"Stolen."

"Yeah," Neswood said. "Stolen." Then he added, with infinite sadness in his voice, "I'll never have another horse like him."

We rode deep into Monument Valley. The buttes slowly crowded and merged into a fantastic landscape of sandstone, the slow sculptures of time poking above the sandy plain. We rode through a series of small, private landscapes, with pinnacles, secret alcoves, hidden arches, and enigmatic cul-de-sacs. Monument Valley is the eroded remains of a fossilized desert, and close up I could see in the sandstone the delicate crossbedded layers laid down by ancient winds. Geologists call this kind of sandstone Aeolian, after the Greek god of the wind.

In almost every canyon, tiny Anasazi cliff dwellings were slotted and tucked into small hollows in the rocks scooped out by wind and water. The place names were exotic: Sun's Eye, Big Hogan Cave, Echo Cave, Hotcake Flats, Moccasin Arch, Ear of the Wind.

We rested briefly at a place called Sand Springs. Behind the spring rose a twenty-foot bank of dune, the bare footprints and handprints of Navajo children scattered across its face. The wind-cut edge of the orange dune carved across the blue sky in a vibrant contrast of color. We lounged in a meadow next to the spring and ate lunch. Down the stream, a group of Navajo kids squealed and splashed about in the water, their voices rising and falling on the wind.

"Those kids make you realize that people actually live here," Christine said.

Neswood nodded.

"Doug," Christine continued, "think what it would be like to live in one of those little cliff dwellings and raise children here. Sitting around the fire telling stories in winter. In summer, going hunting in the mountains. Living and dying among these buttes."

"I can't even begin to imagine it," I said.

Christine looked around. "You know, this area looks familiar." She suddenly sat up. "By god, this was where the last scene in *The Searchers* was filmed, right here!"

Neswood grinned. "You're right. This was it. Sand Spring."

Christine settled back down. "Isn't this the strangest damned place, this country of ours, this America?"

▽ ▽ ▽

Toward afternoon we followed Neswood into the secret mouth of a canyon. We rounded a great mesa and came out on a broad sunny flat covered with sand dunes and blooming globemallow. On the far side was a large cave scooped out of the rock.

"Race you to the cave," he said.

We galloped across the dunes, the sand flying behind us like the wake of a boat.

Neswood was already off his horse by the time we arrived.

"We'll rest here for a moment," he said.

The cave was a large dome, like a great hollow pregnancy in the stone. The floor was carpeted with soft cool sand. I lay on my back, breathing in the perfume of stone and shadow. The intense sunlight reflected into the cave, making the cave glow with a golden light. Beyond the mouth of the cave, a thunderstorm crept across a distant mesa, a black layer of clouds momentarily shot through with flickering light. There was a distant roll of thunder. The cave felt safe.

I leaned back and gazed up at the dome of the roof, thirty feet above. It shone like burnished copper. Then, emerging from the light, I could see a reddish handprint on the stone, and then another, and another. Suddenly there were dozens of handprints scattered across the dome, a riot of waving hands.

It was a powerful and evocative image, this crowd of waving hands. My mind was suddenly flooded with images and memories of hands: a sea of hands on a dock; hands reaching upward to a departing train; the hands of soldiers going off to war; the hands of refugees, of desperate mobs; the hands of panic or farewell. I found myself instinctively listening for the distant cries of joy or sorrow, but there was only a bottomless silence. The Anasazi who painted this cave had disappeared a thousand years ago.

I heard Christine gasp and realized she had seen them too.

Neswood was looking at us, smiling.

"I see you noticed," he said. "Most people don't. House of Hands Cave."

"What if they don't notice?" Christine asked. "Don't you show them?"

"If they don't notice, then they weren't meant to see."

Chapter 12

NAVAJO PAINTING OF
SPANISH FRIAR
—STANDING COW RUIN,
CANYON DEL MUERTO

Agathla Peak
The Center of the World
May 4, 1992

Do walk about on it! Walk on chief mountain!
Now walk on Horizontal Black Belt, walk on chief mountain,
   walk on long life, walk on happiness!
Now walk on Blue Bead, walk on chief mountain,
   walk on long life, walk on happiness!
Now walk on Light Always Glitters on Top, walk on chief
      mountain!
   walk on long life, walk on happiness!
Now walk on Big Mountain Sheep, walk on chief mountain,
   walk on long life, walk on happiness!

—SONG FIRST MAN TAUGHT THE PEOPLE TO SING WHEN HE
GAVE THEM PERMISSION TO CLIMB THE FOUR SACRED
MOUNTAINS[18]

The author trailing his pack horse, Rainbow Plateau

On the edge of Piute Mesa

Doug, Selene, and Frank Fatt on the Moonlight Water Trail

Selene at the edge of Copper Canyon; No Mans Mesa in background

Christine with
Agathla, the
Center of the
World, in
background

Christine, Selene, and Doug in the Lukachukai
Mountains; the Lost City of the Lukachukais is
located in the deep canyon behind.

Selene and Blaze, Mystery Valley

Neswood Begay with Warrior

Doug and Acomita on White Point Mesa; the hobbled horses are in the distance.

Christine and Selene, somewhere in the infinity of the Chinle Valley

(RIGHT TOP) Christine galloping down Chinle Wash, near Many Farms

(RIGHT BOTTOM) Riding toward Mummy Cave, Canyon del Muerto

Moonrise over Navajo Fortress Rock, Canyon del Muerto

Riding past Los Gigantes

Selene mugging on her horse, Mexican Cry Mesa,
Lukachukai Mountains

Christine bonked by hailstones,
Lukachukai Mountains

Aftermath of the
hailstorm

Christine leading her pack horse, coming down out of the
Lukachukai Mountains

Selene, tired of being photographed, sits backwards on her horse, Cove Mesa

Selene with a friend in the Red Valley gas station

Selene looking at Shiprock in the vast distance

Selene, Valerie Walters, and friends, Cove, Arizona

Christine and Shiprock, the sacred Rock with Wings

Early the next morning we left on the second leg of our trip. This journey would take us southward through Monument Valley and down the vast Chinle Valley to Canyon de Chelly, one hundred miles distant. We would be retracing another portion of Monster Slayer's route, his quest to kill an alien god named *Déélgééd*. Canyon de Chelly was also where Monster Slayer and Born for Water found Spider Woman's home and learned who their father was.

Neswood would ride with us as far as Comb Ridge, which marks the southern border of Monument Valley. From there, we would be on our own.

The day dawned cool and still. A few lenticular clouds hung on the southern horizon. We rode southward, past a small butte called Grey Whiskers, and toward noon we entered Mystery Valley. It was a shallow sea of sunlight. Low buttes nudged up from the sand like islands, lapped by blue sky. The dust from our horses' hooves hung in the motionless air.

The floor of Mystery Valley was covered with prickly pear cacti, which sprawled in big patches across the ground, some covering more than 100 square feet. They were at the height of their bloom. The blossoms of the prickly pear are among the most beautiful of all flowers. They unfold like the wings of a butterfly, crinkly and translucent, and they come in a fantastical range of colors, from eye-popping purple and dark bloody crimson to delicate peaches, ivories, and pale greens. The sunlight shone through them as if through jewels strewn about the valley floor.

As we rode south, Mystery Valley narrowed and the red rocks closed in around us. Again, every pocket and beehive in the rock sheltered a ruin, usually a single doorway flanked by two windows. They were like dead faces looking out into the world. The ruins were small, one to four rooms, lived in by a single family. These were not the Anasazi who had built Chaco Canyon or the great cliff dwellings of Keet Seel and Betatakin; these were a more modest Anasazi who lived at the periphery of the ancient world.

"I'm thirsty," Selene sang out, "but the water's too hot to drink *again*."

Neswood grinned and hopped off his horse. He pulled out his knife and cut a thick plant, peeled the stem, and handed it to Selene.

"Dock," he said, cutting some more and passing them around. "Kills thirst. Chew it and then spit it out."

I bit into a piece, and a gush of sour but not unpleasant juice prickled my throat. Selene took one bite and her face became red. As soon as Neswood had turned his horse around she spat out a wad.

"Mom," she hissed, holding it up by her forefingers while making a terrible face, "do I *have* to eat this?"

"I'll eat it," I said.

Neswood stopped at a bush, reached inside, and scooped out a fistful of berries.

"We call this a lemonade tree," he said, popping the berries into his mouth. "You suck on them and then spit them out. Don't chew them."

We raked out fistfuls of berries, which had a sour-sweet, sticky coating tasting uncannily like lemonade.

"Hey, now *this* is good!" Selene cried. As we rode, she stopped at every bush, picking berries and stuffing them into her mouth, until she had fallen behind. Then I could hear her high-pitched voice urging her horse onward. "Arrrgh! You lazy *bum!* Get *going!*"

I looked back. Selene was bouncing up and down in the saddle and kicking his ribs as best as she could with her short legs, but Blaze was damned if he was going to respond. The expression on his face was one of utter disdain.

"Cut yourself another switch!" I called back. "But tap him *gently!*"

Soon Blaze came trotting up, looking put out. Selene was wielding a long prickly branch of lemonade tree like a medieval knight, with a grin on her face.

We reached the end of Mystery Valley and vanished into a warren of intimate canyons, like rooms in an endless desert palace, one opening into the other. The canyon floors were thick with sego lilies and primroses wilting in the heat. Slow heavy bees droned about in the sunlight, fumbling from flower to flower. For the first time in over a week I began seeing grass, tufts of Indian ricegrass and blue grama. There were even some gambel oaks and shaggy cottonwoods buried in the coolest recesses of the canyons.

In one canyon we found a spring. The water flowed out at the base of a cliff, cold and delicious, and sank into the sand, its invisible course marked by a line of cottonwoods. We watered our horses and rode along the shadowy canyon bottom. The sun was tangled up in the green crowns of the cottonwood trees and as the breeze freshened and subsided the leaves chattered softly, like the rising and falling of distant applause.

We gained altitude, following the complex maze upward to some unknown plateau. In late afternoon we finally emerged, topping out on a vast plain, the wind suddenly in our faces, clouds passing across the sun. So different was the landscape in front of us that it was like passing through gates into another world.

We stopped to rest the horses and looked at the landscape in silence. Three miles away rose a black volcanic plug called Agathla. It stood ragged and proud on the plain, fifteen hundred feet high, frozen in a violent upward motion to the heavens. Surrounding Agathla the grasslands were dappled with light coming through a swift, broken cloud cover. The light kept striking the peak and vanishing, making it look as if it were on fire. Beyond Agathla stood another spire of rock, Chaistla Butte, a mafic witch's finger pointing skyward. A mass of sand dunes, a small Sahara Desert, lay to the southeast of us. Directly to the south stood the northern wall of Black Mesa, piled on top with thunderheads and rain. Comb Ridge, a low spine of rock about eight miles off, curved around us and ran to the north.

I noticed something moving in the foreground. An old bent woman, wrapped in a shawl, appeared, walking slowly through the scrub, stopping to lean on a stick at every other step. She was driving in front of her a small flock of sheep, their fleecy backs just visible above the chamisa and snakeweed.

Christine edged her horse next to mine and we waited, holding our horses still so as not to disturb the sheep. The woman continued on and slowly disappeared into the landscape.

"I wonder where her hogan is?" Christine asked. We looked about, but there was no trace of human existence anywhere. It was as if she had materialized out of the fabric of the earth itself, and then dissolved again into it.

"She was like a ghost," Christine breathed, "a ghost of a timeless, ancient way of life."

"A way that won't last much longer," I said.

▽ ▽ ▽

We had reached a place of deep sacredness. Agathla is believed to lie at the geographical center of the world, and it is one of the

Sun Pillars which First Woman and First Man set into place to hold up the sky. All around us, the body of the Earth herself was exposed: Navajo Mountain, her head, was just visible above the northern horizon; Comb Ridge was her backbone, and Black Mesa her body. These linked formations are also known to many Navajos as a sacred female being called Pollen Mountain. Three distant mountain ranges in the east—the Carrizos, Lukachukais, and Chuskas—formed the body of a sacred male being and they are said by some to lie side by side, making love. Others say they lie head to toe, the traditional sleeping position of a comfortably married Navajo couple. Chaistla Butte, the precarious volcanic plug we saw trembling in the distant heat, is the world's dooms-day clock: it will fall when the end of the world arrives.

Monster Slayer had traveled through here on his way east-ward to the Chuska Mountains, but it was a place of peace, where he found no enemy gods. Later, when the People had increased on the Earth, they made a great discovery on this windswept plain: they learned how to use masks to decoy deer in the hunt. They made a tremendous kill and camped near the base of Agathla, not far from where we were standing, to scrape the hides. The wind plastered the fur all over the base of the mountain, so they called it *'Aghaałá*, meaning "Much fur."

▽ ▽ ▽

The horses stood quietly, the wind ruffling their manes. We viewed the landscape in silence. It was a landscape fearful in its indifference, a place which assaulted one's very sense of self. Seeing this, I could understand why the Navajos believe human-ity is only a small part of the natural order.

Christine reached across the saddle and took my hand. I could see the same unease in her face that I felt in myself.

"This landscape kind of shrinks you," she said, "makes you smaller and smaller until there's nothing left. I sit here and I feel like I'm going to disappear just like that old woman."

"I don't like it," Selene said. "It's so big it's scary."

I thought how true that was. The landscape did make us feel small and scared; it reminded us that in the end nature would not bend to our will. It was a place that challenged our version of creation; it questioned the very idea that we should, or even could, have dominion over all the Earth. There could be no taming of this landscape, of these massive buttes, these mountains buried in thunderclouds, these thirsty mesas and mute deserts.

To the Navajos, and probably to the Anasazi before them, this was a landscape of awe and affirmation. The land was not against them, as it seems to be against us. They lived subtly within the landscape, like the old woman tending her flock, while we live hard upon it. I wondered why we felt the land had to be subdued and conquered, or, as René Dubos put it, humanized, before we could call it ours.

▽ ▽ ▽

Some months later, I met with a Navajo medicine man named John Begay.[19] He explained in more detail the Navajo relationship to the landscape. He repeated the same phrase that James Fatt had used. "You have the Bible," he said. "We have the land. The land is our Book." The four sacred mountains and other landmarks were, he said, the physical proof of their origin as a people. The mountains are what maintain *hózhó*, balance, in the world. "Everything we have as a people came from those mountains," Begay said. "They give us our physical and mental health. They give us long life and happiness. Every day, when I pray, I think of those mountains just pouring blessings and health into the Navajo people.

"You find your origin in words," he said. "We see our origin in those mountains. They exist, so we exist. If someday they die, we die too."

Timbering, mining, road construction, skiing, rock climbing, and other activities on the four mountains disturb their inner beings. The inner beings might flee, and then the mountain will die. This has already happened, Navajos say, to certain sacred places. Some medicine men believe the two inner beings of Rainbow Bridge—a male and female rainbow—fled because of the boating, picnicking, and tourism caused by the rise of Lake Powell under the arch. When some rock climbers scaled Totem Pole Rock in Monument Valley, which the Navajos believe is a frozen *yé'ii*, or god, the inner beings may have left, which is why there is less rain in Monument Valley than there used to be. When developers wanted to expand the ski area on the San Francisco Peaks, they were surprised at the angry reaction from the Navajo Nation. They could not understand that to the Navajos, putting the Fairfield Snow Bowl on *Dook'o'oosłííd*, Light Always Glitters on Top, the Sacred Mountain of the West, threatened the Navajos' very existence as a people.

A Navajo leader named Tall Bitter Water was once asked to sign papers that would open the Carrizo Mountains to mining. He objected, saying that "the mountains have arms and legs and a head and everything. . . . Carrizo is the legs. . . ."[20] What is it going to stand on if we turn it over to you? How are we going to live? . . . This mountain is our forefather. He is taking care of all the Navaho. He helps us get the sick well and after he gets the people well we are happy again."

Note that Tall Bitter Water said "how are *we* going to live?" The mountains protect the *Diné*, and keep them sound in body and mind.

It is unfortunate that in a country founded on freedom of religion, native people have had to sue the government again and again to prevent the defilement of their most sacred places. None of the four sacred mountains, for example, is today inside the Navajo reservation. In many of these cases the Indian people have lost these lawsuits, because judges do not understand that a pristine mountaintop can be just as sacred as the Dome of the Rock is to Muslims, the Western Wall to Jews, or the Church of the Nativity to Christians. Somehow, our laws recognize only man-made structures as being "sacred"—a truly strange idea if you think about it.

Despite recent laws guaranteeing religious freedom for Native Americans, the American legal system as a whole has not come to terms with the native relationship between religious freedom and land. Deeply entrenched in the American law of torts is the idea that money is an acceptable compensation for injustice, including the theft of land. Thus, even when a tribe wins a land claims case, it is usually given money instead of the land back. When the Lakota proved that the sacred Black Hills had been stolen from them, the U.S. Supreme Court affirmed an award of several hundred million dollars in damages, in lieu of returning the Black Hills. (Most of the Black Hills are still federal land and could be returned without infringing on private landowners.) The Lakota, a desperately poor tribe, considered their "victory" in court a great loss. Despite their poverty, they have never touched the money and it sits idle in an escrow account. Meanwhile, the Lakota are still fighting for the return of the Black Hills, which will now take an act of Congress.

▽ ▽ ▽

As John Begay said: we find our origin in words—whether the words of the Bible or the equations of the cosmologists. Our God expelled us from the Garden of Eden and forced us to wander the Earth. In doing so, our God, in a way, charged us with a mandate: to wander the Earth, to explore and settle new lands. We have done very well by this mandate. We have planted the flag at the North Pole and explored the abyssal plains of the oceans and scaled the highest mountains and landed men on the moon.

The creation of America and the idea of Manifest Destiny were the crowning expressions of this biblical directive. We worship the voyages, the explorers, and the very trails that carried us into new lands. Our discoveries in science and technology are an extension of this biblical mandate, and even though science has long since parted from religion, scientists still, unconsciously, follow the values of the biblical mandate—the values of exploration, discovery, creation, invention—the values of technology. These are values that spring directly from our creation story and they infuse our attitudes toward geography in a profound way.

The Navajo idea of geography is very different. In the Navajo creation cycle there is no equivalent to the Judeo-Christian myth of expulsion. Indeed, it is the opposite. The Fifth World and the sacred mountains were created expressly for the People. The *Diné* are still living in their Garden of Eden.

Of course, archeology and linguistics show that the Navajo wandered down from Alaska and northwest Canada, arriving in the Southwest not long before the Spanish. The important distinction is this: the Navajo carried their sacred geography with them. When we went wandering, we left it behind.

▽ ▽ ▽

We built our government from words; the Navajos built theirs from geography. A Navajo told an anthropologist once: "The white people all look to the government like we look to the sacred mountains. You . . . hold out your hands to the government. In accord with that, the government, you live. But we look to our sacred mountains. . . . According to them we live—they are our Washington."[21]

Most traditional Navajos keep a compact with the sacred mountains through an object called a mountain soil bundle. Traditionally, a Navajo family should have a mountain soil bundle hidden in a special place in the hogan.

In the 1970s and 1980s, when elderly Navajos at Big Mountain were being forcibly relocated during the Navajo-Hopi land dispute, some of the old women met the government evicters in their bulldozers, weeping and holding out their mountain soil bundle as proof of their right to be where they were. It was more than a property deed: it was their physical connection to the land dating back to the time of creation itself. The bundles, however, were brushed aside and the bulldozers did their work.

Some months after the journey we met a Navajo woman, Katherine Smith, in her hogan near Big Mountain, Arizona. She lived on land that had been awarded to the Hopi tribe in the Navajo-Hopi land dispute. She was fighting to remain on her land in the face of government pressure to relocate, and told me through an interpreter that the mountain soil bundle was for her like the Constitution was to us. The center of her bundle contained soil from Big Mountain itself. Such a bundle, she said, was the proof, the highest authority, of her right to the land. As she spoke, this seventy-year-old woman gripped a rifle and said that, just as the white people would defend their Constitution, which was, after all, just a piece of paper with words on it, so she would defend her Constitution, which was the land and the mountain soil bundle that gave her the right to it.

The mountain soil bundle is a bundled buckskin about the size of a fist. The buckskin used to make the bundle must be from a deer that has been chased down, roped, and suffocated with sacred pollen by men "praying to the animal as their brother, asking that he understand their need."[22]

The bundle is folded in such a way as to form four pouches, and tucked inside each pouch is earth gathered from the summits of the four sacred mountains. In the middle of the bundle might be soil gathered from the nearest sacred mountain. The bundle also contains white shell, turquoise, abalone shell, and jet. These four materials represent the diurnal rhythm of the world itself, a rhythm of four pulses: dawn, day, evening twilight, and night. This rhythm is personified by the four directions, the four sacred mountains, the four sacred colors, the four sacred materials, and the four natural phenomena, all symbolically and literally

surrounding the *Diné Bikeyah*, the Land of the People. A diagram
would look like this:

North
Dibé nitsaa
Big Mountain Sheep
(Hesperus Peak)
Color: Black
Material: Jet
Natural phenomenon: Night

West
Dook'o'oosłííd
Light Always Glitters on Top
(San Francisco Peaks)
Yellow
Abalone Shell
Evening Twilight

East
Sisnaajiní
Horizontal Black Belt
(Sierra Blanca)
White
White Shell
Dawn

South
Tsoodził
Blue Bead Mountain
(Mount Taylor)
Blue
Turquoise
Daylight

This Navajo sand painting from the Blessing Way illustrates the same thing: the four sacred mountains surrounding the *Diné*

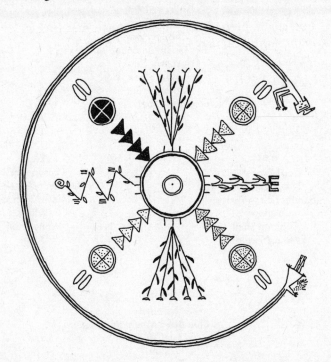

Bikeyah. The center point is the Place of Emergence. Radiating from it are cloud symbols, rain, corn, and other plants associated with each sacred direction. The four circles with crosses in them are the four sacred mountains: Sierra Blanca (*Sisnaajiní* or Horizontal Black Belt) in the east, Mount Taylor (*Tsoodził* or Blue Bead Mountain) in the south, the San Francisco Peaks (*Dook'o' oosłííd* or Light Always Glitters on Top) in the west, and Hesperus Peak (*Dibé nitsaa* or *Big Mountain Sheep*) in the north. Surrounding the whole of the *Diné Bikeyah* is a rainbow figure, a symbol of protection, long life, balance, beauty, and happiness. The rainbow being is always open at the east. This figure was copied from a drawing in an early missionary's notebook; in the original, the four mountains wear their sacred colors: white in the east, blue in the south, yellow in the west, and black in the north.

These linkages are embodied in the very first lines of the Navajo creation story. And now we can finally understand the symbolic meaning of these lines:

*White arose in the east, and they regarded it as day
there, they say; blue arose in the south, and still it was
day to them, and they moved around; yellow rose in the
west and showed that evening had come; then dark arose
in the north, and they lay down and slept.*[23]

Thus is everything in the world connected in a dynamic
four-count pulse that began on the first day and will end on the
last day. The four mountains are the prime maintainer of this
rhythm. Monster Slayer's final and most important test by the
Sun was whether he could name the four sacred mountains: it
was the ultimate catechism.

Chapter 13

NAVAJO YE'II FIGURE
—CANYON DE CHELLY

White Point Mesa
May 4–6, 1992

Slayer of Alien Gods brings for me:
A piece of lung he brings for me.
Déélgééd's lung he brings for me
Our People are restored.

Child of the Water brings for me:
A piece of wing he brings for me.
Nináhálééh he brings for me.
My People are restored.

Enemy Slayer he brings for me:
A lock of monster hair he brings for me.
Monster of the cliffs he brings for me.
His people are restored.

Monster Slayer brings for me:
Monster eyes he brings for me.
Bináá' yee aghánii he brings for me.
Our people are restored.

—Song that Changing Woman sings when her sons
bring home trophies from their battles with the enemy
gods[24]

The sun hung low over Agathla. We gathered our reins and rode across the plain, through a cluster of gray hills and toward a low mesa in the east. We were sore and tired, and a late-afternoon chill was settling in the air.

We found a sheltered camp in a hollow behind a low ridge. As the sun set, I walked to the ridgeline and looked out again at Agathla Peak, the center of the world, and Chaistla Butte beyond (which was looking none too steady) and the body and backbone of the Earth. The wind momentarily brought to my nostrils the faint perfume of woodsmoke from some invisible hogan, and I had a sudden sharp feeling of loss. We have, somehow, forgotten about the sacredness of landscape. We have desacralized the world to the point where we've disconnected ourselves from the vast complexity and mystery of life itself.

According to a new theory advanced by the Harvard biologist E. O. Wilson, called the biophilia hypothesis, the sacredness of the landscape is not some nebulous religious idea. It is rooted in our very genes. We do not love the beauty of the natural world by accident; we *evolved* to love it. This love is so profound that it is actually encoded in our genes, and it helped us survive in the landscape. If we continue to destroy the landscape that we love, our species will carry forever the dull ache of that loss.

▽ ▽ ▽

The next morning, before dawn, Christine and I climbed the ridge behind our camp and watched the sun rise. The desert was so still we could almost touch the silence. The darkness sank into the ground, and then the sun burst over the horizon, moving fast, throwing its light across Black Mesa and Agathla Peak.

We rode southward, toward the plunging fold of Comb Ridge. Our route took us across the sea of sand dunes, where the horses floundered and sank to their cannon bones. The dunes ended at an alkali flat covered with saltbushes and tumbleweeds. We rode to a corral built up against Comb Ridge itself, where we turned loose our horses and set up camp.

Comb Ridge marked the southern boundary of Monument Valley. From this point on we would be on our own until we reached Canyon de Chelly. Our yellow line—Monster Slayer's route—would soon be entering the white maps, the pieces of paper that showed almost nothing on them at all. This was the vast Chinle Valley, the area between the Chuska-Lukachukai Mountains and Black Mesa. It was in this valley that Monster

Slayer had battled *Déélgééd*, and where later his father the Sun had celebrated his long-delayed wedding to Changing Woman, his mother. The Sun had given Changing Woman so many animals as a wedding gift that the vast herds trampled the valley flat, as it remains to this day.

▽ ▽ ▽

The next morning dawned cold and windy. We said goodbye to Neswood and watched him turn his horse northward, back toward the Visitor Center. He loped across the dunes, the sand kicked up by the hooves, and disappeared into the land. We watched, then mounted our horses for the long ride south.

I sat on Redbone, looking down Comb Ridge for a gap we could pass through. Christine came riding up on Chaco, trailing Roscoe.

"We're on our own," I said.

"Yes," she said. "It's kind of exciting. I'm looking forward to riding with just the three of us." She took my hand.

Selene climbed aboard Blaze and began fussing with her reins and makeshift crop. "How far to the next town?" she asked.

"About eighty miles," I said.

"Eighty miles?" Selene cried. "Oh my God! *Eighty?* And I'm almost out of candy! Geez!"

We rode along the spine of Comb Ridge looking for a gap. An immense 440-kilovolt set of high-tension lines loomed in the distance, the steel towers ten stories high, looking like a row of alien gods striding across the Earth. Under the powerlines we passed an old Navajo man on horseback, herding sheep, with a furled umbrella dangling from his saddle strings.

The powerlines went through a gap in the ridge, which we also took. The gap acted as a kind of wind tunnel, and the blast of air was so powerful that we rode hunched over, our eyes half-closed, letting the horses pick their way on their own. The powerlines were directly above us, and I could hear the gusts of wind humming and moaning past the wires, mingling with the buzzing of electricity. It was an infernal sound, like some wounded, dying monster.

These particular powerlines carried electricity from the coal-fired power plant at Page to the immense strip mine on Black Mesa. There, the electricity powered the huge conveyor belts that carried coal to the railroad, from which it was taken back to Page and burned to create more electricity. It was a self-feeding monster, and it struck me as ironic that these howling tension lines should retrace a part of Monster Slayer's mythological route. It reminded me again of the prophecy James Fatt had told us, about the ruins of the white man. How long would these steel towers stand after we were gone? A hundred years? A thousand?

▽ ▽ ▽

Past the ridge, we found ourselves in a barren plain. Long wobbly lines of green tumbleweeds sprouted from the cracked crust, their seeds deposited by earlier tumbleweeds rolled across by the wind. A dead horse lay on an alkali flat, salt crystals sprouting from the eye sockets, the bones poking through the shrunken skin, the lips drawn back in a rictus of desiccation.

"Yuck!" cried Selene with relish. "That's gross!"

"Ride upwind of it," I said, "or your horse might spook."

In the late afternoon we crossed a paved road and approached White Point Mesa, a long grassy scarp with an outcropping of gypsum rock at its point. A herd of wild horses, perhaps fifty or sixty, grazed along the base of the mesa, moving nervously and pausing to watch us approach.

For some time a storm had been building in the south, and now we saw a dead-black wall of weather rearing up behind the mesa. The front passed the mesa and began closing in on us at high speed, pushing an opaque curtain of dust a thousand feet high in our direction.

I rode up alongside Christine.

"That looks bad," I said.

"I know. I've been watching it."

Selene caught up. "Why are we stopping?"

"I think we better put on our slickers," Christine said. "Look at that."

"Darn," said Selene. "Something bad always has to happen."

We stopped and untied our slickers from behind our saddles. As we remounted, the wind began to quicken and a low vibration filled the air. The grass flattened, and then hundreds of tumbleweeds came flying past us, bouncing, spiraling upward. There seemed to be some kind of wind shear above us, because when the tumbleweeds reached a certain height they were suddenly whipped about and shredded to pieces. The wall of dust advanced, its top arching over our heads, buried in the boiling clouds. The herd of horses had turned to watch the storm approach. As the wall of dust bore down, the lead stallion whirled and ran, and the others followed, the entire herd disappearing into their own cloud of dust, driven back over them like a blanket.

I took a compass reading in the direction we wanted to go, a small cut in the side of White Point Mesa. The storm struck. A cloud of gravel and sand whacked us across the face and we were enveloped in a roar of wind. The air temperature plunged twenty degrees. The blast carried along an intense humidity and an overpowering odor of crushed vegetation. I hunched over in the saddle, with my eyes closed, drinking in the heady smell of bruised sages and grasses, flowers, wild buckwheat, wet sand, and static electricity, all mixed together into one intoxicating fragrance.

I felt Redbone stiffen under the blast and I had to fight him back around into the wind. I rode blind, keeping Redbone pointed in the direction indicated by the compass, because I could not raise my eyes to see past his ears. There was no sound from Christine or Selene, but I kept glancing around and could see their dark shapes behind me, two muffled figures hunched over their horses.

In fifteen minutes the wind began to abate, and a few heavy drops of rain slapped the ground around us. We climbed through a cut in the side of the mesa and came out on a vast plain, thick with wildflowers and grass. A windmill poked over the far horizon. The rain came harder, and finally Selene started to cry. We stopped, brought our horses together, and held hands.

"First the dust, and now it's raining, and I'm cold," she wailed.

"I know," said Christine.

"It's not *supposed* to be this cold," Selene wept. "I was *so* hot back there and now I'm *freezing*. It's not fair."

"We'll snuggle down in the sleeping bags as soon as we get to camp," I said. "We'll camp at that windmill."

"That's too far away," Selene cried. "Let's camp here."

"There's no water here," I said.

Selene didn't answer and we rode on. The rain was fitful and gusty. We camped about a quarter mile from the windmill, on the grassy plain. There wasn't anything from horizon to horizon, not a bush, not a twig, just gray rain.

We unpacked and I brought the horses over to the windmill and watered them. I hobbled three of them with sidelines and staked the two others on fifty-foot ropes attached to picket pins driven into the ground. I strapped a cowbell around Redbone's neck, so I could find them in the morning. I had learned that this kind of flat landscape was deceptive; there could be a hollow somewhere where a whole herd of horses could be grazing, and two hundred yards off it would seem like empty, level ground from horizon to horizon. The grass was excellent, a mixture of sideoats grama, dropseed, and Indian ricegrass, high in vitamins and protein.

Christine and Selene cooked dinner on our tiny backpacking stove, which they set up at the door of the tent. When I came back, they poked their heads out and greeted me.

"Dinner's ready!" shouted Selene. "Come on in. It's nice and cozy. We'll eat dinner and then play Crazy Eights."

We finished a delicious dinner of tuna-noodle casserole and lay in the tent, wrapped in our sleeping bags. It was cold and the rain hammered away, but we were dry. I could hear the comforting sound of Redbone's bell in the distance. We played Crazy Eights and Selene won every game.

"Doug!" she finally said, "tell a story!"

So I began a story, a very long tale about a boy on a distant planet who had forgotten who he was and where he came from. In order to discover his identity, he had to make a dangerous journey across a wilderness of mountains and deserts. Along the way he met various supernatural beings, good and evil, who taught him many things. It was a kind of variation on the story of Monster Slayer. Selene hung on to every word, and begged and howled in protest when I stopped, leaving the boy lost in the desert, dying of thirst.

"I'm too tired to think anymore," I said. "I'll finish it tomorrow."

Selene snuggled in between me and Christine. I felt her hand burrow around and grab mine tightly.

"Are you glad you came along?" I asked.

Selene snorted. "Are you kidding?" she asked. "I'd *much* rather be home with my friends. Why would anyone *want* to be out here in the rain?"

"Us, for example," Christine said.

"Not me!" Selene said.

"Do you really hate it all that much?" I asked.

"Well," she said, and there was a long silence. "Maybe it's the kind of thing I'll be glad I did when it's over."

"*I'm* glad you came along," I said. "You're a great kid."

The rain drummed on the tent for a few moments.

"I love you," Selene said. For a moment I thought she was talking to her mother. "Who?" I asked.

"You! Geez!"

"Oh. I love you too," I said.

I was extremely embarrassed.

▽ ▽ ▽

As dusk fell we heard the grinding of gears. I looked out the tent and saw the headlights of a truck creeping over the prairie toward us. I dragged on my wet slicker and went outside. The rain had stopped.

A Navajo man got out, thin, neatly dressed, wearing a hat that said Show Low Construction. He was perhaps sixty years old. He shook my hand and introduced himself as Art Longpasture.

"Is this your land?" I asked, a little nervously.

"Yes," he said, "but you're welcome to stay here. I'll bring you some hay for your horses."

"That's very kind of you," I said. "Please let me buy it from you."

"Oh no! This is on me. I'll be right back."

Art returned a half hour later in the dark. He refused any kind of payment or gift.

"I like to see horses well fed," he said, leaning on the open door of his truck. The dome light cast a dull glow for a few feet into the blackness.

"This is beautiful grass you've got around here," I said.

"Yeah," he said, "I used to have three hundred cows but they was a lot of trouble so I got rid of all of them but sixty-five. Got some good quarter horses. I'm semi-retired." He laughed, because sixty-five cows were still a lot of work.

"Is this all yours, this land?"

"My family's been on this mesa forever," he said proudly. "They call us Longpasture because of it. It's a natural pasture, thousands of acres of grass. There's fifty-foot cliffs all around except where you came up and over there and where you'll go down on the other side. Those're the only two ways up and down at this end. The cows and horses can't go anywhere, they stay right here. There's no place like it anywhere else."

"So you worked cattle all your life?"

"No!" he said, offended. "I worked for Show Low Construction. And then I was a supervisor for the Arizona D.O.T."

He opened a wallet and removed an old, greasy business card. In the wallet I caught a glimpse of a picture of Jesus, praying with shining blond hair, his tear-filled blue eyes turned to heaven. He handed the card to me. It said "Arizona Department of Transportation, Art Longpasture, Supervisor."

"That's great," I said, returning it.

He accepted it and carefully slid it back in the wallet, a treasured possession. "It was a *good* job. Like I said, I'm semi-retired. But I'm up for this job removing those uranium-contaminated tailing piles over there at Bluewater. Pays thirty-two dollars per hour, and it would last twenty-four months. What I'd be doing is just blading the road they're taking it out on. Thirty-two an hour. I figure that's worth going back to work for, wouldn't you say?"

"That's incredible pay," I said. "Why so much?"

"It's because of all this fear of radiation, they have to pay extra. But it doesn't hurt you, because if it did the government sure wouldn't let you work on it. Right? Thirty-two an hour for twenty-four months. Then I'm going to buy a travel-trailer, do some sightseeing, see America. That's what I want to do: see America."

I pointed to the windmill in the distance. "Is the water there drinkable?" I asked. "We need to fill up our canteens."

He shook his head. "I never drink cow water. That's why all these Navajos got gallstones, drinking water like that. I haul my water from Baby Rocks."

"So," I asked, "have you heard anything about those riots in Los Angeles? Were people killed?"

"Yeah. It's a mess over there. They killed fifty, sixty people I heard. All the blacks and Mexicans went on riot because those policemen got off. Well, if you ask me, anyone who's speeding could kill someone, right? So that guy deserved getting beat up. All this rioting, it's just an excuse to rob some stores and get a free TV if you ask me."

Suddenly Acomita had leapt up and was barking savagely at something in the darkness.

"What is it?" I called out.

A voice answered "Hello" from the darkness.

Art shifted uncomfortably.

"How you doing?" the voice said, slurring the words.

I dragged Acomita back but she continued to growl.

"Hello!" I said. "Who are you?"

"I live up here," the voice said.

Art spoke loudly: "Don't pay any attention to him. He's a drunk and a thief."

There was silence in the darkness. I couldn't even see the man's silhouette. It was a disembodied voice.

"What you guys doin'?" the small sad voice asked, a bit unsteadily.

"Don't answer him," Art said. "He'll come back and steal everything to buy liquor."

There was a long silence. "Hey," the voice said, "whatever you guys are doin', good luck."

The voice did not come out of the darkness again.

"Who was he?" I asked. I wondered where in the world he had come from.

Art scuffed his shoe in the dirt. "He's nobody," he said quickly, "just a drunk and a thief."

We shook hands and Art departed in his truck.

▽ ▽ ▽

That night, lying in my sleeping bag, I could not stop thinking about the rioting in Los Angeles. It was true then, that fifty people had died. I lay awake in the darkness in a distant place called White Point Mesa, listening to Christine's slow breathing, listening to the rain and wind buffeting the tent, and I could not shake the image of Los Angeles burning, the smoldering ruins of the white man.

Chapter *14*

SHIPROCK

▽
▽
▽
▽

Chinle Valley
Where the Mountains
Descend Upon a Broad Plain
May 7 and 8, 1992

It was the morning after a rain, with the smell of turf-root and
wildflowers, and the grasses sagging under drops of water. The
sky was a sweet clean blue speckled with cumulus. We found
ourselves in another world, soft and green, a great contrast to
the harsh splendor of Monument Valley.

We lugged our dishes, canteens, and dirty clothes to the
nearby cattle tank and began washing everything. The water
tasted like it came from a mountain spring, not at all the usual
water you find in the desert. We drank deeply and filled our
canteens.

Then we stripped off our clothes and dumped buckets of
water on each other's heads, laughing and splashing about. Even
Acomita went for a swim in the cattle drinking trough. Suddenly
Selene gave a squeak and retreated behind us.

"Somebody's coming!" she hissed, dancing around, trying to
get on her pants.

A four-wheeler ATV was approaching from the west. For a seemingly deserted mesa, I thought, things were rather busy. We got as much of our clothes on as we could before the vehicle pulled up. A lady sat on it. She was stout and well dressed, with a designer scarf looped stylishly around her neck.

"I'm Glenda, Art's wife," she said.

"Hello!" we said heartily, standing there, dripping, holding our clothes up in front of our nakedness.

"Art wanted me to tell you how to get off the mesa. There's only one way down." She stood up in the seat and pointed. "See that little dip about two miles away? Just head straight for that. When you get there, you'll see tire tracks going southwest. Follow those. There's a drift fence and a wire gate in some sand dunes blown up against the mesa. Just close the gate when you go through, and ride the dunes to the bottom."

"Sure, thanks!" I said.

She looked us up and down. "I'll leave you to your washing up," she said, with a smile, and drove off.

Selene was bright red. "I'm sooo *embarrassed*," she hissed, "and I've got all this sand in my jeans."

▽ ▽ ▽

We rode across White Point Mesa with a breeze in our faces. A swaying profusion of wildflowers crowded the ground at our horses' feet: coral-red globemallows, red penstemons, Indian paintbrush, great eruptions of purple locoweed, sego lilies, prickle-poppies, and delicate morning primroses blooming white and then wilting to purple. The land was so vast and treeless that riding through it was like sailing through the ocean, the wind luffing in waves through the grass, the horses rocking with the rhythmic swell.

The heavy form of Black Mesa lay across the horizon to our right, and on our left the Chuska Mountains glowed amethyst in the morning light. We soon arrived at the southern edge of White Point Mesa, where we could look down on Chinle Valley, thirty miles broad and so long it vanished over the southern horizon.

At the base of the mesa we entered another infinity of grass. As the sun climbed in the sky the landscape dissolved into fields of color, the long green prairie interrupted by low mesas of blood-colored sandstone or white gypsum. Above us was an inverted landscape, valleys and canyons made from billowing clouds. Here and there the clouds were dropping distant columns of rain speckled with silent lightning. Every so often we glimpsed a hogan hidden in a swale or hollow, a wisp of smoke curling from the smokehole, a dozing horse in a corral. Occasionally we saw a Navajo, usually an old person or a child, on horseback or standing, quietly watching a flock of sheep. Once we saw an old woman herding sheep with a pickup truck, far from the nearest road, whistling out the open window at two dogs who were doing the work.

▽ ▽ ▽

Monster Slayer killed the savage alien god *Déélgééd* out here somewhere, at a place called Where the Mountains Descend Upon a Broad Plain. From a low hill he spied the grotesque creature lying asleep near the foothills, a massive four-legged beast with a rack of horns like a giant deer.

While he observed the beast, Gopher came walking up. "I greet you my friend!" said Gopher. "Why have you come hither?"

"Oh, I am just wandering around," replied Monster Slayer.

Gopher was suspicious and asked him again what he was doing, and added, "I wonder that you come here; no one but I ever ventures in these parts, for all fear *Déélgééd*. There he lies on the plain yonder."

"It is him I seek," said Monster Slayer, "but I know not how to approach him."

"Ah!" said Gopher. "If that is all you want, I can help you, and if you slay him, all I ask is his hide."

Gopher disappeared into a hole in the ground. While he was gone, *Déélgééd* suddenly rose, walked around sniffing in the four directions, and then curled up and lay down again.

Soon Gopher reappeared.

"I have dug a tunnel to *Déélgééd*," he said. "I have made a hole upward from the tunnel to his heart." He had also dug four side tunnels, one east, one west, one north, and one south, for Monster Slayer to hide in.

Monster Slayer crawled through the tunnel, carrying the great bow and arrow that the Sun had given him. He soon came up underneath the beast's heart, which he could see beating strongly. He drew back the bowstring, and let fly an arrow of chain-lightning.

Déélgééd leapt up with a roar of rage and pain, and plowed the ground with his horns, back and forth, trying to reach his tormenter. The Slayer of Alien Gods dodged from tunnel to tunnel, just keeping ahead of the horns. Finally the creature writhed and lay still upon the plain.

Monster Slayer fled back through the tunnel and observed *Déélgééd* from his distant hill. While he was standing there, wondering if *Déélgééd* was really dead, an old creature approached wearing tight leggings and shirt, with a jaunty cap and feather on his head. It was Ground Squirrel.

"What do you want here, my grandchild?" he asked. "Do you not fear the *anáye* that dwells on yonder plain?"

"I think I have killed him," said the Slayer of Enemies, "but I am not certain."

Ground Squirrel volunteered to inspect *Déélgééd* to make sure he was dead. "He never minds me," he explained. "I can approach him any time without danger."

And soon, Monster Slayer saw the tiny old animal dancing and singing on the topmost horn. In his exuberance, Ground Squirrel had decorated his face with streaks of *Déélgééd*'s blood, which can be seen on Ground Squirrel's face to this day. Gopher, as his reward, gnawed off a piece of *Déélgééd*'s skin and put it on his back, saying, "I shall wear this in order that, in the days to come, when the people increase, they may know what sort of skin *Déélgééd* wore." It would always be a reminder of the days when the Earth was out of balance.

Monster Slayer took as trophies a section of the creature's bowel filled with his blood and a piece of the creature's lung. He brought both back to Changing Woman, to prove to her he had indeed killed *Déélgééd*, the fearful Horned Destroyer of the Fifth World.

Chapter 15

SOUTHERN BUTTE
—LOS GIGANTES

Chinle Valley
Many Farms
May 9–11, 1992

I am indeed its child.
Absolutely I am Earth's child.
Now I am the child of long life, of happiness,
I am the child of the sky,
I am the child of the mountains, of the waters,
I am the child of the darkness, of the dawn,
I am the child of the twilight of evening,
I am the child of the Sun,
I am the child of white corn, of yellow corn,
Now I am the child of long life, of happiness.

—A SONG TAUGHT TO THE PEOPLE BY THE TWO INNER FORMS
OF THE EARTH [25]

For days we traveled through a landscape of Zen-like emptiness,
a great yellow plain bounded by blue mountains. It was more a
state of mind than a landscape. Riding through it, hour after

hour, day after day, became a form of meditation; we could feel nothing but the swaying of the horse and the wind, hear nothing but the rhythmic creak of leather and the croaking of the vultures that sometimes circled overhead. We saw coyotes slinking away, grinning back at us with their tongues hanging out, and pronghorn antelope running against the horizon. One time we surprised a herd of wild burros in a dry wash, who took flight in high panic, careening like pinballs across the plain.

The long hours of riding did peculiar things to the mind. The landscape around us became mirrored by a similar emptiness within, an internal landscape of silence. We human beings have so little idea of how loud the clamor of the world is, how much deafening busyness is happening in our minds and in our lives, that when true silence does arrive it is a revelation.

Over the past few weeks, all the false complications and worries of life had fallen away like rotten scales. It was a great housecleaning of the brain, leaving only those stray thoughts and memories that mysteriously resisted moving: the smell of rain blown against a screened porch, the melody of a Chopin prelude, the motion of my brother's arm as he cast his flyline across the lake at evening, a dog's bark echoing through a snowy wood, frozen puddles on the path to school. These things, somehow, mattered terribly. The rest was irrelevant.

We hardly ever spoke during these endless hours. The frantic human need to talk over a silence had disappeared. We were utterly alone, three people in a nothingness, and that was enough. For all we knew, the rest of the world could have ceased to exist.

▽ ▽ ▽

We began to have serious trouble finding water. The only water we had seen since leaving White Point Mesa was a poisonous spring, marked with a crude skull and crossbones and the words, "Water Not Fit for Human Consumption. No Drinking, Washing, or Bathing." By this time the horses had been without water for twenty-four hours, and they were starting to show it, becoming restless and irritable.

Several miles beyond the poisonous water, dusk caught up with us and we stopped to make our second waterless camp in a row. It was in a sandy depression, covered with clumps of sacaton grass, where we felt hidden from the disconcerting vastness of the prairie.

We were woken up at first light by the sound of thunder.

"What's that?" Christine asked.

I listened for a moment. "Wild horses," I said, climbing out of my sleeping bag. Wild horses meant trouble.

I pulled on my boots and stepped out, in time to see a herd of six horses gallop over the ridge and run straight through our camp, their nostrils flaring and ears laid back, and make a wide circle around the camp. They were true mustangs, short and stout, with shaggy manes, Roman-nosed faces, and thick necks. They were all undoubtedly related: dark sorrel in color, each had a white line down the face and white socks. The stallion stopped where Redbone was picketed about two hundred yards away, and in a fury spun around and whaled Redbone in the chest with both hind legs. It made a sickening sound, like a brickbat whacking a side of ham. I ran toward them shouting and whirling a rope. Most horses, even wild ones, know what a rope is, and the stallion flattened his ears and plunged away, slinging his head back and forth and kicking behind him.

Meanwhile, the other horses were circling around to make another pass. Roscoe, who was hobbled with a side-line, became so excited that he got tangled up and fell down. As the wild horses disappeared behind the rise, Brazos, incited by thoughts of freedom, tried to follow at a gallop. When he hit the end of his picket rope, the steel bullsnap at the picket pin shattered and he kept on going past me, dragging the rope. I stomped on it as it went by; the rope zinged under my boot as I bore down, finally arresting him.

Soon all was quiet. I unbuckled Roscoe's side-line and got him back on his feet, and then I went to look at Redbone. He had two perfect hoofmarks on his fur where the stallion had kicked him. I felt around and saw that he was bruised but otherwise unhurt.

I heard Selene's delighted laughter pealing across the prairie. She was poking her head outside the tent.

"Doug! What're you doing out there, running around naked, yelling your head off?" And she laughed and laughed.

I looked down. All I had on was a big pair of cowboy boots and the underwear I had been sleeping in. I cut a perfectly ridiculous figure.

▽ ▽ ▽

We hurried through a breakfast of oatmeal, anxious to resume our search for water. At the conclusion, without thinking, Selene filled up her cup to rinse it out.

"After you've cleaned that cup," Christine said, "I want you to drink that water."

Selene was aghast. "What?" she cried. "Drink *dishwater?*"

"We can't afford to throw it away."

"No!" said Selene defiantly. "I *won't* drink dishwater. I'd rather die of thirst."

"You have to."

"I won't! I won't!" And then she burst into tears.

Christine and I drank the water.

We brought out the canteens and took stock. We had about two quarts left, not a lot when we found ourselves needing twelve to sixteen quarts a day. What was worse, the horses had been without water for thirty-six hours—an extremely serious situation.

We set off, moving at a good pace. My map showed a windmill and cattle tank about seven miles off, and we headed in its direction, navigating as if by sea, using the compass and dead reckoning. We came upon it around noon, sitting in a large bowl, in its own world of sky and grass. Something was not right, however; hundreds of horses and cattle were angrily milling about.

We rode up. The windmill was broken and the water trough was dry. A large bull, his testicles dangling like two melons in a sack, cast a pair of red eyes in our direction. A stallion stood guard at the water trough, screaming and kicking at any other horses that tried to shove past. I shook my trusty rope in the stallion's face and he backed off.

I turned on the lever, hoping there might be some residual water in the system; it squealed with dry rust and a single drop of water swelled at the lip, hung for a moment, and fell: and that was all. Redbone crowded by me and mouthed the pipe with his fat lips as if to suck water out of it. At the sight, the other horses crowded forward and a fight erupted between two stallions, with kicking and rearing and teeth snapping like gunshots. I led our horses off to safety.

"I can't believe this," Christine said. "These animals look like they've been without water for days. They could die."

"They're obviously desperate," I said.

"Does this mean we're going to die of thirst?" Selene asked.

"Of course not," Christine said. "We'll just have to keep riding until we find some water, that's all."

We were lucky in the weather, at least: the day was cool and moist.

We rode on. With each passing hour, as their thirst augmented, our horses became increasingly bad-tempered and unruly. Christine's temper deteriorated apace. Her two horses were nipping at each other and prancing about, and I could hear her behind me, muttering threats that became louder and more dire as the day wore on.

She suddenly issued a loud expletive and cried, "Why, you're no better than a bucket of rotten guts! Ugh, I can't ride you any more."

Selene giggled. "What'd you say?"

"Be quiet," Christine said.

Christine dismounted and started hauling them along by their lead ropes.

She caught up to me. "When is this flat country ever going to end? What's the point of this? We've been riding three days and we've gone absolutely nowhere."

"This was the country trampled down by the great wedding feast between the Sun and Changing Woman," I began. "It—"

"I didn't ask you what the hell it was. I just want to know when it'll end."

"According to my map we've gone sixty miles," I said.

"I don't believe it. This is awful. We haven't seen a tree or a bush in two days. We haven't been able to have a nice fire in the evening. Everything is filthy and we're drinking dishwater. I'm so dirty I'm getting rashes."

"At least the riding is good," I said, trying to be encouraging.

"You call this *good* riding? These horses are impossible. Totally impossible."

"I'm not enjoying it very much either," I said.

"Yeah right. You *love* it. You just think it's so wonderful with all this dirt and no water."

"Now why would I think that?" I asked irritably.

"I can just see it in your face. You think it's just a big, wonderful, macho *adventure.*"

"I'm glad I'm marrying a psychiatrist," I said, "who can psychoanalyze people by their faces."

"Don't be a wiseguy with me," Christine said.

"I'm not the one complaining and cussing out my horses."

"Oh, listen, this coming from the man who *never* swears at his horses."

"Hey!" Selene shouted. "You two *quit* it. Right now! Geez, you're like two *kids*."

There was an embarrassed silence.

"Now Mommy," Selene said. "Cheer up, look at the bright side."

"What bright side," Christine said.

"Well, why don't you two do what I'm doing?" Selene said.

"What are you doing?"

"I'm thinking about a big huge piece of strawberry-rhubarb pie at the Zia Diner."

We were both silent.

"With two scoops of vanilla ice cream," she added.

"When we get home," I said, "we'll go to the Zia and you can have your pie."

"*With* ice cream? Promise?"

"I promise," I said. "And then we'll go to El Nido's and I'll have an ice-cold Bombay gin martini with a twist followed by a steak, medium rare, covered with garlic and cracked pepper, a baked potato, sour cream, and chives, and a huge salad with blue cheese dressing."

"I want twin steamed lobsters," said Christine, "with drawn butter and lemon. And mussels steamed in a white wine and garlic sauce. With fresh oysters on the half shell. For dessert, a Linzer torte piled with whipped cream."

There was a silence while we digested our thoughts.

"Actually," Christine said, "I'd settle for a glass of cold water and a bath."

We came over a rise and there, a mile away at the bottom of the next draw, was a windmill, turning merrily in the breeze. We had found our water.

We camped five miles beyond the windmill. As usual, there was no wood or brush to burn, but I found some cow chips and clumps of dry grass and started a fire of sorts. A plume of fragrant smoke drifted into the empty sky. I stirred up some brownie mix, poured it into the Dutch oven, and set it on the fire to bake. I piled the smoking cow chips around and on top of it. The brownies took forever to cook, but they emerged from the pot gooey and delicious, with a faint but not displeasing taste of smoke. We ate ravenously and then washed our dishes. Selene watched with tremendous satisfaction as we poured the dirty water into the sand.

"I *knew* we weren't going to die of thirst," she said scornfully.

After dinner we spread the horsepads on the prairie, and wrapped ourselves in blankets, huddling together against the chill. A great twilight peace had settled down. I lay on my back and examined the inverted world: the empty, abyssal sky, surrounded by the blue peaks of the mountains, and arching over everything the darkening plain of the earth. What a beautiful world, I thought, and how quickly we are losing it.

"Where are we, exactly?" Selene asked.

"Another ten miles to Many Farms," I said, "and then fifteen more to Chinle."

"No, I mean, like, *where?* What state?"

"Arizona, of course! You silly," Christine said.

"How was I supposed to know? I thought we were in Utah. I didn't see any signs at the border!"

We laughed.

"Doug, tell me more of the story," Selene said, snuggling up beside me.

I resumed the story, with the boy in the desert finding a magic well, and the water bubbling up over the top, and soon it was night and we went into our tents to sleep.

▽ ▽ ▽

The town of Many Farms lay alongside Chinle Creek, a collection of bleak HUD houses at a crossroads, with two gas stations, a convenience store, and a laundry.

We tied our horses in a trash-strewn lot behind the store and bought french fries and tacos. A few suspicious-looking men, drunk, loitered around the back door of the gas station, and as I walked by one of them slipped a silver belt buckle out of his pocket and offered it to me for ten dollars. We ate and got out of town as quickly as we could.

On the outskirts, we passed a house trailer surrounded by a barbed-wire fence. A young man stood at the gate. He waved us over.

"Where you guys going?" he asked. "You camping out?"

"We're going to camp past the lake," I said.

"Big storm coming," he said. "*Big* storm. You better stay here in my hogan."

"Thanks," I said, "but we really wanted to get another few miles of riding in today."

"We'd love to stay!" Christine said firmly. "How kind of you!"

"But it's only two o'clock," I said.

"Yay, Mom!" Selene cried. "Let's stay in the hogan!"

The man smiled. "You can put your horses in the corrals over there. We got hay and water. You guys look like you need a rest."

"We could make at least five miles—," I began again.

Selene turned to me. "Sorry, Doug," she said, "but we're staying here, and that's *final*."

I knew when I was beaten.

The young man introduced himself as Dwayne Betonnie.[26] He was about twenty-four, wearing a black T-shirt under a nylon warm-up jacket. His voice was so quiet and mellifluous that a hush seemed to fall when he spoke. He was unaccountably pleased by our arrival, as if he were expecting us, and he bustled about, showing us the corrals, where the feed and water were, and our new quarters.

The hogan sat in his backyard, an eight-sided hut made of plywood painted a cheerful blue with white trim. We unpacked our gear, and Dwayne advised us to lock everything inside as there were many thieves in the area.

It was cozy. The door faced east toward Chinle Wash, and the interior was lit by a single naked lightbulb run in on a wire from the house trailer. The floor was hard-packed dirt. A pile of mattresses covered with an old Pendleton wool blanket lay in a corner. The usual stove—half an oil drum—sat in the middle of the floor, with a stovepipe running up through the smokehole in the center of the roof. A large plastic banner of stars and stripes was tacked up around the inside walls. Bundles of herbs hung from the rafters.

"What's the flag doing in here?" Selene asked Dwayne.

"We had special ceremonies here for soldiers returning from Desert Storm," he said.

"What kind of ceremonies?" Selene asked.

"Navajo ceremonies," he said.

"With a *flag?*" Selene asked.

Dwayne looked surprised. "Why not? We're all Americans, right?"

He left us to get settled.

After we unpacked, Christine and I rode our horses across Chinle Wash to see Many Farms Lake. It was a typical desert lake, brown and desolate. We found a large Anasazi ruin, utterly leveled, on a rise above the lake. It was, apparently, a parking place for teenagers from Many Farms. Thousands of prehistoric potsherds and sandstone blocks littered the ground, mixed with broken beer bottles and aluminum cans.

We rode down to Chinle Wash and galloped along the sandy bottom, having a grand time and glad to be rid of the packhorses. Christine indulged her love of speed once again, goading her horse into a terrifying pace, churning up a rocketplume of sand and dust behind, hollering and brandishing her hat above her head. When we stopped to rest, we saw on the far side of the wash an old woman with iron hair walking slowly up a hill. She drove a flock of sheep toward a hogan tucked in the lee of a bluff. A small, yapping mongrel nipped at the heels of the laggards, turned to bark at us, and then went back to work. A rising wind signaled the approach of the storm and the woman's dress whipped about her. She clutched at her collar, bent over to temper the force of the blast, and opened the gate to the sheep pen. The sheep streamed in, expertly hustled along by the capable dog. Then she disappeared into her hogan.

Back at our hogan, I started a fire with lumps of coal from a pile in the yard, while Christine washed our clothes in a pail behind the trailer.

The wind picked up, and around five o'clock a few drops of rain came spinning down. A mountain of black thunderheads advanced from the south, boiling with electricity, and slowly covered the sky like a great dark eyelid. The wind steadily increased until it was screaming through the cottonwoods along the wash, pressing the trees nearly horizontal, sending twigs and brush flying across the yard. It felt like the beginning of a hurricane. The hogan vibrated from the blast.

Selene spread out her sleeping bag on a mattress and snuggled inside, playing Gameboy, with her journal, Polaroid camera, candy, postcards, and pencils arranged neatly around her.

▽ ▽ ▽

Around six o'clock, Dwayne knocked at the door and came inside with a plate heaping with fry bread.

"Thought you folks might be hungry," he said, passing the plate around and sitting on a stump inside the door. "Storm's gonna hit at any moment. I could see it coming up the wash."

As if on cue, there was a sound like machine-gun fire on the roof. A shower of hailstones came flying through the smokehole, rattling and bouncing off the inside walls of the hogan. Some were more than half an inch in diameter.

"If you were out there in your tent," Dwayne said, "there wouldn't be much left of you. That hail would tear you to pieces."

Selene looked at me, aghast. "And *you* wanted to ride on! If we'd listened to you, Doug, we'd be *dead!*"

"I'm glad you insisted," I said, feeling the hogan shudder.

Selene burrowed deeper into her sleeping bag. "I'm so happy," she said, giggling to herself. "It's like *paradise* in here."

I thought, we human beings really don't need as much as we think.

A particularly large hailstone ricocheted off the wall and landed in Christine's lap. She popped it in her mouth and we laughed.

The wind shifted and the fusillade of hail swiveled on top of us. We jumped up, dragging away our sleeping bags, fending off the stinging blows. A bolt of lightning then struck in the yard, and the flash was followed instantly by a crash of thunder like a blow to the gut. The lightbulb dimmed, flickered, and winked out. We could see the fire shining through cracks in the rotted barrel, the light playing about on the walls like demons dancing by firelight. The stove glowed cherry red, throwing out a wonderful infrared warmth.

"So what you guys doing?" asked Dwayne.

I told him about our trip, where we'd been, where we were headed. He asked a few questions while munching on fry bread. There was a pause in the conversation.

Then he said, quietly: "You gotta be careful. These skin-walkers gonna be out tonight."

There was a short silence. We all knew what skinwalkers were. Selene had been falling asleep but she quickly woke up.

"What, around *here?*" she asked.

He looked at me steadily. "You believe in skinwalkers?"

I said, "Yes."

He watched us without speaking, the fire playing off his

face. There was a white blast of lightning through the smokehole and a wallop of thunder.

"Why, you know something about witches?" I finally asked.

Dwayne nodded. "Yes," he said quietly, "I know quite a bit."

There was another flash and a crump of thunder. I thought, if this guy is going to tell us about witches, he picked the right night.

"Lot of witches live north of here, down Chinle Wash. They come through here every night. Every single night."

"Where?" Selene demanded to know.

He gestured toward the door. "Right there," he said, "through the yard."

I could barely hear his voice over the noise of the storm.

"No *way*," said Selene. "Get out of here."

"Shhh," Christine said. "Don't interrupt."

Dwayne continued, softly. "You hear the dogs start barking and going Oooooo, Oooooo, and you know they're there. Your dog, that yellow dog, is she outside?"

"She's under the eaves."

"Tonight, when they come through, you'll hear her start making a sound like *nothing* you've ever heard before. The rain'll stop at midnight, and they'll come through around three in the morning."

There was a long pause, broken only by the roaring of the wind and the hammering of hail on the roof. The hail abruptly stopped, giving way to a torrential rain which came down through the smokehole at such an acute angle it was hitting the wall, the water running over the dirt floor. We had to adjust our position again.

"What kind of witches?" I asked.

"Naked men and naked women, spotted all over with white clay. Some of them are covered with jewelry. And some are these wolf-skin runners. They lay wolf skins on either side of their body, and get down on all fours. And say an evil prayer. And one of those skins just *shhhtuck!*" He smacked his hands together. "It just *sucks* on to their body. Then they move like the wind, seeing in the dark with these glowing red eyes. But the worst are the naked ones covered with jewelry. Totally naked, loaded down with jewelry."

"Jewelry? What kind of jewelry?"

"Jewelry of the dead. Say an old man dies, a respected person. They put him in a nice suit, put him in a coffin. Then you bring jewelry, all kinds, and lay them down on top of him. Everyone brings jewelry. Then you close it up and bury him. That skinwalker, he comes at night, and un-digs that coffin. And he wears that jewelry when he goes out. Sometimes if he needs money, he'll go to Gallup or Flagstaff, and he'll pawn that jewelry. You see all that stuff up there, all that dead pawn? That's what those skinwalkers been selling. When you wear that stuff, you're wearing a dead person's jewelry and if you don't have the skinwalker power, it'll kill you."

He paused and looked into the fire. It was burning yellow-hot and the sulfurous smell of coal smoke hung in the air.

I wondered why he was telling us all this. My previous experience had been that most Navajos were extremely reluctant to talk about witchcraft. But he seemed positively eager, almost obsessed, as if he'd had it bottled up inside and we, being perfect strangers, suddenly presented him with the opportunity to let it all out.

"My uncle," continued Dwayne, "that happened to him. He was an old, respected person. When he died the skinwalkers un-dug his grave, took the jewelry. Then they cut pieces off his body to make corpse powder."

"Corpse powder?" Christine asked.

"Dry some of the dead flesh, grind it up. Then they blow it on you, *phoooo*, and you get ghost sickness."

"Who are these skinwalkers?" I asked.

"They live north along Chinle Creek. During the day they're people, just like me. You'd never know, except they always seem to have money. Always got a new pickup in front of the house."

"Do you know who any of these skinwalkers are?" I asked.

There was a long pause after the question. Then he said, "Lot of my relatives are skinwalkers."

He let that sink in.

"Your *relatives?*" Christine whispered.

"My aunt, who lives just across the wash."

"You mean the old woman with the little hogan against the hill? With the sheep?"

He nodded, his eyes slowly traveling around the room.

"We saw her when we were riding," I said. "She was wearing a shawl. She looked like a nice little old lady."

"That's the one," he said. "She's a witch."

Selene had gone rigid in her sleeping bag and she took my hand and just about crushed it.

"I don't understand," Christine said. "Why would anyone want to become a skinwalker?"

"Power," he whispered. "Power over nature. Power over people. Money."

"How do you become one?" I asked.

Dwayne Betonnie was silent for a long time, and just when I thought he had decided to stop talking, he shifted on his elbows and looked up.

"You got to kill someone you love. It's got to be a brother, sister, father, or mother. You got to *make* that sacrifice to get the power."

"You mean, murder?" I asked. I could feel Selene's hand bearing down on mine. She was terrified.

"A kind of murder. But you don't go shoot someone or anything like that. You *wish* the death. You *decide* in your mind that you want to become a skinwalker, and you *wish* that person's death. Then, a week later, maybe he's driving to Gallup, gets in a head-on wreck. Or he rolls his car. Everyone thinks it's an accident. But *you* know different. When that happens, the pact is sealed, and then you can get the ability, the power. You've started down the path to the dark side. There's no going back."

Dwayne shifted on his stump, and the light flickered on the walls.

"There's an initiation ceremony," Dwayne whispered. "You got to find someone who's already a skinwalker and pay them. It's very expensive. Then you have this ceremony. If you don't do it exactly right, the ceremony will kill you."

"What kind of ceremony?" I asked.

"They use traditional Navajo ceremonies but turn them around. Reverse them. Say the prayers backwards. Reverse the spiral windings on the prayer sticks. Like, say, with the stick they use in the Squaw Dance? You have to wind the string around the prayer stick in a certain direction. Like this."

He demonstrated the direction with his hand.

"You mean, clockwise?" I asked.

He nodded. "Clockwise. When you enter a hogan for a ceremony, you got to walk clockwise to your seat. Same with a sweat. The skinwalkers, they reverse that direction, wrap it the other way. It turns the power in the other direction. Like what the Anasazi did, like in Canyon de Chelly, with these reversed spirals and all that other stuff carved into the rock. They were turning the power in the other direction."

He paused for a moment.

"You know Black Mesa over there? Where that big coal mine is?"

I nodded.

"The coal company stripped that land. There's nothing growing, no life at all. Nobody lives there anymore. It's all deserted. That's where the skinwalkers get together, have those ceremonies, take new people in. It's like a witches' convention."

He laughed suddenly and hard.

I had once visited the Black Mesa strip mine, the second largest in the world. The word *hellish* describes it well; the devastation covered thousands of acres. Much of the land had been reconstructed and reseeded, but nothing had taken and the land was dead. The artificial landscape was strangely unsettling, because the dip and course of the ground had no logic to it; it showed no erosional or geological history; it was just a bulldozer operator's idea of a landscape. Because traditional Navajos (and Hopis) believe that Black Mesa is the body of the Earth itself, they feel the coal mine is literally digging into her heart and killing her. It seemed like a logical place for witchcraft activity.

"Sometimes," Dwayne continued, "when these skinwalkers come through here, they shoot a bone into you. They have a little bow and arrow. You get up in the morning and *ahhh!* you got a pain in your back. I go to this medicine man, he says a prayer and extracts that bone. Cuts it open and sucks it out. One time he took a deer's tooth out of my back. He lets you look at it but you can't touch it."

"Why would they shoot this bone into you?" I asked.

"They get jealous of me, because I've got a good job and a new pickup. But I go to a medicine man I can trust. A lot of these medicine men, they work together and one'll make you sick and then the other takes your money to sing a cure.

"Sometimes the skinwalker, they get on top of the hogan, and look down the smokehole. Wait for a flash of lightning, and see where everyone's sleeping, then shoot a bead into someone or blow corpse powder down the hole. You got to look up through the smokehole, see if anything is moving against the stars, blotting out the stars. Then you know he's there. When it flashes, then you can see him with these red eyes looking down at you.

"Tonight, when you hear them dogs start barking, if you go outside you might see these dark shapes, *whooosh*, running away into the darkness. Or maybe not, because you're white. White people can't usually see them. But I've seen them. . . . I've seen them."

There was another very long silence. It had grown cold in the hogan and the fire glowed dully inside the stove. I threw a few more lumps in and we all sat watching the flickering light behind the cracks in the barrel.

"Well!" Dwayne suddenly said, getting up. "I guess you folks gotta get some sleep, after that long riding you done. Don't worry about the weather; it'll be clear tomorrow."

We thanked him again for the hogan. We shook hands and he departed into the dark.

There was a long silence after he left.

"That was some story," I said.

"There's *no such thing* as witches," Selene said firmly, with a derisive snort, but still crushing my hand.

"I'm afraid to look up into the smokehole," said Christine. "I think I'll see some skinwalker with red eyes staring down at me."

"Oh Mommy," Selene said, "please, *please* be quiet."

Around midnight the rain stopped, and gradually the thunder and lightning died away into a deathly stillness.

▽ ▽ ▽

At three o'clock, we were all startled awake to hear Acomita let loose a terrible savage barking which trailed into a drawn-out howl. Suddenly all the dogs in Many Farms were screeching, their barking and howling erupting across the stillness of the night.

"The skinwalkers!" Selene screamed, bolting up in her sleeping bag. "Oh my *God*, it's the *skinwalkers!*" She grabbed me around the neck in a chokehold, sobbing with fear, her whole body shaking. I managed to pry her hands loose, but she scrabbled and grabbed at me like a drowning person, pulling my hair and clutching my ears. I had to pin her arms down.

"Don't worry," I said. "There aren't any skinwalkers. That's just a story. And anyway they won't hurt white people. I'll hold your hands."

"They're killing Acomita!" she cried.

Acomita was shrieking in a kind of frenzy, a sound I had

never heard her make before. It was highly unnerving. All the dogs in town seemed to be involved in one unholy chorus.

"The skinwalkers!" Selene screamed again.

I sat up and began to pull down my bedroll.

"Don't you dare go outside," Christine said.

"Oh my God no!" Selene cried, clutching me again.

"Okay, okay, I'm not going anywhere."

We waited, wide awake, in the darkness. Selene buried herself against my side and squeezed my hands every time Acomita let loose another round of ferocious barking or howling. When she thought I might be drifting off to sleep she would shake me and cry out, "Don't go to sleep! Doug! Wake up!"

After about thirty or forty minutes, the barking rapidly subsided. Selene finally became quiet and her grip relaxed and she fell asleep.

▽ ▽ ▽

We woke late. The sun was streaming through the tiny window. Selene sat up in her sleeping bag, and she had a sheepish look on her face. The horrors of the previous night seemed very far away. We all felt a little silly.

"Mom?" Selene said in a small voice.

"Yes?"

"Promise you won't be mad?"

"Mad? Why?"

"Well," she said, "I can't believe I'm nine years old and I did what I just did."

"What did you do?"

Selene covered her mouth with her hand. "I was really scared last night," she said.

"So was I," said Christine.

"I was so scared, I peed in my sleeping bag." She dropped her head into her arms. "I'm *so* embarrassed."

"Come over here," Christine said, gathering her daughter into her arms. "Don't worry about it. Unzip it and we'll air it out in the sun. I was scared too. But look what a beautiful morning it is, and all the witches have gone back to bed. The storm's over, the sun's shining."

When I opened the door to the hogan, the sun roared in and I could feel the pressure of solar radiation bearing me back into the dimness. Acomita came sniffing over, subdued and bedraggled but unhurt, and we gave her breakfast. I looked into her little black eyes, wondering just what it was she had seen.

The sky was impeccable and great sheets of muddy water lay across the ground. It was a glorious morning; the earth had been washed clean and the storm had shaken the fragrance out of the Russian olives along the wash. Behind the trees I could hear the swift rumble of Chinle Creek, swollen to the size of a river.

We were starving. I cooked a big breakfast of oatmeal on the stove, and we sat around eating.

"Doug?" Selene asked. "Do you really believe in witches like you told Dwayne last night?"

"Yes," I said slowly. "I do."

"Really? Get *out* of here."

"Well," I said, "I don't mean to say that I literally believe a man can put on a wolf skin and run sixty miles an hour. But there's no doubt in my mind there are skinwalkers like Dwayne said. There are always people who want to take what's good, like the Navajo healing ceremonies, and turn them around. Witchcraft is a very real force."

"But the red eyes? And the corpse powder?"

"Who's to say those things can't possibly exist? Maybe they exist for real, or maybe they exist because people believe in them. All societies have something like witchcraft. An ultimate perversion of their values."

"What's perversion?"

"Something strange and unnatural."

"Witchcraft," Christine said, "is just another way of describing evil. It exists everywhere."

"So what's our witchcraft?" Selene asked.

"It's the same thing Dwayne talked about," I said. "The same old desire for money, power, and control over other people. When I lived in New York City, I met plenty of people who were sort of like Navajo skinwalkers. Only they wore suits. There's not much difference between digging up the dead to get their jewelry and making a business deal that ruins a thousand people's lives."

"Well," Selene said firmly, "I hope *I* never meet a skinwalker."

"I think," I said, "that there's a little bit of skinwalker in each one of us. There's a part that craves power and money.

There comes a time in everyone's life when they have to face that skinwalker inside."

"Not me!" said Selene. "No way! There's no skinwalker in me!"

▽ ▽ ▽

We spent the day in Many Farms, and that afternoon walked down the road to a local Mother's Day rodeo. Everyone sang "The Star Spangled Banner," and the announcer spoke in Navajo and English over a buzzing PA system. In the hills behind, Navajo kids were riding horses, three per horse, their shrill laughter floating over the arena. All the people sat in and on their cars and flashed their lights when someone made his eight seconds.

After the rodeo I talked to one of the bull riders, who had been thrown and was walking back to his truck, coiling and uncoiling his bullrope. We stood for a while next to his pickup in the hot sun, while Selene and a group of Navajo children had a race across the arena, to a place where apples and oranges had been scattered. All the kids had taken off their hats and were filling them up. Selene was the only white kid out there, but she didn't look out of place, being sunburned and covered with dust.

"Those were tough bulls," he said. "You see that Brahma? He broke his back throwing his rider."

"Broke his back?"

"Yep. He was a green bull. Cost that stock contractor a lot of money, losing a bull like that."

I could see the animal lying in the far corrals, surrounded by men in white cowboy hats. There were a lot of raised voices in Navajo and a stock trailer was backing up to the scene.

"How did you do?" I asked.

"I just couldn't get the rhythm of that bull," he said. "Right out of the chute he started spinning, and I lost it in the well."

"The well?"

"They call the inside of the spin the well."

I asked if he could give us a ride back to Dwayne's.

"Sure," he said. "I know Dwayne. Haven't seen much of him since his brother's accident, though."

"What happened?" I asked.

"Rolled his car going to Gallup."

Chapter 16

NAVAJOS, UTE RAID PANEL
—CANYON DEL MUERTO

Canyon de Chelly
August and September
1849

A certain people are going to come to us.
From below where the sun constantly rises,
They are going to come to us.
Their ears are wider than anything.
They extend down to their ankles.
And these people at night,
Covering themselves with those ears of theirs,
Lie down to sleep.

—FROM AN OLD STORY THAT CIRCULATED AMONG THE NAVAJO
TRIBE IN THE LATE 1840s[27]

We rested a day in Many Farms and then continued south, along
Chinle Creek, to the mouth of Canyon de Chelly, the great
stronghold of the Navajo people.

The opening to the canyon was sudden and narrow. Passing through the high sandstone portals was like entering the gates to a different world. Chinle Creek was flowing full bore out of the canyon, swelled by the recent storm, a sweep of chocolate water rippling below the red bluffs.

Canyon de Chelly lies at the center of the *Diné Bikeyah*, and it is in many ways the spiritual home of the Navajo. It was also here where so much of the tragic history of the *Diné* played itself out.

In 1848, the United States annexed the Southwest from Mexico after the Mexican-American War. At the time, the U.S. government had only the barest notion of the Navajo. The *Diné Bikeyah* was mostly unexplored territory, where the laws of the United States did not penetrate.

The United States could not permit such a large area to remain outside its jurisdiction. In 1849, it launched a military expedition to Navajo country. The expedition would explore this vast new territory and go to Canyon de Chelly to bring back pieces of paper suitably marked by the *Diné*, acknowledging the sovereign power and glory of the United States of America over their persons, property, and land. It was the first significant contact between the Americans and the Navajos.

▽ ▽ ▽

In the cool of the morning of August 16, 1849, the military expedition left Fort Marcy on the outskirts of Santa Fe. They followed the old Spanish Camino Real to the edge of La Bajada escarpment. From the rim, they had their first glimpse of an 11,000-foot peak known to the Spanish as San Mateo. This was the mountain the Navajos called *Tsoodzil*, Blue Bead Mountain, the Sacred Mountain of the South. It marked the southern boundary of the *Diné Bikeyah*. For the Americans, it marked the edge of the unknown.

Along with the troops was a young man, James H. Simpson, a lieutenant of the Corps of Topographical Engineers. Simpson was under the vague orders to make "such a survey of the country as the movements of the troops will permit." He had arrived in Santa Fe a few months before, a short man with a blunt, pragmatic face, a builder of roads and improver of harbors. The expedition was commanded by Colonel John Macrae Washington, the new military commander of New Mexico, a rigid and coldly correct Virginian.

In signing the treaty with Mexico, the United States had unwittingly inserted itself into a bitter, two-hundred-year war between the Navajos and the New Mexicans.[28] The new U.S. territorial officials in Santa Fe did not understand this conflict, and interpreted Navajo raids on New Mexican villages as open defiance of the United States government. What they did not realize was that the New Mexicans were also raiding Navajo settlements far from the eye of the government and were holding hundreds—possibly thousands—of Navajo slaves.

Thus, when John Macrae Washington set out, he was in a belligerent mood: he was itching to teach the Navajos a lesson they would never forget. In going to Canyon de Chelly, Washington did not intend to nibble at the edges of the *Diné Bikeyah*; he would eat its heart.

▽ ▽ ▽

In several days, the troops passed the northern flank of Blue Bead or San Mateo Mountain; Simpson, on the return trip, would rename it Mount Taylor in honor of the president and hero of the Mexican War. And thus would the renaming of the landscape, the final act of conquest, begin.

They did not know the significance of the mountain or even that they had passed into the *Diné Bikeyah*; all they knew was they had entered unknown territory. The *Diné*, for the time being, were keeping hidden.

As the Americans pushed deeper into the unknown land, they found themselves in a long yellow-toothed landscape interrupted by low mesas, surreal badlands, and curious outcroppings of rock like the droppings of a beast. Except on a few high mesas, there were virtually no trees. Just past the Continental Divide the troops struck the headwaters of a wash which their Pueblo Indian guides called the Río Chaco. They headed down it, still moving northwest. Chaco Wash in August is implacable, flanked by sand dunes, grasslands, and long thirsty horizons of endless blue.

As they rounded a bend in the wash, Simpson was amazed to see, on a slight elevation, "a conspicuous ruin." It was a huge wrecked building that once stood several stories and contained hundreds of rooms.

Simpson and the troops had become the first Americans to gaze upon the vanished civilization of Chaco Canyon. His guides called it Pueblo Pintado, "Painted Village."

Simpson did not know that Pueblo Pintado was sacred to the Navajos, a place they called *Kin nteel*, or Broad House. According to the Navajo creation story, Broad House was one of the hiding places of the First People during their flight from the alien gods. At that time Chaco Canyon was under construction by a powerful and evil despot who had enslaved all the Pueblo people in the region, forcing them to undertake huge building projects for his pleasure and greater glory.

Now Broad House lay in massive ruin, and Simpson was awed by its size and grandeur. He was particularly impressed by its masonry. In it he found a "combination of science and art" which must have belonged to a "higher stage of civilization and refinement." He added: "Indeed, so beautifully diminutive and true are the details of the structure as to cause it, at a little distance, to have all the appearance of a magnificent piece of mosaic work."

Pintado was just the beginning. As they moved deeper into the canyon, ruin after ruin came into view, many four stories high and still roofed. As Simpson explored the ruins, he recorded their names as given by his guides, a jumble of Spanish, Navajo, and Hopi words: Chettro Kettle, Hungo Pavie, Una Vida, Wijiji, Pueblo Bonito.

The entire canyon was sacred to the Navajos, the center of the *Anaasází bighan*, the Home of the Ancient Enemy. Many important events of the Navajo creation took place here. Wijiji, for example, was where the Navajos first learned how to weave. A Pueblo Indian slave of the Navajos, the story goes, came across Spider Woman weaving the first blanket in this pueblo. Spider Woman showed the Pueblo woman how to weave, and she in turn taught it to her Navajo masters.

Each turn of the canyon revealed yet more ruins, as well as rock faces covered with strange "hieroglyphics"—animals, stick figures, and spirals. Simpson became almost eloquent in his descriptions. But what impressed him most of all was seeing American troops firmly ensconced in this savage and remote place: "Another and more splendid view burst upon us as we turned an angle of the cañon, just before reaching camp. The chief object in the landscape was Mesa Fachada, a circular mound with a tableau top, rising abruptly midway in the cañon to a height of from three hundred to four hundred feet. The combination of this striking and beautiful object with the clear sky beyond, against which it was relieved, in connexion with lesser mounds at its base, the serried tents of the command, the busy scene of moving men and animals in the vicinity, and the curling smoke from the camp fires, which made up a picture which it has seldom been my lot to witness."

Fajada Butte, Simpson's Mesa Fachada, is a sacred monument to the Navajos, who call it Holy Rock, just as it was once sacred to the Chaco Anasazi, who created on its flank the famous Sun Dagger solstice marker. Everywhere the Americans trod, they trod upon holy ground.

▽ ▽ ▽

On August 29, just west of Chaco, they saw "fresh tracks" belonging, Simpson presumed, to "Navaho spies who had been dogging us." As they continued toward the blue outline of the Chuska Mountains, they finally met their first *Diné*: fifteen men and women on horseback. They were friendly and rode alongside the soldiers. The women, Simpson noted delicately, "bestrode their horses *à la mode des hommes*."

On the morning of the 30th they were joined peacefully by a larger group of mounted Navajos, splendidly dressed in buckskin caps and eagle feathers, their bodies smeared with red and white pigment. "I could see," wrote Simpson, "the whole body of Indians . . . moving in a cloud of dust in advance of us. A dark, portentous cloud was hovering at the time over the Tumecha Mountains[29] beyond, the forked lightning ever and anon darting vividly athwart it; the beautiful peaks of the Ojos Calientes lay quartering to the right; and in the rear could be seen the main command—first the packs, then the infantry, and last the artillery."

Early in the afternoon they came to the brow of a valley, carpeted with luxuriant cornfields. The corn was nearly at peak ripeness and ready for harvest. They set up camp above this valley, somewhere south of Two Grey Hills. Washington ordered the cornfields cut to supply fodder for the animals. He justified this theft of the Navajos' critical winter food supply by noting that the Indians would be required to reimburse the government for the costs of the military campaign against them anyway. In case the Navajos did not appreciate this exquisite turn of logic, Washington sent an armed detail with the corn cutters to "enforce the order."

The Navajos watched, impassively, the destruction of their fields.

That afternoon several Navajo headmen rode into the camp, and promised to return the next day with other chiefs to "hold a council with the United States."

The council began at noon. Representing several Navajo bands were five Navajo headmen: Archuleta, José Largo, Armijo, Pedro José, and an aged but revered chief named Narbona. (We have their Spanish nicknames only, as the Navajos did not reveal their real names to strangers or enemies.) As a sign of their good intentions, the chiefs brought with them a number of sheep, mules, and horses, which they turned over to Washington.

Narbona was the most imposing and important of the chiefs at the conference, and he greatly desired peace. Over eighty years old, he had, according to Simpson, "a grave and contemplative countenance not unlike, as many of the officers remarked (I hope the comparison will be pardoned), that of General [George] Washington." Narbona's white hair hung loosely to his shoulders, and his carefully tended fingernails were more than two inches long. A gorgeous chief's blanket hung over his large frame. At the time Narbona was so crippled by arthritis that he could barely sit a horse.

There was a reason, unknown to the Americans, why the Navajos wanted peace so badly, even to the point of signing an unfair treaty. According to Navajo oral history, the Navajos had been impressed by the easy victory of the Americans over their longtime enemies, the *Naakai*, or Mexicans. Shortly after the American conquest of the Southwest, Narbona undertook a secret journey to Santa Fe to observe and evaluate the "New Men," as he called them. In the foothills above Santa Fe, Narbona found a vantage point overlooking Fort Marcy and its parade grounds, and was able to watch the soldiers drilling, parading, and firing cannon. He returned to the *Diné Bikeyah* deeply impressed. These New Men were vastly more powerful than the *Naakai;* to fight them would bring ruin to the tribe.

Not all the Navajos felt that way. The *Diné* were composed of many bands ruled by independent headmen. There was no overall chief: each headman could speak only for himself and his band. Narbona, therefore, had had to persuade the other headmen to accept peace by putting his own prestige and wealth on the line.

At the peace talk, Colonel Washington explained to the chiefs that he was heading for Canyon de Chelly, where he would make a formal treaty between the Navajo people and the United States. Narbona explained that he was too infirm to journey to de Chelly himself, but that he would appoint two younger chiefs to act for him. For now, though, the assembled headmen wished to hear the substance of the treaty that was being taken to Canyon de Chelly.

Agent Calhoun, through interpreters, began to explain the treaty. The exchange was recorded by Lieutenant Simpson.

MR. CALHOUN: Tell them they are lawfully in the jurisdiction of the United States, and they must respect that jurisdiction.

INTERPRETER: They say they understand it . . .

MR. CALHOUN: [Tell them] that the people of the United States shall go in and out of their country without molestation, under such regulations as shall be prescribed by the United States.

INTERPRETER: They, very well.

MR. CALHOUN: Tell them that, by this treaty, the government of the United States are to be recognized as having the right to establish military posts in their country wherever they may think it necessary, in order to [assure] the protection of them and their rights.

That the government of the United States claim the right to have their boundaries fixed and marked, so as to prevent any misunderstanding on this point between them and their neighbors.

INTERPRETER: They say they are very glad.

MR. CALHOUN: For and in consideration of all this, and a faithful performance of the treaty, the government of the United States will, from time to time, make them presents, such as axes, hoes, and other farming utensils, blankets, &c.

INTERPRETER: They say it is all right.

The council broke up. As the Navajos were preparing to leave, one of the New Mexican volunteers went to Washington and complained that a Navajo in the crowd was riding a horse that had been stolen from him some months or years back. Washington immediately ordered the Navajos to turn over the horse. (This was absurdly unfair, since a large percentage of all the Navajos' and the New Mexicans' mounts had been stolen from each other.) The chiefs responded that the man in question had fled with the horse. Washington then ordered the officer of

the mounted guard, Lieutenant Torez, and his men to charge
the Navajos and seize any horse in reprisal. When Torez and his
men surged forward, the Navajos, thinking they were under
surprise attack, wheeled their horses about and fled.

Washington cried out to his troops to *fire, fire!* at the backs
of the retreating Navajos. A fusillade of shots rang out and Narbona, who was in the rear, fell, along with six other men. When
the Navajos regrouped out of rifle range to recover their
wounded, Washington ordered the six-pound cannon into action. "Major Peck," Simpson wrote, "threw among them, very
handsomely—much to their terror . . . a couple of round shot."

Narbona was rolled on his stomach by some soldiers and
scalped, and two scientific members of the expedition were "later
furious with themselves" because in all the excitement they had
forgotten to decapitate Narbona and send his head to a colleague
of theirs, the distinguished Dr. Samuel George Morton of the
Philadelphia Academy of Natural Sciences, who was greatly
desirous of obtaining Indian heads for study.[30]

▽ ▽ ▽

Far from bringing peace, Colonel Washington had managed, in
one stroke, to start a war. He seemed, however, quite unaware
of what he had done. As if nothing untoward had happened,
Washington ordered his troops over the Chuska Mountains and
on to Canyon de Chelly to proceed with the signing of the peace
treaty. Washington picked up an old Navajo trail through the
mountains, which went through a gap the Navajos called *Béésh
Líchi'ii Bigizh*, or Red Flint Summit. The renaming of the landscape continued: Simpson called it "Pass Washington" in honor
of their commander, the name it bears today. At the top of the
pass they boxed a spring with stones[31] to water the livestock; the
spring has been left untouched by the Navajos ever since.

Over the mountains, the troops arrived at Canyon de
Chelly.[32] "We found it to more than meet our expectations,"
Simpson wrote, "so deep did it appear, so precipitous its rocks,
and so beautiful and regular its stratification. Its probable depth
I estimate at about 800 feet. At its bottom a stream of water
could be seen winding its way along, the great depth causing it
to appear like a mere riband."

The Americans camped on a rise a few miles from the canyon mouth, near where present-day Chinle is, where they set up
shop, ready for the Navajo chiefs to come and sign the treaty.

Not surprisingly, the important chiefs stayed away, and only a few minor headmen showed up. The only other appearance was made by a worried New Mexican man who had heard the treaty required the return of all captives; he had come to beg Washington to allow him to stay with the Navajos.

Unknown to Washington, the Navajos had already begun a campaign of revenge for the killing of Narbona. An American, Charles Malone, carrying mail to Colonel Washington from the command at Santa Fe, was attacked and killed near Chaco Canyon, and his mailbags opened and scattered about the ground.

▽ ▽ ▽

Washington returned to Santa Fe with the pieces of paper covered with worthless marks, well satisfied with the success of his expedition. Looking back, we can only term it a mission of deliberate provocation; but even as a military campaign it was singularly incompetent. Washington had not only succeeded in killing the one Navajo leader most dedicated to peace, but he had provoked the Navajos into carrying war from *Naakai* the Mexican to *Bilagáana* the American.

In the following months, Navajo bands swooped out of the *Diné Bikeyah*, descending on Hispanic villages and Indian pueblos with renewed fury. "Not a day passes," Agent Calhoun would write less than a month later, "without hearing of some fresh outrage, and the utmost vigilance of the military force in this country is not sufficient to prevent murders and depredations and there are but few so bold as to travel alone ten miles from Santa Fe. . . ." The Navajos, he concluded, would not be pacified until they were placed on a reservation, with "their limits circumscribed, and distinctly marked out, and their departure from said limits be under certain prescribed rules. . . . Even this arrangement would be utterly ineffective unless enforced by the military arm of the country."

It was a chilling observation.

Chapter 17

NAVAJO PLANETARIUM SITE
(DETAIL)
—CANYON DE CHELLY

Canyon de Chelly
May 13, 1992

That flowing water! That flowing water!
My mind wanders across it.
That broad water! That flowing water!
My mind wanders across it.
That old age water! That flowing water!
My mind wanders across it.

—A PRAYER TO THE WATERS OF THE *DIBÉ NITSAA*, THE SACRED
MOUNTAIN OF THE NORTH, FROM THE MOUNTAIN TOP WAY
CEREMONY[33]

Canyon de Chelly was busy and alive. Navajo children ran and
splashed through the shallow water, their laughter and shouts
echoing and distorted by the high cliffs. There were teenagers
revving the engines of pickup trucks and driving them recklessly

through the stream; there was a large family barbecuing a sheep; there were young couples in bathing suits holding hands, and others lounging in deck chairs listening to loud rock music on boom boxes. It was a powerful reminder that, despite the soaring sandstone cliffs, the vast Anasazi ruins, and the endless flow of tourists, this was a place where people actually lived their lives.

The freshly washed cottonwoods shook their leaves in the passing breeze, and a river of cool air seemed to pour out of the canyon on top of us. Our horses pranced and splashed through the water, drinking deeply, while Acomita raced across the shallow riffles, throwing up water like a speedboat. We were all exhilarated to see so much water after weeks of parched desert.

We stopped at a stable owned by Justin Tso, and he put up our horses for the night in an empty corral. To ride through the canyon complex we were required to hire a guide, and the next morning Justin introduced us to a man named Terrill Spencer. Terrill's large bulk was fitted onto the back of a small Navajo pony named Linx Cookies. He rode so lightly and balanced that he seemed weightless. He was silent, and wore a checked shirt and a black cowboy hat. He had a serious, melancholy face that looked older than its years.

We packed up under the cottonwoods and set off, Terrill leading the way, Selene in front, Christine and I bringing up the rear with the two packhorses.

We rode up the wash, splashing through the water. Canyon de Chelly is infamous for its quicksand, but Terrill led us in a complicated pattern of crossing and recrossing the stream that avoided it.

Selene's horse Blaze was delighted by the sight of water. Indeed, he was so overcome by it that he decided to roll; he accordingly jettisoned his load (Selene again) and lay down in the stream, with a look of pure bliss on his face.

Selene sat in the stream, dripping, her hair full of wet sand. There was a choking silence and then an outraged howl rose up the canyon walls and into the blue sky.

"He dumped me right in the water!" she screeched.

Christine had jumped off her horse and was splashing toward her daughter. "Selene! Are you all right?" she cried out.

"I'm gonna *kill* that horse," Selene said.

"You're all right, then?"

"No, I'm *not* all right. Do I look all right? I'm all wet

and full of sand. I'm never getting on that horse again. I'm going back to Durango right now." Her voice dissolved into a wail.

Realizing that Selene was not hurt, I rode over and punished Blaze, interrupting his lovely bath with a few sharp cuts of the lead rope across his rump. (Immediate discipline is necessary with horses; otherwise they cannot connect the deed with the punishment.) He leapt up with a look of surprise and hurt and ran, with me galloping after him through the shallows, cursing foully. Terrill headed Blaze off and caught him by the reins.

An open lorryload of tourists rumbled past us through the stream, the people in pastel hats swaying and bumping in unison, staring at us with shock blooming on their pink faces.

"You better get up," Christine said, "your Gameboy is under water."

Selene leaped up. "Oh no!" she cried, rummaging in her fanny pack. "What will I do if it's broken? This is *it*. I'm going back to Durango."

"No," said Christine, "you're getting right back on that horse and coming with us."

"I am *not*," she replied firmly, crossing her arms, still standing in the stream.

"I think maybe Blaze has learned his lesson," I said, bringing him over. "I don't think he's going to do that again."

"I don't *care*, I'm not coming, and that's *final*."

There was a long silence, interrupted only by Selene's sniffles and hiccoughs.

"Selene," Christine said gently, "take the reins of your horse from Doug, and let's go."

She took the muddy reins. "Somebody help me up," she said in a small voice.

I wiped the mud and sand off her saddle and gave her a boost.

She gave Blaze a good kick and we moved forward. "You ugly, stupid horse," she said, "I hope you break a leg."

"If you keep his head up," I said, "he's less likely to lie down. If he starts nosing around near the ground it means he might be getting ready to roll. Kick him and pull his head up if he does that."

"But he just all of a sudden lay down," Selene said, starting to cry again. "I can't watch him *all* the time."

"Yes you can," I said. "You have to. That's what riding's all about, paying close attention to your horse."

"If that's what riding's all about then I *hate* it."

We rode along in silence, crossing and recrossing the broad stream. We rounded a bend and came face-to-face with an enormous cliff face covered with petroglyphs, Newspaper Rock. There were tall shamanistic figures with horns, Anasazi spirals, and figures of antelopes, deer, flying birds, and snakes. Near the bottom the Anasazi hunchbacked figure Kokopelli danced and played a flute. Incised on top of the Basketmaker and Anasazi petroglyphs were Hopi clan markings dating from the seventeenth century; and on top of these were eighteenth- and nineteenth-century Navajo drawings of Yei dancers and men riding horses and carrying guns.

It was an extraordinary document, a palimpsest of canyon history going back fifteen centuries.

Terrill was serious and professional. He had a job to do. He reined his horse at the panel and launched into a memorized spiel, as if straight out of a textbook, reeling off all the facts, dates, and petroglyph styles. He concluded and looked at us. "Any questions?"

It was rather disconcerting, because it made us feel like the tourists we were.

Several miles up the canyon we came to the junction of Canyon del Muerto and Canyon de Chelly, two immense corridors of rock coming together at a forty-five-degree angle. Just above the fork we stopped at a beautiful fenced pasture, where Terrill told us we would camp. We dropped off the packhorses in the field and continued on unencumbered.

Our destination was Spider Rock, the mythical home of Spider Woman, ten miles up the canyon. This was where Monster Slayer and Born for Water had learned who their father was, and where they had received prayers and knowledge to use in their fight against the alien destroyers.

We continued up the canyon, crossing and recrossing the stream. Blaze started to fall behind so Selene cut herself another riding crop. I heard a shrill expostulation behind me and the sudden sound of thundering hooves.

I turned around in time to see Selene racing through the stream at a dead run, sending up glittering cascades of water.

"Selene!" I called out as she blasted by.

I heard something as she passed, sounding like either a cheer or a scream. I was horrified; it looked like Blaze was running away with her. I put my heels to Redbone and quickly passed her, getting in front of Blaze and crowding him to a stop.

I turned around in the saddle. Selene's face was red and her hat was dangling again by its stampede straps.

"Hey!" she said, scowling at me. "What's the idea?"

"Are you all right?" I asked.

"I'm fine!" Selene said. "We were just doing a little galloping. It's fun!"

"What do you mean, 'just doing a little galloping'? You were going about thirty miles an hour."

"Well," said Selene, "I just got bored with how slow everyone was going, so I whacked Blaze with my stick and off we went!" She held up her makeshift crop with a grin.

Christine came up on Chaco, followed by Terrill. Both Terrill and his horse looked considerably surprised to see how fast we were moving.

"Look," I said. "I think you're a little inexperienced to be galloping. You might not be able to stop him."

"I can stop him just fine," said Selene. "I've been sitting on this stupid horse every day, all day long for two weeks. I *think* I should've *learned* how to ride by *now*."

We started walking, with me in front, Selene second, Christine third, and Terrill behind.

Soon Selene was pleading to gallop again. "It's so *boring* just plodding along like this!"

"Galloping is too dangerous."

"No it *isn't*," she said. "Come on, let's go. This is boring. You ride in front, and stop when I yell stop."

"We'll do a little slow loping," I finally said. "But you stay behind me, all right? Don't you dare pass me, and you stop when I stop."

I urged Redbone to a lope, and I could hear Selene shrilly goading Blaze along.

"Faster!" Selene yelled at me.

I looked back. She was riding beautifully: centered and balanced, with a quiet seat. She really had learned how to ride.

"*Faster!*" she cried again.

I moved Redbone into a hand gallop.

"Wheeee!" Selene cried. "This is fun! I love riding!"

We galloped for a while and I slowed Redbone down to a walk.

I turned around and found Selene leaning on her saddle horn, crying.

"What happened?" I asked.

"When he slowed to a trot, he knocked my wind out!"

"I knew we shouldn't be galloping," I said. "That's a rough transition, when a horse drops back into a trot."

Selene quickly dried her tears.

"Let's gallop some more," she said.

"No," I said, "that's enough."

Soon we saw ahead of us an open truck full of tourists, inching along the sandy track, grinding its gears, the people shading their heads with guidebooks and newspapers.

"Let's run past them," said Selene.

"I don't think—"

But she had already whipped Blaze into a gallop and raced by me. I quickly followed, and I could hear Christine and Terrill thundering behind me, Christine yelling to Selene to stop. Selene passed the truck, whooping and waving her hat and yelling "get a horse!" to the consternation of the tourists and the great amusement of their Navajo guide. I raced past, trying to catch up with her, and was finally able to pass her and force Blaze to stop.

"Selene!" I said, "I don't want you doing that anymore!"

"Aw, come on."

"It made you cry back there, remember?"

"I did *not* cry."

"It's too dangerous."

Christine finally rode up. "Selene, you're going *way* too fast," she said.

"I am *not!*"

"Yes you are."

"Geez! He's my horse and I'll do anything I want with him."

"No, you won't," Christine said.

Terrill finally caught up with us on Linx Cookies, who looked less than thrilled to be forced to gallop. "If I'd known who I was riding with, I'd have taken a faster horse," he said, breathing hard and looking at us curiously.

▽ ▽ ▽

Canyon de Chelly was a gentle place on a human scale. The warm sandstone cliffs created an intimate space, watered, green, and shaded, a secret garden between stone walls. The braided creek wound from canyon wall to canyon wall along a bed of sand, enclosed by thickets of willows and Russian olive trees. Beyond that lay farmers' fields freshly plowed to the upthrusting stone. Every turn of the canyon brought a hogan into view, nestled up against the cliff or hidden in a stand of trees.

The sun angled into the canyon, cutting through the treetops, which glowed like stained glass against the dark canyon wall. When the heat came up, the cottonwoods released clouds of fluff, dazzling motes of captured sunlight drifting against the shadowed stone. They swirled around us as we rode.

Toward noon, we rounded a sharp bend in the canyon, and there, wedged in the cliff face, was White House Ruin, a cluster of towers mortared into a shallow alcove in the rockface. They looked like broken teeth in an ancient mouth of stone.

A dozen or more tourists clustered below the ruin, photographing, talking, and buying jewelry from several Navajo women who had spread their wares on velvet blankets on the dusty ground. Selene rushed off to inspect the jewelry while we tied up the horses.

A lady had arrived on horseback with her Navajo guide, and I was struck by the difference between the way Anglos and Navajos relate to their horses. She talked constantly to her horse, animadverting on his every disobedience. "Oh so you want to turn around in circles, do you? Well, now, what good did that do you? Huh? Aha, you want to trot now! Well no thanks I'd rather walk. Walk! I said *walk!* All right, go ahead and trot then, you'll just tire yourself out you silly horse. Oh so *now* we're walking. It's about time." But the horse paid absolutely no attention to her and did exactly what he pleased. Her Navajo guide rode up silently behind her, his horse beautifully behaved, all communication between them nonverbal. I thought with shame of my own tendency to rant at my horses.

Terrill gave us his set speech on White House Ruin, and then we ate off to one side, munching on beef jerky and nuts and drinking warm water from our canteens.

Terrill lounged back in the sand, propped up on an elbow.

"So where've you ridden from?" he asked.

"We started at Navajo Mountain about two weeks ago."

Terrill sat up. "Navajo Mountain? You're kidding."

"No, we really did."

He let out a long whistle and settled back. "Why?" he asked.

I tried to explain what we were doing.

Terrill nodded when I finished speaking. "This is something really good you're doing. With your family."

He was still staring into the sand, lying on his side, propped on an elbow.

"Horses are the right way to travel," he said. "I grew up at Spider Rock, and I've been riding all my life in this canyon. I never had a saddle, just rode bareback. But when I got this job they said I had to ride with a saddle. Insurance or something. I'd never sat in a saddle before. So I got in the saddle and rode these tourists out to Spider Rock, and when I got back I was *so* sore, I could hardly walk. I was as sore as they were."

He laughed once, like a hiccough.

"My grandmother," he said, "was the one who taught me how to ride. Just put me on the horse's back, gave me the reins, and slapped him. He ran away and I fell off."

He smiled.

"So she just did it again, and again. And finally I could stay on. She taught me by experience. Not by telling me what to do, saying I had to do this or not do that. That way I learned in a good way, the right way, by experience. Like what you're doing."

We talked some more and then he looked curiously at my hat. "Where'd you get that eagle feather?" he asked.

I took off the hat and handed it to him. "Is it really an eagle feather?" I asked.

He balanced the hat in his hand, turning it slowly. "It sure is. And it's not just any eagle feather; this comes from the longest feather of the wing."

"It was given to me by a friend in Monument Valley," I said. "He said it came from a live eagle."

He handed the hat back to me. "He must be a really good friend, to give you something like that. That's very powerful, it'll keep you and your family completely safe."

We packed up our lunch and rode on.

Just beyond White House Ruin Terrill took us up a side canyon to a place called Pictograph Cave: hundreds of painted figures and designs were crowded into an alcove in the canyon wall. There were handprints with spirals inside them, armless figures, painted rainbows, flute players with rainbow headdresses, a figure of a shaman with power lines and spirits emanating from his head, as well as lightning, dogs, turkeys, and deer. The ceiling of the cave was covered with painted stars, a night sky, deeply mysterious. It was a rare Navajo star ceiling, connected with the Navajo Blessing Way ceremony. Terrill did not give a speech this time, and we observed the cave in silence.

We passed a rock Terrill called Rock Struck by Lightning, opposite a dangerous trail going out of the canyon, called Ladder Trail. Many years ago, Terrill said, the rock had been struck by a tremendous bolt of lightning that left streaks down it. In 1864, this rock was the site of a massacre of Navajos by U.S. soldiers.

A mile below Spider Rock we stopped and tied up the horses. We walked with Terrill over to where some men were plowing a field. One man rode a John Deere tractor from the cliff wall to the creek and back, turning over the brick red soil, while a skinny fellow carrying a coffee can of corn walked in the glossy furrow, pushing each kernel into the earth. They were relatives of Terrill's, and he chatted with them in Navajo for a few minutes while we rested our horses. Soon the relatives went back to work and Terrill leaned against the fence, squinting into the sun, with a distant look on his face. The chugging of the tractor echoed off the cliff wall and bumblebees droned among the wildflowers along the fence. I could smell the overturned earth warmed by the sun.

Terrill pointed to a ruined hogan against the cliff, hidden in shadow. The roof had fallen in and the sides were leaning outward, ready to collapse. An empty windowframe had sagged into a crooked parallelogram, the adzed timbers sprung from their sockets.

"When I was a boy, I spent my summers in that hogan," he said quietly. "I used to work in this field right here. Just doing what these guys are doing, plowing, planting corn, harvesting."

He propped a boot on the fence. "It was really beautiful here in the summer. I spent a lot of time with my grandmother. Over there was the hand-and-foot trail we used to take out of the canyon. It was pretty steep, you couldn't ride a horse or drive stock along it. And over there is another trail we call the Ute Trail. A long time ago my great-granddad and some others cornered a Ute against the cliff there. He'd snuck into the canyon to steal livestock. So they thought they had him trapped and were shooting at him, but the next thing they knew, the Ute was on the top of the canyon yelling and waving goodbye." Terrill smiled. "He had climbed up through that crack in the rock. That's how the Navajos discovered there was a way out."

▽ ▽ ▽

We rode deeper into the canyon, arriving at Spider Rock in the afternoon. It was a double spire of sandstone, eight hundred feet high, standing alone at the junction of Canyon de Chelly, Bat Canyon, and Monument Canyon. We tied our horses up in a cottonwood grove and lay down on the grass, in the shade, looking up at the pinnacle that appeared to be poking the sun itself.

"Why do they call it Spider Rock?" Selene asked.

"That's where Spider Woman lives," said Terrill. "We call it *Tsé na'ashjé'ii*. She used to weave her web across the gap. Spider Woman was the one who told Monster Slayer and Born for Water who their father was. And she taught weaving to the Navajos too. But when we were kids, my parents used to tell us that Spider Woman would get us if we weren't good. I was really scared of meeting her and I was afraid to look up, because I thought I'd see her hanging up there." He chuckled. "She's still there, somewhere. If you believe in her."

He stood up. "I'm going for a short walk," he said. "I'll be back in a few minutes." He took the lariat off his saddle and walked off, swinging and playing with it, zipping the rope through the hondo, whirling it about his head and dropping the loop over a fencepost or log. He meandered through the cottonwoods and across a fallow field and disappeared.

We sat in the shade and passed around the canteen. The low murmuring of the creek created a pleasing sotto voce to the wind rustling through the cottonwoods and the humming of crickets and bees.

▽ ▽ ▽

Terrill returned in twenty minutes. It was already late afternoon, and we trotted the ten miles back to camp, arriving just as the light was dying on the eastern wall of the canyon. Our camp was in a lush meadow surrounded by cottonwoods, with a twenty-acre pasture for the horses, fenced on one side, with the cliffs as a natural barrier on the other.

The canyon wall in front of the camp curved upward, forming a perfect echo chamber. While we were relaxing by the fire, Acomita, hearing the murmuring echo of our voices, stood and growled menacingly, a ridge of hair on her spine bristling up. When the same growl came echoing back she began to bark, and when her own barks came bouncing back she rushed forward, enraged at the effrontery of the unseen dog, barking hysterically. Naturally her invisible adversary responded in kind, and Acomita lost her nerve and beat a hasty retreat back into camp, her tail between her legs.

Terrill built up the fire and we cooked dinner. We talked for a while and I told Terrill about my own grandmother, who was, I thought, like his, a woman of great wisdom.

"I used to spend a lot of time up there at Spider Rock," Terrill said. "I really loved my grandmother a lot. She taught me everything I know, how to live a good life, how to live the *right* kind of life."

He gazed into the fire. "The rest of my family didn't help me when I was growing up," he said. "They didn't care about me. My grandfather was a big medicine man and he was always away. Out curing everyone else and going around with important people, but he was never at home with his family. My paternal grandparents didn't help me either, they were drinkers. And my parents. . . ."

He shoved a stick into the fire.

"Anyway, my grandmother was the only person I could really talk to in my family. I don't know what would have happened to me if it wasn't for her."

"What was she like?" I asked.

"She had this ability to see the future. She knew *my* future. I didn't realize it then. It wasn't like she would tell me, 'This or that is going to happen to you.' Instead, she would just mention things. Like she would say, 'Don't marry a woman with painted nails and blue makeup around the eyes.' At the time I just thought she was giving me advice, but later I realized that there were *reasons* why she said that. She could see my future; she was warning me of certain things."

Terrill spoke in a whisper. "I still talk to her sometimes. I talked to her today even, you remember when I went out walking up at Spider Rock? I was talking to her. I needed to ask her about some things and she helped me."

I was surprised, believing that the grandmother had died. Terrill had seemed to talk to her in a very short period of time; I hadn't seen any sign of a nearby hogan. "She must be quite old now," I said.

There was a long silence. "My grandmother," Terrill whispered, "passed away a long time ago. But she still lives there, at Spider Rock."

He was silent for a long time, staring at the fire. "When my grandmother got sick, I was really scared. They sang over her and she didn't get better, then they took her to the hospital, and then they came back and told me she was dead. She was the only person who cared about me. I just went walking out there in the cornfields, walking around crying. I felt so bad, I just wanted to die. Everyone said I'd feel better in a little while, but a long time went by and I didn't feel any better. So I went to this medicine man and he said that I should go up to Spider Rock. He said, 'She's not gone, she's still there. You can talk to her and she'll answer. You'll see.' So I went up there and talked to her. And she was there, she talked to me. Now when I need help, I go up there and talk to her. You know, she told me some things about you."

"She did?"

He nodded, but didn't say anything.

"What did she say?" I finally asked.

Terrill remained silent.

It was night. Crickets and frogs sounded across the cool air. We were quiet for a while and then we turned in for the night.

Chapter 18

SPIDER ROCK
—CANYON DE CHELLY

Canyon del Muerto
May 14, 1992

The next day we packed the horses and moved our camp up Canyon del Muerto. The early-morning sun slanted into the canyon, bursting through the tops of the cottonwoods and shimmering off the surface of the creek. The two red rims of the canyon rose up on either side, holding in between the lapis sky. We moved slowly, trailing the packhorses, stiff from our long ride the day before.

A few miles up the canyon we heard whoops and shouts, along with the sound of hoofbeats. A herd of horses came thundering around the bend, being driven by three Navajo cowboys waving coiled lariats and shouting *Heeyah! Hup! Líí! Hi!*

They drove the horses across the stream in front of us, the water cascading through the morning light like fragments shot off the sun. The muscled flanks of the horses were raked aslant with mud, and their eyes were wild. In an instant they passed, the sounds dying behind us in a confusion of echoes.

Every turn of the canyon revealed new wonders: Two Spiral Shelter, a small ruin in a cove of rock, with painted humans, turkeys, handprints, and several prominent reversed spirals; Kokopelli Cave, with seated and recumbent flute players; Ceremonial Cave, with an extraordinary sixty-foot-long painted panel showing lines of dancers, humans with bird heads, handprints, lightning, and painted animal tracks.

A few hours of riding brought us to a long sandstone wall under an overhang, partly hidden behind willows and salt cedars. We rode close to the stone and Terrill armed aside the brush, revealing a long painted mural: the Ute Raid Panel. The panel recorded a fight between Ute Indian raiders and Navajos that took place in the canyon in January of 1858, and it was perhaps the most extraordinary example of Navajo rock art in the canyon. In the mural, forty mounted Ute warriors come galloping in from the left, carrying guns, fringed shields, and feathered lances, some with horned helmets and warbonnets. They are being met in fierce combat on the right by Navajos with guns and bows and arrows. The lower part of the panel shows what appear to be frightened Navajo women and children fleeing the invaders. The Utes are shown large and fierce and depicted in great detail, down to the feathers decorating their horses' heads, while the Navajos are small and weak-looking and sketchy—perhaps an attempt to magnify the enemy and thus mitigate the Navajos' defeat. During the raid, the Utes killed an important Navajo chief and made off with a number of horses.

We stopped at the mouth of Black Rock Canyon and turned our horses loose in a large pasture belonging to a relative of Terrill's. The grass was knee high and so rich I worried it might colic the horses after their sparse desert diet. We set up camp under a lone cottonwood nearby.

It was still early afternoon. Terrill disappeared for a long walk up the canyon while Christine, Selene, and I went down to Tsaile Creek, the creek in Canyon del Muerto, for a swim. There was a sharp bend in the stream, where it came up against the northern wall of the canyon, and the current had carved out a deep elbow in its bed. It was screened by thick willows. We took off our clothes and lay down in the water, rolling around and letting it wash off the dust of the last weeks. We got out and lay in the sun but Selene continued to wallow in the water on her stomach, squealing and laughing. She did some cartwheels through the water and a handstand, her wet red hair flopping down over her face.

Suddenly we heard a shrill scream.

"Spiders!" she shrieked. "Help, Doug, I'm being attacked by spiders!"

I came rushing down. The wet banks of the stream were crawling with spiders, thousands of them. Selene stood in the middle of the stream, dripping and yelling.

"Help! Carry me out!"

I waded in and swung her out over the swarms of spiders.

She retreated into the willows and put on her clothes, and came back out. "That was a close call. They almost killed me."

"You silly," said Christine. "Those spiders are harmless."

"Yeah, then *you* go walking through them barefoot."

"No thanks."

"See."

▽ ▽ ▽

We went back to camp, and I gathered wood while Christine lit a fire. Terrill was still gone. We spread out some horsepads and put a pot of beans and rice on to boil.

The sun had fallen below the rim and a twilight silence gathered in the canyon, where even the smallest sounds seemed to carry for miles. A plume of fragrant smoke drifted out of a distant grove of cottonwood trees, marking a hidden hogan. The smoke rose to some invisible barrier in the air and flattened out, drifting in sheets up the canyon. Selene lay on a nearby blanket, reading a book.

Christine and I sat next to each other. It became chilly, and we snuggled closer to the fire; she rested her head in my lap. I kissed her.

"Hey!" Selene said. "None of that stuff!" She came over and wedged herself between us. I bent down to kiss Christine again and she clapped her hand over my mouth.

"I'm going to tickle you if you don't move," Christine said.

"I'm not ticklish. I have Buddha control," Selene said.

"We'll see about that," Christine said, and started to tickle her knees. Selene went as rigid as a board for a moment and then doubled up and began to shriek. "Help! Doug, help!"

"Some Buddha control," Christine said, laughing. "You

can't fool me. I knew all your tickly spots from the time you were six months old."

"I *have* no tickly spots," Selene declared.

Christine flexed her hand into a vicious tickling claw and reached toward her. Selene began to shriek and squirm away. "No! Please! Wait!"

"Admit it, you're ticklish," she said, inching closer.

"I'm ticklish! I'm ticklish!" Selene hollered.

We laughed and rolled around a while, and then inched closer to the fire to get warm.

"Tell more of the story," Selene asked me. And so I began to talk.

Terrill returned at dusk. The air was cold and thin, and felt like a veil drawn against the infinite vacuum of space. After dinner, we stretched out by the fire, keeping warm. There was a peculiar smell of winter, of crows and cornhusks, in the air.

"See that bluff?" Terrill asked, after dinner. "That's called Navajo Fortress. When Kit Carson and his troops came through here, rounding up all the people to take them to Fort Sumner, my ancestors went up on top of that rock with a couple hundred people. To get up there, you have to cross those gaps with poles."

The rock was separated from the rim of the canyon by a series of large crevasses.

"The soldiers surrounded the rock and camped right here, right where we are. The Navajos stayed up there for a long time. It was in the winter, so they had a little snow that could be melted in potholes, but they didn't have any food. They could smell the cooking food of the soldiers at the bottom and it nearly drove them crazy. In the end the sun melted all their snow and their water ran out and they had to surrender. They were taken on the Long Walk down to Fort Sumner, and a lot of them didn't come back. In the daytime, you can still see some of those poles, propped up on that ledge."

Terrill spoke quietly, and the grasshoppers chirruped in the meadow beyond. The silvery moonlight grew in strength as the moon climbed into the night sky. I looked for the poles but could see nothing.

"You know, Terrill," I said, "you've been saying a lot of things that I don't want to forget. Do you think it would be all right if I turned on my tape recorder?"

Terrill's face broke into a broad smile. "I knew you were going to ask me that."

"You did?"

"That's just what my grandmother said you were going to ask." He chuckled knowingly.

"Really? Did she say it would be all right?"

"She said to tell you no, no taping."

"No taping?" I was becoming a little irritated at this ghostly, interfering grandmother.

Terrill nodded.

"Why not?" I asked.

"Because the truth can't go on a tape."

"I don't understand."

Terrill smiled indulgently. "She said that if that tape is on, what I say will go on the tape instead of into your heart."

"How so?"

"Without the tape going, you *have* to remember what's being said. If you forget it, then you weren't ready to know. It didn't go into your heart. When someone says something important to you, if you have to write it down or tape-record it in order to remember it, then it means you didn't understand it. The only really *good* things are those things you can never possibly forget. They become part of you. A thing doesn't become truth until it goes into your heart. Before that, it's just words."

I was silent. It made a certain amount of sense.

Terrill was in his usual reclining position, propped up on one arm, looking into the fire. Christine had fallen asleep. I could hear the distant murmuring of the stream, like someone breathing in the dark.

Terrill shifted. "In the books," he said, "they tell you the Anasazi left the canyon because of drought."

I nodded. This had been one of Terrill's earlier set speeches.

"To be a canyon guide," he continued, "you got to get this card, and they make you learn all these things out of the books. About the Anasazi, who they were, where they came from, why they left. They give you a test, so you can repeat it to the tourists. Like the things I was telling you yesterday."

He picked up a twig and began stripping off the bark, throwing each piece into the fire, where it flared up and died away. "A lot of this stuff isn't what I heard growing up. Like about the Anasazi leaving because of a drought."

He peeled another piece off, and his face glowed briefly.

"What did you hear?" I asked.

"The people who came here, my grandmother said, they came from Chaco Canyon. There had been evil things done at Chaco Canyon. A terrible kind of witchcraft was practiced, things against nature. I don't really know what. They fought with each other, there was a war, and that's how everything got destroyed. Some went other places, but a group or a clan sent two runners over here. These two guys stopped at the mouth of Canyon de Chelly. They saw how beautiful it was. So they shouted into the canyon, asking the goddess of the canyon to allow their people to live there. And the goddess said yes, but on one condition. She gave them a sack of corn to plant and said they could live there only as long as the corn would grow.

"So the first year they planted the corn and it grew tall. And the next year it grew, but a little lower. And many years passed and they built those cities in the rocks, but the corn kept getting smaller and shorter and the leaves were yellow. And then one year, it didn't grow at all. And so they had to move on."

Terrill shifted again and threw the twig into the fire.

"That's why they left," he said in a low voice, "and they never came back. Nothing but ruins now. That was a long time ago, they say."

He became silent. The story reminded me again of the ruins of the Anasazi and the ruins of the white man; what, I wondered, was the connection? What was this terrible kind of witchcraft? But Terrill had said enough, and remained silent.

The temperature had dropped past the dew point and a sharp, wintery smell gathered in the air. The full moon lay bright upon the side of Navajo Fortress Rock, and it was falling into the deserted ruins of the White House and into the crumbling rocks of Two Spiral Shelter, which would never be lived in again. It was shining softly over Spider Rock and falling, too, on the broken hogan where Terrill spent his boyhood. It was falling like mercury across the backs of the sleeping horses in the field and it was falling into the murmuring waters of the creek beyond the cottonwoods.

Chapter 19

NAVAJO YE'II
—LARGO CANYON

 Canyon de Chelly
The Long Walk
January 1864 to
June 1868

Let us go home to our mountains.
Let us see our flocks feeding in the valleys, and let us ride again
where we can smell the sage and know of the hidden hogans
by the smell of piñon smoke.
Let us go where we can build our homes in solitude and privacy
and live again as men, not animals.
Let us be free to build a better way of life and learn to live in
peace where the red buttes rise from the desert sands, and
eagles sweep across the sky. . . .
Here we have nothing. Our children grow up in ugliness and
death.
Let us go home.

—GANADO MUCHO, A NAVAJO CHIEF, CAPTIVE AT FORT
SUMNER, ASKING FOR THE RETURN OF HIS PEOPLE TO THE *DINÉ*
BIKEYAH[34]

Life in the canyon had not changed much in the centuries since the Navajo first came here. There were no powerlines or paved roads, gaslines or water mains. The people who lived here still lived in the old way, in dirt-floored hogans heated by wood. Navajos still herded their livestock through the canyon on horseback, and they still planted the same soil with corn. It was a closed world, out of place and time. The vast antiquity of human life in the canyon almost made the world outside seem fleeting and ephemeral.

I woke as the sky was lightening, and lay in my sleeping bag looking at Navajo Fortress. I could suddenly see the poles that Terrill had mentioned the night before, wedged in a protected cleft in the rock. I thought then of Kit Carson and his troops camping where we were camped, waiting for the sun to melt the snow, waiting for thirst to drive the Navajos off the rock.

Kit Carson's attack on Canyon de Chelly took place in 1864. It broke the back of the Navajo Nation and precipitated the Long Walk,[35] the most calamitous event in the history of the Navajo people. So horrifying was the Long Walk that it will remain branded on the collective memory of the *Diné* for eternity, or at least as long as there are *Diné* to remember.

The chain of events leading to the Long Walk began in 1862, when Colonel James Carleton took over as commander of the Department of the Army for New Mexico Territory. Photographs of Carleton show a truculent, intelligent, cruel, disheveled-looking man. He had a streak of ethnocentric utopianism, common to men of his time, that led him to believe that "savage" Indians should be transformed into decent, God-fearing white folk. He was incapable of admitting wrong. It would prove a most dangerous combination.

In his first year as commander, Carleton shrewdly concluded that it was the land itself that gave the *Diné* their protection. They would never be crushed, he wrote, until they were ferreted out of the "haunts, and hills, and hiding-places of their country" and transferred to a distant reservation, under the eye of the army.

Carleton immediately set his plan into action. He set aside a forty-square-mile piece of land along the Pecos River in eastern New Mexico, at a place called Bosque Redondo, to be the new "reservation." It would be dominated by a fort, which he named Fort Sumner. Instead of engaging the Navajos directly, Carleton decided to direct his attack on the land itself. Through a scorched-earth campaign he would render the *Diné Bikeyah* itself uninhabitable. This would be followed by a crushing attack on Canyon de Chelly. He chose the ruthless and capable Christopher "Kit" Carson to execute the plan.

In the late summer of 1863, just before the harvest, Carson and his soldiers went into action. Using Fort Canby (later called Fort Defiance) as a base, they laid waste to 7,500 square miles of the *Diné Bikeyah*, including the most productive grazing areas and farmlands of the Navajos. The soldiers drove the Navajos off their farms, slaughtered thousands of Navajo horses and sheep, burned hogans, and destroyed two million pounds of grain standing ripe in the fields. As a bitter winter closed down, Carson sent troops around to harass the Navajo families and bands to keep them on the move. Still, the Navajos refused to surrender.

▽ ▽ ▽

On January 6, 1864, two columns of troops left Fort Canby to deliver the final blow to the *Diné* in their stronghold, Canyon de Chelly. Carson's plan was simple: he would trap the Navajos in the canyon complex with a pincer movement, one column entering the head of the canyon, the other the foot.

The day dawned bright and clear, and the snow lay heavy on the ground. The soldiers headed northwest through the heavy piñon-juniper forest of the Defiance Plateau in high spirits, singing a song especially composed for the occasion:

Come dress your ranks, my gallant souls, a standing in a row.
Kit Carson he is waiting to march against the foe;
At night we march to Moqui, o'er lofty hills of snow,
To meet and crush the savage foe, bold Johnny Navajo,
  Johnny Navajo! O Johnny Navajo!

The first column, led by Captain A. W. Pheiffer, entered the top of Canyon del Muerto. (At the time, they did not know there were two canyons.) The other command, some four hundred troops led by Kit Carson himself, blocked the mouth of Canyon de Chelly at its western entrance near Chinle. Pheiffer's troops had struggled about eight miles down the canyon when a group of Navajos appeared on the rim, "whooping and yelling and cursing, firing shots and throwing rocks down upon my command." The troops fired on the Navajos and, according to Pheiffer, "killed two (2) Buck Indians in the encounter, and one

Squaw who obstinately insisted on hurling rocks and pieces of wood at the soldiers."

This is almost certainly a gloss of what really happened. Oral histories collected from Navajos themselves indicate it was a massacre of much larger proportions. An old Navajo man named Eli Gorman recalled one version that had been passed down in his family. His ancestors heard gunshots at a place called *Tsébo'osni'í*, Rock Struck by Lightning. They took refuge in a cave above the rocks, and the soldiers began firing indiscriminately at the cave opening. "The firing gradually picked up," Gorman said, "and soon it sounded like frying, with bullets hitting all over the cave. This went on nearly all afternoon. Then the firing ceased, but, by that time, nearly all the Navajos were killed. Men, women, children, young men and girls were all killed on the cliffs. Some just slid off the cliffs down into *Tsébo'osni'í*. . . . Blood could be seen from the top of the cliffs all the way down to the bottom."

Another woman recalled that after the fight, the company commander surveyed the gory scene. "It frightened him," she said. "He broke down and wept, saying, 'What a terrible thing we have done to these people!' "

Meanwhile, Carson's command killed a number of Navajos at the southern end of the canyon.

The plan was devastatingly effective. On January 14, sixty Navajos who were in extremis surrendered to Carson. He gave them a bundle of white flags and ordered them back into the canyon to distribute the flags and tell the people that they all had to go to Fort Canby and surrender.

To underscore his demands, Carson ordered Captains Pheiffer and Carey to lay waste to the canyon. Pheiffer moved through Canyon del Muerto while Carey moved through de Chelly, burning hogans and destroying corrals. Most of the Navajos' livestock had already been destroyed, but what animals were left were rounded up and slaughtered, their bodies left in frozen piles.[36]

When the *Diné* who had fled returned and saw the devastation in their canyon, they lost heart and began surrendering in huge numbers. This was when Carleton's first mistake quickly became apparent: he had grossly underestimated the population of the tribe. By the end of February more than two thousand starving and "quite naked" Navajos had come into Forts Canby and Wingate. Carleton was utterly unprepared to feed and clothe them, and in one week 126 had died of exposure and dysentery. In a high panic, he hastily ordered the emaciated and weakened survivors to Fort Sumner, three hundred miles away on the Pecos River.

Without horses, the only way for them to get there was to walk. And thus the infamous Long Walk began, a three-hundred-mile journey of death through snowstorms, freezing rain, icy rivers, and waterless deserts. The few wagons they had were filled to overflowing with the elderly. Those who dropped behind—the sick, pregnant women, children—were shot by soldiers in the rear, or kidnapped or murdered by marauding Utes and New Mexicans. At night they had no shelter, clothing, or blankets, and were forced to endure temperatures that dropped into the low twenties or teens. Many campsites had no wood even for fires. Many, many hundreds of Navajos died; exactly how many we will never know.

When the Navajos arrived at Bosque Redondo a month later, they found absolutely nothing. None of the things they had been promised was there. There was no shelter, no tools, clothing, blankets, irrigated farmland, livestock, or wagons. Having occupied more than fifty thousand square miles in their old homeland, the Navajos found themselves required to start over with nothing on a piece of land less than one-thousandth that size.

Not all the Navajos surrendered. *Hashkéniinii* and his band were the most famous resisters, but others disappeared into remote areas of the *Diné Bikeyah*, notably Gray Mountain and in the Tzunjejin Badlands just north of Chaco Canyon. Man of Blackweed, the son-in-law of Narbona and inheritor of his mantle of leadership, fled into the Grand Canyon itself and sent a message to Carleton: "It is the tradition of our people that we must never cross the three rivers [to live]—the Rio Grande, the San Juan and the Colorado. . . . I shall remain here. I have nothing to lose but my life, and that they can come and take whenever they please, but I will not go there." Despite these brave words he later surrendered, a broken man. Years later he died in misery, a victim of *Tódiłhił:* white man's whiskey.

At Fort Sumner, the Navajos went to work putting in crops. With only fifty spades, they dug an irrigation ditch twelve feet wide and six miles long. The land they were to cultivate was covered with thorny mesquite bushes with deep, hard roots. They grubbed up the mesquite by hand, beating out the roots with stones. They busted the tough virgin sod with digging sticks. In the first year at Fort Sumner they managed to put in an astonishing 3,000 acres of irrigated crops. They were excellent farmers and by mid-summer a bumper crop was on its way. Then cutworm ravaged the corn, and a series of storms battered the wheat crop into the mud. The crops failed again the next year, and the next. The soil, irrigated by the highly alkaline water of the Pecos River, became impregnated with salt.

Conditions at Fort Sumner went from unspeakable to worse. It was a concentration camp in the true sense of the word. For housing, the *Diné* could only dig holes in the ground with their bare hands and cover them over with a few thorny mesquite branches and dirt. There was a critical shortage of food. Carleton wrote letters pleading with various government officials to send rations. What little did arrive was rotten and unfit for human consumption. The U.S. cavalry horses were fed better than the Navajos, and the Indians were reduced to scouring the corrals, picking through the horses' manure for undigested pieces of corn. The soldiers guarding the *Diné* raped the women and spread venereal disease through the tribe. One old Navajo shepherd told me, "Some of the ladies came back with white kids and with black kids." The number of Navajos at Fort Sumner climbed until, by March of 1865, nearly nine thousand were crowded there.

Despite the horrors, Carleton refused to admit his grandiose plan was a failure. He blamed everyone but himself. He feuded with the Indian superintendent and became embroiled in disputes with local landowners. He was pilloried by the Santa Fe newspapers, not over humanitarian issues, but over what the Navajos were costing the government. Carleton had managed to reduce a fiercely independent people to abject (and expensive) dependency. The *New Mexican* newspaper complained about Carleton "making one of our most fertile valleys an asylum for Indians of another territory; removing them from 300 to 400 miles east against the current of emigration and improvement."

Meanwhile, the Navajos silently endured.

Word of the frightful conditions spread, and various commissions investigated. They dutifully journeyed to Fort Sumner, gathered information, and reported back to Washington. The Navajo headman spoke eloquently of their plight to these commissions, and their words were duly recorded. "Cage the badger," one headman said, "and he will try to break from his prison and regain his native hole. Chain the eagle to the ground—he will strive to gain his freedom, and though he fails, he will lift his head and look up to the sky which is home—and we want to return to our mountains and plains."

Still nothing happened; no one could break Carleton's stranglehold on Fort Sumner.

Navajo oral history tells a curious story. In early 1868, the leader of the imprisoned Navajos, *Yichi'dahyiłwóh* (more commonly known as Barboncito), conducted a sacred ceremony called Put a Bead in Coyote's Mouth. He and a group of *Diné* fanned out across the prairie and spread into a huge circle. Slowly they walked together, tightening the circle up, until it was about fifty feet in diameter. A female coyote had been caught in the sweep, and she cowered in the center of the circle, facing east. Barboncito caught the animal and placed a piece of white shell, tapered at both ends with a hole in the center, into her mouth. When he released the coyote she turned clockwise and walked off toward the west. He then announced to the assembled *Diné:* "We'll be set free." Because the coyote had rotated in the sacred direction and then had gone west, the Navajos, Barboncito explained, would be allowed to go back to their homeland.

On May 28, 1868, representatives of yet another commission, the Peace Commission, arrived at Fort Sumner to negotiate a new treaty with the Navajos. Lieutenant General William Tecumseh Sherman himself led the delegation. Sherman had in the back of his mind the idea that the Navajos should be sent to Indian Territory in Oklahoma.

Even after four years in captivity, the Navajos had not learned English, just as they had not given up their traditions, become Christians, and in general turned themselves into white people. Therefore, two interpreters were required to communicate between the Navajo headmen and General Sherman: Jesus Arviso, a man who spoke Navajo and Spanish, and an American named James Sutherland, who spoke Spanish and English.

Sherman opened the meeting. "The Commissioners are here now for the purpose of learning and knowing all about your condition and we wish to hear from you the truth. . . ."

Barboncito began to speak, secretly holding under his tongue a turquoise bead dusted with sacred pollen so that his words would be true. He gave one of the great speeches in Native American history, whose eloquence shines through the awkwardness of the double translation. He tried to explain to the

white people the profound relationship between the Navajos and
their homeland.

▽ ▽ ▽

"The bringing of us here has caused a great decrease of our
numbers, many of us have died, also a great number of our
animals. Our grandfathers had no idea of living in any other
country except our own and I do not think it is right for us to do
so. . . .

"When the Navajos were first created, four mountains and
four rivers were appointed for us, inside of which we should
live, that was to be our country, and was given to us by the first
woman of the Navajo tribe. It was told to us by our forefathers,
that we were never to move east of the Rio Grande, or west of
the San Juan rivers and I think that our coming here has been
the cause of so much death among us and our animals. First
Woman, when she was created, gave us this piece of land and
created it especially for us and gave us the whitest of corn and
the best of horses and sheep. . . .

"It is true we put seed in the ground but it would not grow
two feet high, the reason I cannot tell, only I think that this
ground was never intended for us. We know how to irrigate and
farm. Still we cannot raise a crop here. . . . There are a great
many among us who were once well off. . . . My mouth is dry
and my head hangs in sorrow to see those around me who were
at one time well off, so poor now. . . .

"Outside my own country we cannot raise a crop, but in it
we can raise a crop almost anywhere; our families and stock
there increase, here they decrease; we know this land does not
like us, neither does the water. They have all said this ground
was not intended for us. . . . I believe now it is true what my
forefathers said about crossing the line of my own country. It
seems that whatever we do here causes death. Some work at the
acequias, take sick and die; others die with the hoe in their
hands; they go to the river to their waists and suddenly disappear; others have been struck and torn to pieces by lightning. A
rattlesnake bite here kills us; in our country a rattlesnake before
it bites gives warning which enables us to keep out of its way
and if bitten, we readily find a cure—here we can find no cure.

"When one of our big men dies, the cries of the women cause
the tears to roll down to my mustache. I think then of my own
country. . . . Before I am sick or older I want to go and see the

place where I was born . . . I want to go and see my own country. If we are taken back to our own country, we will call you our father and mother. . . . I am speaking for the whole tribe, for their animals from the horse to the dog, also the unborn. All that you have heard now is the truth and is the opinion of the whole tribe. It appears to me that the General commands the whole thing as a god. I hope therefore he will do all he can for my people. This hope goes in at my feet and out at my mouth.[37] I am speaking to you now as if I was speaking to a spirit and I wish you to tell me when you are going to take us to our own country."

General Sherman replied: "I have listened to what you have said of your people, and I believe you have told the truth." He was so moved by the speech that he later dropped the idea of sending them to Indian Territory. They would be allowed to return home. Barboncito's eloquence had saved the Navajo people.

On June 1, 1868, the treaty between the Navajos and the U.S. government was drawn up and signed by the Navajo headmen. It delineated a reservation straddling the Arizona–New Mexico border, only a fraction of the size of their original territory. Later the reservation was added to and now it stands at 25,000 square miles, the largest Indian reservation in the United States, but still only about half of the original *Diné Bikeyah*.

According to Navajo oral tradition, Sherman had one more lesson he wanted to teach the Navajos. He ordered a billy goat tied to a wooden post, and forced the Navajos to watch while a soldier struck the goat repeatedly in the midsection with a stick. In fear and pain the goat butted his head again and again on the post until his brains burst out of his skull. One Navajo recalled: "the general turned to the Navajos and said, 'Nowhere, at no time in the future, whatever you do, don't break this treaty. If you get into trouble with Washington or the U.S. Government again and do the things you should not do, this is what is going to happen to you people.' "

At dawn on June 18, the Navajos left Fort Sumner, heading back to the *Diné Bikeyah*. They formed a ragged line ten miles long. They were deeply impoverished: from their vast herds of 310,000 sheep and horses, only 2,500 wormy, starving animals survived. Many thousands of Navajos—perhaps a quarter or more of the entire tribe—did not return.

Twelve miles east of Albuquerque, at the mouth of Tijeras

Canyon, the Navajos had their first glimpse of the low outline of *Tsoodzil*, Blue Bead Mountain, the Sacred Mountain of the South. It was a transcendental moment for them all. At the mere sight of the sacred mountain some of the old leaders of the tribe —men who must never show emotion—fell to their knees and wept. One Navajo man became deranged and had to be tied to a wagon. No matter that they were going back to a wasted land; no matter that the fat herds once covering the prairies and mesas were now white bones among the grass; no matter that the valleys once rustling with corn and dotted with hogans were now scorched and rutted; no matter that the cool peach groves in Canyon de Chelly were now rotting stumps; no matter: the *Diné* were returning to the *Diné Bikeyah*, the Land of the People.

Many years later, an old Navajo chief recalled that moment: "When we saw the top of the mountain from Albuquerque we wondered if it was our mountain, and we felt like talking to the ground, we loved it so . . ."

Chapter 20

ATTACKING UTE, UTE RAID
PANEL
—CANYON DEL MUERTO

Canyon del Muerto
Mummy Cave
May 15, 1992

The following day we moved deeper into Canyon del Muerto
and set up camp at the junction of Twin Trails Canyon, where
we rented a fallow field from one of Terrill's relatives for our
horses. In the corner of the field was a rickety "shade" built from
discarded pieces of plywood where we stowed our gear and set
up our kitchen. Then we took four horses and continued up-
canyon to a great ruin called Mummy Cave.

As we rode in the warm sun, the canyon gradually changed
character, becoming wilder and less populated; the fields and
stately cottonwoods gave way to rocky talus slopes with gnarled
piñons and junipers, and the canyon walls became higher. The
creek burbled over a pebbled bed, the water no longer laden
with brown silt, but running clear and glistening like honey in
the sunlight. The only life we saw were some stray horses and a

herd of burros, peering suspiciously at us from behind a cluster of junipers.

It was a long, exciting ride, with Selene shrilly urging us along. Like a teenager with a new car, she had learned how to gallop and now the very idea of walking the horse was intolerable. Whenever we slowed she would be yelling, "Get a move on! Go faster!" And then I would hear the drumming of hooves on the ground and a whoop of excitement as she came running up. We raced through every stream crossing, the icy sting of the water wonderful in the heat, emerging wet from head to toe.

Selene shouted out the number of each crossing. "Forty-five!" she cried as we loped across the stream, up a cutbank, and back down to the next bend, then "Forty-six!" Her horsemanship improved dramatically. In addition, somewhere along the way she figured out how to imitate the tongue clicks I used to communicate with Redbone, and would sneak up behind me and make clicking noises, wreaking havoc with my control of Redbone. I had one click that was as effective as a good jab with spurs in getting him into a gallop. She snuck up behind me while I was admiring the scenery and clicked loudly, and before I could react Redbone was off and running. Selene ran along behind, squealing with delight.

"Don't do that," I said, slowing to a trot. "You caught me unawares. I nearly went over the saddle backwards."

Selene laughed. "Now Doug," she lectured, "you're *supposed* to be *aware* of your horse at *all times*."

Christine came up and rode alongside of me, and we talked while Selene rode behind us, complaining that she had been cut off and that we were too slow. "You up ahead! Slowpokes! Quit yakking and get a move on! Beep beep!"

"God," Christine whispered, "I hate to think what's going to happen when she gets her first car."

Thus we continued noisily upstream.

After eight or ten miles the stream made a broad turn through a meander scar. When we came around the bend we reined our horses in and fell silent with astonishment. The canyon had widened into a deep bowl. Built into an alcove in the opposite cliff, perhaps a half mile away, was a great Anasazi city: two massive towers flanking a broken wall and surrounded by wrecked kivas and roomblocks. Whole sections of the ruin had tumbled down a talus slope to the canyon floor. From the distance, the city looked like a sleepy face under a heavy brow of rock. It was the most spectacular Anasazi ruin we had seen in the canyon.

"Mummy Cave Ruin," Terrill said.

"It's incredible," breathed Christine.

"We call it *Tséyaakiní*," said Terrill, "the House under the Rock."

"Wow," said Selene. "Cool. It's like a castle."

We rode down the hill toward the ruin. A pair of crows flapped away as we approached, and a golden eagle, whistling a lonely cry, traced a semicircle and vanished beyond the canyon rim.

Terrill lounged in the shade while I walked up to the cliff face below the ruin and stared up at the great tower with its black windows and vigas projecting from the stonework. I laid my cheek against the cliff, feeling the gritty warmth and smelling the fragrance of stone. The cliff arched above me like a cresting wave.

For years I had wanted to see this place, ever since a peculiar experience I'd had during my years working at the American Museum of Natural History. Arriving one morning, I found my office redolent with the smell of mothballs. When I complained, I discovered that the museum's mummy storage room was located on the other side of the drywall from my desk. That morning the mummy cases had been unsealed and were receiving a new dose of paradichlorobenzene preservative. The largest source of these mummies—dozens and dozens of them—came from here: Mummy Cave. Indeed, for years I had lived not ten feet from the collected dead of Canyon del Muerto—the Canyon of the Dead—itself. Over the next few years I paid several visits to the mummy storage room. The place was packed with mummies from floor to ceiling, stored in black tin boxes and sealed glass cases. The curator who showed me the collection opened several of the tin boxes. Most of the mummies had been unwrapped, and they fascinated me, with their curling fingers like cheroots, their delicate fingernails and braided hair. Some wore leggings and moccasins and shell bracelets. Their lips were drawn back with the anger of desiccation, and their eyes were open and cloudy, staring at a world they could not see and could never have imagined. So fresh were some of the mummies that the archeologist who dug them up, Earl Morris, said that upon exhumation the irises of their eyes still retained their color.

Other mummies were bundled in a flexed position as they

had been found, wrapped in woven mats or gorgeous robes of rabbit fur, some with large baskets over their heads. One carried his most prized possessions: a spear thrower, a bag of dice, a pipe and tobacco.

Earl Morris excavated Mummy Cave for the museum in the 1920s. The vast overhang of the cave created an environment drier than the Sahara Desert, naturally mummifying the dead buried there. Morris had a strange sense of humor, and he propped the mummies up around his camp before crating them and shipping them back to New York. The museum's photographic archives contain several photographs of Morris in his camp surrounded by cross-legged, grinning mummies, like some macabre party of the dead, while Navajo workmen sit uneasily nearby.

The Navajos in the canyon were aghast at Morris's treatment of the dead. In an age when museums and archeologists were not terribly sensitive to the feelings of indigenous peoples, Morris and the American Museum of Natural History were among the worst. Indeed, the American Museum was already notorious for its destructive excavation of Chaco Canyon, where the museum's chief archeologist, Richard Wetherill, had been murdered by Navajos.

After Morris finished each season of excavations, some of his Navajo workers had to undergo curing ceremonies and sweat baths to purge them of the taint of death. One Navajo had a powder given to him by a medicine man, which he sprinkled over the mummies as they were uncovered. Even so, a few simple rites could not provide protection against the dead, and it is probable that any Navajo who worked on the excavation had to undergo an elaborate, three-day Enemy Way curing ceremonial.

Not all the mummies Morris removed were Anasazi. I remember vividly one drawer being opened, to reveal a corpse wrapped in a gorgeous black-and-red Navajo blanket, its hair tied in a bun. Morris, in his diggings, sometimes uncovered relatively fresh Navajo burials in the ruin. He secretly removed some of these burials at night, after his Navajo workmen had left, and shipped them back to the museum.

When Earl Morris's discoveries at Mummy Cave were shown back at the museum in New York City, they brought him instant fame and led to the creation of the Canyon de Chelly National Monument.

There is no doubt that the cavalier white attitude toward the dead shocked the Navajos deeply. Most of the ruins in the canyon are considered sacred, and some of them, such as White House Ruin, figure in the chant ways and may only be entered by medicine men after careful preparation. To some *Diné*, the activities of the archeologists and the activities of witches may have looked uncomfortably similar.

Perhaps it is not surprising then that the coming of the archeologists is part of the prophecy told to us by James Fatt—the "sign" which marks the end of this world and the beginning of the next. It was the archeologists who were among the first white people in the *Diné Bikeyah*, and their interest was in the digging up of the dead. It was they who first came around asking the Navajos about the Anasazi ruins. It is fitting, and ironic, that the Navajos believe that in a distant future, new archeologists will come around asking about the ruins of the white man.

▽ ▽ ▽

We rode beyond Mummy Cave to a place called Massacre Cave, where Spanish troops killed over a hundred Navajo women and children in 1805. The Navajos call this cave *Adah aho'doo'nilí*, Place Where Two Fell Down, because a Navajo woman and a soldier fought at the rim of the cave, both falling to their deaths. The cave is still full of the human bones of the massacred, although white looters have removed their skulls, clothing, blankets, and possessions.

We rested in a pleasant grove of trees below Massacre Cave, and went swimming in the creek. Terrill showed Selene how to make drip castles with sand while Christine and I drowsed in the warmth. We loped back to camp and arrived as dusk folded the light away behind the rimrock. Blackness filled the canyon and when the moon rose it was as bright as a second dawn. It was our last night in the canyon.

Chapter 21

NAVAJO CHARCOAL
DRAWING
—CANYON DEL MUERTO

Tsaile
May 16–18, 1992

In my thoughts I approach,
The Sun God approaches,
Earth's end he approaches,
Changing Woman's hearth approaches,
In old age walking
The beautiful trail.

—SONG THE SUN SINGS WHILE HE JOURNEYS WESTWARD EACH
DAY TOWARD HIS HOME AND HIS WIFE, CHANGING WOMAN[38]

The next morning we rode out of Canyon del Muerto. It was a
difficult climb, and by the time we reached the rim the horses
were creamy with sweat and winded. We stopped for a long
rest.

For the first time we could see the scale of the canyon we had spent the last four days in. It was an immense gorge, carved into the flat Defiance Plateau like a savage cut into the red flesh of the Earth. Eight hundred feet below, Tsaile Creek looped between the canyon walls. The floodplains on either bank were neatly tiled with cornfields and pastures. A massive cottonwood tree stood alone in a field, casting a long shadow, next to a hogan with a wisp of smoke climbing into the morning light. It looked like a lost world buried in the desert, glowing with life.

"I'm going to miss that place," Christine said. "It was so nice to have unlimited water and green grass."

"Me too," said Selene. "I hope we don't have to go back to being dirty all the time and drinking our dishwater."

"It really is a beautiful place down there," Terrill said. "I'm always sad when I have to leave it. The rest of the world looks so ugly by comparison." He solemnly shook our hands and wished us luck, and then reined his horse around and rode toward the rim and back down into the beautiful canyon of light.

▽ ▽ ▽

We rode across slickrock and over hot sand and soon hit the paved road to Tsaile. It was lined on either side by barbed-wire fences. The roadside was littered with countless empty bottles of Garden De Luxe Tokay wine as well as aluminum cans, used diapers, motor oil containers, and cigarette packages.

"Look at all these bottles!" Selene said.

A car whizzed by at sixty miles an hour, buffeting us with its backlash, leaving grit in our faces and a faint odor of internal combustion in our noses. Selene's horse stepped forward and there was a pop as his hoof exploded a wine bottle.

"Watch out for the glass!" Christine said. "You could cripple your horse!"

"Welcome back to civilization," I said.

It was a long, ugly ride to Tsaile. Acomita was nearly hit by a car and Brazos picked on Roscoe the whole way, looking for every opportunity to bite or kick him. My temper became badly frayed and I found myself hurling the most shocking epithets at the horses. We could find no water, and the barbed-wire cross-fences forced us to travel alongside the road next to a constant stream of speeding cars. The bottles of Tokay were so numerous it was impossible to keep the horses from occasionally breaking them with their feet.

We stopped for lunch under an old piñon alongside the road and watched the cars go by.

"This is the worst riding of the whole trip," Christine said grumpily. "Civilization and horses don't mix."

"You're telling me," said Selene. "And Doug's in a *really* bad mood."

"Be quiet," I said, "I am not."

"Yeah, right," said Selene, with a snort.

"And even if I were, I don't appreciate it being pointed out."

"Doug, you really ought to control your language," said Christine. "Some of the things you're saying to those poor horses are so awful I've never even *heard* them before."

I expressed my opinion of their advice and stalked off to eat my lunch alone.

We rode down the hot road, the heat shimmering off the tarmac. In late afternoon we left the ugly road and arrived at Tsaile Lake, a sheet of blue water lying among reeds, surrounded by meadows and ponderosa pines. We had been steadily climbing and were now at over seven thousand feet. We rested our horses by the lake. An old man sat on a stump at the edge of the woods, watching a flock of sheep, and he smiled and waved as we went by. A stream flowed from the southern end of the lake, over a waterfall and into the head of Canyon del Muerto. Tsaile comes from the Navajo word *Tséhílí*, meaning Where Water Enters a Box Canyon.

The Chuska Mountains rose up behind the lake, silhouetted against a sky covered with white thunderheads. From our vantage point, almost every peak and butte was sacred. Directly behind the lake a great stump of basaltic rock pushed out of the top of the mountains, a sacred butte called *Tsézhin dits'in*, Standing Black Rock, recorded on American maps as Tsaile Butte. After killing *Déélgééd*, Monster Slayer passed this way going to Shiprock Pinnacle, to kill a brood of birdlike alien gods. Behind Tsaile Butte he encountered two giant snakes sunning themselves. He crept up to them and then skipped lightly over their backs, so as not to wake them, and continued on his way. The snakes continued to drowse in the sun, slowly turning to stone, where they remain to this day.

To the south of Tsaile Butte we could see two strange little hills which the Navajos call Slender Female Sandpile and Slender Male Sandpile, respectively, which Anglo maps designate as White Cone and Little White Cone. Medicine men climb these two peaks to obtain herbs to heal women who have been the victims of incest. Beyond Little White Cone were two high, rounded mountains, heavily forested in ponderosa. These were the Sonsela Buttes, the remains of the stars that fell back to Earth during the creation, when Coyote, in his impatience, threw First Man's blanket of stars skyward. Beyond those rose Chuska Peak itself. It is believed to be the head of the sacred male being, the counterpart to the female being whose head is Navajo Mountain. In this sense it is the male aspect of the Earth, as Navajo Mountain is the female.

▽ ▽ ▽

At Tsaile we planned to stay with friends, Marci and Jim Matlock, before heading on the last leg of our trip across the mountains to Shiprock. We rode past the lake and headed toward the town. Selene was beside herself at the prospect of a hot shower, cold soda, and sleeping in a bed. She sang and hummed and whistled all the way to the Matlocks' house.

The Matlocks were gone, and we met a young Navajo couple, Norman Tulley and his wife, Sara, who were housesitting. Norman and Sara were both students at Navajo Community College in Tsaile. Norman was Navajo and Sara was White Mountain Apache. We spent several days in Tsaile, resting the horses and waiting for the Matlocks to return.

That night, I told Norman and Sara about our trip. Norman was in his mid-twenties, and he spoke a strange kind of English, peppering his convoluted sentences with sudden phrases of beauty and wisdom. He was round and soft-spoken, with a long black braid down his back, but there was nothing soft in his way of looking at the world; indeed, I felt, talking to him, a kind of unspoken challenge.

Norman was a born leader. He once traveled across the United States, visiting Native American tribes, and from there went to Europe and Asia meeting with indigenous and oppressed peoples. In March he had organized and led a horseback ride—a kind of religious pilgrimage—from Tsaile to Big Mountain, Arizona. The ride publicized the plight of the elderly Navajos living in the Big Mountain area who were resisting government eviction orders to leave their land. Along the way the riders, most of whom were teenagers or in their twenties, stopped at a Navajo nursing home in Chinle and visited the residents. It caused a sensation among the older men and women, who

thought the young of the tribe had forgotten all about them and
Navajo traditions. They wept and laughed and told stories.

"Our parents," Norman said, "they got taken away to boarding schools and they got Christianized and lost a lot of traditions.
So what we wanted to do is skip that generation, go back to the
elderlies and learn about Navajo ways from them."

After dinner we sat around and played gin rummy. Selene
lost and got very grumpy and began reading through a stack of
Reader's Digests. Christine went to bed. Norman and I talked and
I finally hauled out my tape recorder.

Norman started to laugh. "What is it about the *Bilagáanas,*
they always got a tape recorder hidden somewhere!"

I told Norman what Terrill had said about using a tape
recorder.

"What he said was right," Norman said. "But if I know you,
you're gonna use it anyway. Right?"

"Only if you don't object."

"I don't object. But you should try *listening* too."

"I will," I said. "Tell me about your life."

Norman laughed. "I was born in Ganado, in a hospital. Is
that what you want to hear?"

"Whatever," I said.

"Let's see. Went to boarding school at Little Mountain. I
never graduated from high school. I don't know how I got into
college. See, for me, it's like I really don't know how to read or
write. I don't know how to do math problems. But I know how
to ride a horse, so now I'm learning how to write 'a horse.' "

He laughed at the pun, a low musical kind of chuckle, like a
bronze temple bell.

"When I was growing up all my brothers said I was stupid
and crazy."

"Were you?" I asked.

"What's stupid and crazy is when you start talking about
how you're better or smarter than someone else. I got a very
simple philosophy: nobody's stupid, everybody's good."

We talked about conditions on the reservation, and I mentioned economic development and jobs.

Norman snorted. "The white people, the government comes
out here. 'Look at this,' they say. 'Look at this poor old woman
living in a hogan. Look, it's got a dirt floor, and there's no
electricity or running water. We got to *help* this *poor* old
woman!' "

He looked at me. "Right? We got to *help* her."

"You don't think she should get assistance?" I asked.

Norman expelled some air. "See, that's the problem. She got her sheep, she got her family, and she's self-sufficient. She's happy and she don't feel poor. This is the way she lived all her life. And this is the way her mother and grandma lived. But the government says, look, this is terrible, you're *poor*. We're going to *relocate* you where there's electricity and water, and build you a nice house. So they relocate her. She loses her sheep and she's moved away from her family. And pretty soon maybe a bill arrives for the water or electricity, and she's never seen a bill in her life and she can't speak no English. So the electricity gets cut off, and maybe the water. So she has to get assistance, fill out papers. Nobody to help her because her family's somewhere else. And nothing to eat because her sheep are gone."

He gave me a penetrating look. "So what happens? The government has to support her! She's a welfare case. The government's taken a totally self-sufficient, happy old lady and *made* her poor. *Made* her dependent."

He laughed. "And then they say, 'Look at all these damn raggedy old Indians on welfare! We got to do something. We need jobs and economic development. So let's drill oil wells and cut down the forests and strip-mine, and dig up uranium, and give these poor Indians jobs.' "

He leaned forward. "Hey, I say to you, *Bilagáana*, don't come here and tell *us* we're *poor*. *I* don't feel poor. This old lady who lives in a dirt floor hogan, *she* don't feel poor. She's rich! She got everything she needs. But they think we're poor and so they tell us over and over, 'You're poor, you're poor!' and that's how the government *makes* us poor.

"Take relocation. When you relocate an elderly person, he's gonna think about the land and where he grew up, and think that he can't go back there ever again. And then he's gonna die. That's what happens when an elderly is relocated, he dies of a heartache for the land. When they moved those people from Big Mountain, about seventy-five percent of them died in a year. Died of a heartache for the land."

"That's a terrible statistic," I said.

"It's no statistic. It's people. Take the European-Americans. If they get relocated from their area, it's okay, they don't have any ties. To a Native American Indian person, the land itself, where you grew up, where your birthplace is, there's a lot of prayers in the land there. Even to the small plant, the rocks and sand, and where the ants roam around. All those thoughts and prayers are there in the landscape. Every tree and every rock and every anthill is a memory of prayers. If you really listen to the landscape, you can hear what the spirits are saying.

"The white people, they've been moving around a lot in the centuries. They don't mind moving around. Because Christian people, they don't pray for ants. They don't pray for the rocks and the trees and the mountains and the four-leggeds. For us, the mountains are sacred. You can't explain it in English, but in *Diné bizaad*[39] to say the mountains are sacred means a big amount. Like when you're talking in English, it's impossible to explain the feelings that you have for the mountains. I can't tell you in English how much I love the four mountains.

"Big Mountain, *Dził nitsaa*, over there is the heart of the Female Mountain. Chuska Mountain is the Male Mountain. If you destroy the Female Mountain, like Peabody Coal is doing with that Black Mesa Mine, you will destroy the Earth. You *kill* the heart of the Earth. The Earth, you were born from it, it gave you the sacred flesh. That's how the Earth is: it feeds you, it gives you animals, it gives you plants, it gives you shelter. The Earth is the mother, the Sky is the father. And Peabody Coal is killing the heart of the Earth, killing the mother.

"To us *Diné* there's always a female and a male in everything. In Christianity, there's only one, there's only a man—there's no woman; women are less than men. They say that wine is Christ's blood, but why would Christ's blood be killing the People? Wine is killing the People. The way they talk in the churches, love thy neighbor, the commandments. If they follow that way, why hate other churches? Why put lies in people's minds and tell them they're better than everybody else? Nobody's better. All religions are good. All belief is good. God is everywhere, God is when you feel it, God is when you see it, God is when you hear it. I think Jesus was a wise man, but where'd Jesus come from? He came from a woman. And today the Christians don't have respect for a woman anywhere on this earth."

Norman fell silent, and shifted in his chair. "I don't mean to talk down about Christians. Spirituality is important, but what I don't like is the way Christians say their belief is better than everyone else's."

Suddenly Norman laughed a low laugh. "I've got a story for you. The Mormons came around and kept asking me to go to their church. And some born-again Jehovah's Witnesses came around and asked me to go to their church to be saved, asked me if I knew who God is. Those missionaries are all over the *Diné Bikeyah*. Me, myself, and I, *I* know who God is. I know who she is and what she is."

He laughed again. "But these people, I don't really think they understand who God is so they keep coming around, coming around.

"So one time I said, 'I'll go to your churches, but after that you should come with me to see my belief. The sweat lodge.'

"The Mormons brought me a coat and tie to wear to their church, white shirt, slacky pants, black shoes [laughs]. And I went over there. They said we are the Lammanite people, the Indians, Chicanos, blacks. So all white people are better. Nobody's a real Christian but them. All the other churches are bad. That's what the Mormons believe.

"So then I went over there to the Jehovah's Witnesses. They say that God is one, God is a man. They say they're better than the other churches. They dance around on the floor and if you're a better dancer than everybody, raise your hands! That was Jehovah's Witnesses."

Norman picked up the deck of cards and whiffled through them and they flew all over the place.

"Oops. Anyway, so then they came here," he continued. "We ran a sweat for them. Heated up the rocks, put them in the sweat lodge, prayed. And it was really something. We prayed, praying all the time. They were praying that God is a man, God is something you never see. But I prayed that God is the rocks, God is the mountains, God is life, God is everything that you see. I prayed that everybody is sacred. We are no different from anybody. We all have five fingers and we walk on the Earth.

"The Jehovah's Witnesses, they said it was too hot in there and they beat it out fast. After the sweat was over, one of the Mormons left but the other stayed. He wanted to know more about sweats, about *Diné* belief. And then he quit the Mormon church and now he's running sweats. He was snapped out of it! So I say to them, anytime, I'll go to your churches, if you'll come see my belief. But now they won't come. I guess they don't like that deal any more."

He laughed and started picking up the cards.

We talked long into the night. My tape recorder ran out and

we continued talking. I told Norman about the stories I had heard about the Anasazi and the fate of the white people, and I asked if he had heard anything about that.

Norman was quiet for a moment and then he shifted in his chair.

"What you heard, that's something we don't talk about too much. There's some stories from way back, I don't know how many centuries ago, I heard from an elderly *Diné* that one color is going to conquer. When one color conquers the world, then that's the end of the world. The future of the white people is that they're going to conquer and take all the minerals and destroy the land, and then they're going to say . . ."

There was a dramatic pause.

"*Oops!*" Norman laughed.

"Look at how the Earth came about. How did the creation people, the First People, make this Earth? There was a reason why they made it this way. If we change it too much, it's going to be the end of us. But we've changed it too much already. It's too late. We've created a monster and we can't even stop it. But it's okay. The world, it's drawing to a close. It's out of balance. It's gonna end soon, like the other worlds, because of the bad deeds of people. But then a new world's coming, and there's gonna be new life, a new beginning. So it's okay."

▽ ▽ ▽

By the time we finished talking, the house was dark and silent. I packed away my tape recorder and Norman said that he wanted to introduce me to someone, a relative of his, who might help me and share with me her knowledge.

The next day, Norman and I made a trip to see his relative. I was half expecting to head out into the desert, to some smoky hogan with an ancient medicine woman hovering over a fire. Instead, we turned into a suburban enclave next to the Navajo Community College campus, with paved streets, shade trees, lawns, and garages. We pulled into a driveway. I could hear the blare of a television set from the open window and the shrill laughter of kids. Norman knocked and a young woman with black curly hair answered. She grinned.

"Hey Norman, whatcha doing, come on in."

She was short and plump, and she bustled about with sharp movements. She was wearing designer glasses, a T-shirt, and slacks. She could have been a suburban housewife, except for the fact that she radiated the same kind of high intelligence and unsettling intensity that Norman did.

We settled in the living room, which was painted a light yellow. Two kids were watching Sunday-afternoon cartoons on the television at high volume and eating Rice Krispies.

We sat back on the sofa; nobody seemed to be aware of the deafening noise of the television. I wondered how I was going to record anything with that noise. Norman and his relative talked, and Norman asked her if I could interview her.

She ignored the question as well as me, and she and Norman talked for some time about family matters, switching from Navajo to English and then back again. Norman then told her a little about us and our ride.

She turned to me. "So what's this ride you doing?"

I told her where we had started and what we hoped to do. We talked for a while.

"That's quite a ride. That's something good. When you first walked in, I thought maybe you were just another of those 'researchers' coming to talk to the 'Indians.' You're doing the right thing, doing it that way."

She glanced at my tape recorder. "You can listen, but no tape recorders."

I put it away.

The conversation moved around to the Rodney King verdict and the riots in Los Angeles.

"I wish," she said with sarcasm, "that with all this science and technology they could invent a pill to cure racism."

We all laughed.

"So," she said. "You heard something about the fate of the white man. And you want to know more."

I mumbled that, yes, I did. Did she know anything?

She looked at me with intensity. "The fate of the *Bilagáana*," she repeated.

"I keep hearing," I said, "about how we, I mean the white people, are going to suffer a fate similar to the Anasazi."

"And *I'm* supposed to know something?" she said, looking at Norman.

"Go ahead," Norman said. "Tell him."

There was a long silence. She sighed irritably.

"Well," she said, "a long time ago, when I was a little girl, my grandfather talked about that once. He was a medicine man. I guess it was a very important and sacred piece of information."

She stopped and held her head in her hands for a moment.

"Oh, I *wish* I'd had more sense and asked him what he meant! I was just a kid and I wasn't thinking about things like that. I didn't know anything. And then he died before I grew up and I never did get a chance to ask him what he meant. He was very old and wise, and he knew a lot of sacred things. I never forgot what he said and when I got older I thought about it more and more. It seems like I'm thinking about it more and more these days. Wondering what he meant."

"What did he say?" I asked.

She looked at Norman.

"Well, he said that the white man was going to create an image of himself. And when that happened, the image would turn and destroy the creator."

I sat for a moment on the sofa, listening to the cartoons, to the giggling of the two kids, looking into the kitchen with a sinkful of dirty dishes and out the window to the paved street and a kid wobbling along on a battered bicycle.

"This is the fate of the white people?" I asked doubtfully. "This is how it'll end?"

"Yes," she said firmly.

"Like cloning a human being or genetic engineering or something like that?"

She was silent, looking at her hands. "Maybe. Like I said, I never asked him what he meant. I read about these scientists in Russia implanting a human egg into a gorilla, but I don't know."

There was another pause. "Well," she said, "I'm not sure it was that. He might have meant something else. I think maybe it had something to do with a machine. Something to do with these powerful computers."

"Like what?"

"Artificial intelligence."

I was a little perplexed. This was more like something out of a science-fiction book.

She shifted in the plastic easy-chair and leaned forward. "At Chaco Canyon," she said, "the Anasazi had a deep knowledge of nature and sacred things, and they started to misuse that knowledge. They died out because they abused sacred things, and they tried to control and dominate nature. They wanted power. They made evil and forbidden drawings on the rock that offended the gods, the holy people. They drew the sacred spiral in reverse. You can see it over there, in Canyon de Chelly too, those pictures, the reversed spirals and other things carved in the rock. They were like the white man, inventive and creative. They wanted too much. They practiced witchcraft. And then they made a machine."

"A machine?"

"An evil, magical machine, and it destroyed them. It turned on them and they turned on each other, and there were fires, war, and destruction. And what you see, all those ruins, that's all that's left."

"What kind of machine?"

"Corn," she said. "It was a machine made out of corn."

A machine made out of corn? I hardly knew what to think. It seemed unlikely.

She saw my puzzled look.

"People were created from corn," she said quietly. "Corn is what gave us life. First Man and First Woman were created from two ears of corn, in a sacred ceremony. The Anasazi abused that ceremony. They created false life in a witchcraft ceremony using the sacred corn. Which is just what the white man is doing today with this artificial intelligence and genetic engineering."

I suddenly understood. In the Navajo creation story, the four Talking Gods created First Woman and First Man by placing the two ears of corn between buckskins and allowing the Wind to enter and give them life. The Anasazi of Chaco, according to her, duplicated this ceremony and tried to create false life of some kind. Tried, in short, to create something artificial in their image. Like the mind in a machine. Now I suddenly saw the connection.

"The white man," she continued, "is a creator, an inventor. From the very beginning he creates and invents and creates. He sees a river, and he builds a dam. He sees coal, so he strips. He finds uranium, and he makes a bomb. He drills for oil and he sends messages through the wires and the air and makes cars and planes. He messes with nature, but he never thinks about what's going to happen because of those creations. Nobody ever stops and thinks what's going to happen. This messing with nature, all this *inventing*, we're heading for something terrible. Someday one of these inventions'll destroy us.

"My grandfather said the white man would create something

in his own image. I'm not sure, but I think he meant the image of a human *mind*, put into one of these super-powerful computers. My grandfather didn't know anything about computers, he couldn't even speak English, but that's what I think it meant. I've thought a lot about it for many years since. That's what it was about. This wasn't just his idea, but a prophecy that the medicine men knew about or had been given, like in a dream or vision.

"So you see, it's the same thing. The Anasazi and the *Bila-gáana*. Messing around with the essence of sacred life, using inventions and machines, turning everything into something else, trying to overcome nature."

"So this image," I asked, "will turn on us? This artificial intelligence?"

"Yes. Because you'll lose control of it. It'll be a mind in a machine, and you'll lose control. Like you've lost control of all your inventions, the atom bomb, gasoline, electricity, cars. The whole world is out of control. So this artificial mind, you can't find it, it's invisible, going here and there. It goes over wires and flies through the air. Like a witch. It's smarter than anyone. And to survive, it'll have to turn on its inventor."

"But what about the Navajo people? Will they survive?"

She smiled bitterly. "Oh yes. We'll survive. We always survive. All we need is our land; we don't need the white man's technology. We know the plants and the animals and the springs. We'll be here . . . we'll always be here."

She suddenly jumped off the sofa. "Now wait!" she said. "You can put it in the book, but don't say who told you this. All this stuff I'm telling you is very sacred. Okay? But I think maybe you need to know it. And now look at the time! I've got to start dinner."

Chapter 22

BASKETMAKER SHAMAN
—CANYON DE CHELLY

Lukachukai
Los Gigantes
May 19 and 20, 1992

I usually walk where the rains fall
Below the east I walk
I being the Talking God
I usually walk where the rains fall
Within the dawn I walk
I usually walk where the rains fall

Among the white corn I walk . . .
Among the collected water I walk
Among the pollen I walk . . .
By means of the white corn darkness is cast
Over it dark clouds cast a shadow
Over it male rain casts a shadow
Among it zigzag lightning hangs suspended here
*   and there . . .*
Among it is a gentle spray of rain . . .

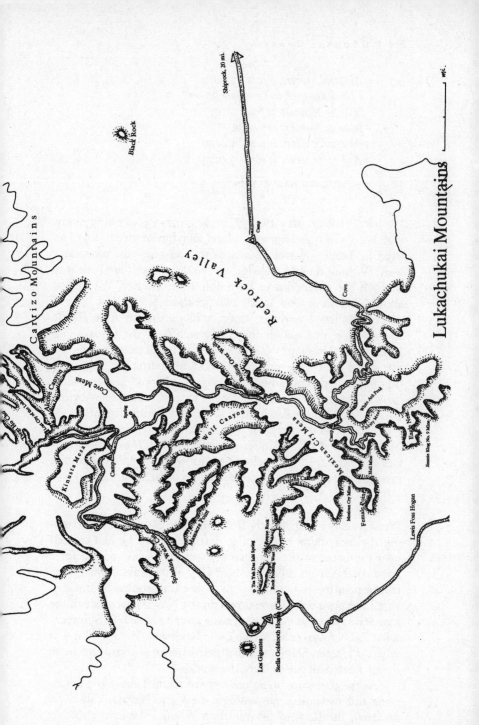

Shiprock, 20 mi.

Black Rock

Carrizo Mountains

Redrock Valley

Camp

Cove

Lukachukai Mountains

Cove Mesa

Wolf Canyon

Kinusta Mesa

Mexican Cry Mesa

White Ash Peak

Los Gigantes

Stella Goldtooth Hogan (Camp)

Lewis Foss Hogan

mi.

As I walk where it usually rains
I being the good and everlasting one
It being pleasant in front of me
It being pleasant behind me
As I walk where it usually rains
As I walk where it usually rains

—Song for making rain[40]

We left Tsaile on May 19, 1992, riding into a cool sunny morning. We were traveling with Marci and Jim Matlock, who had lived in Tsaile for over twenty years and knew the mountains well. Without their knowledge we could not have found our way through the mountains or been able to find water. We carried about ten days of food on our two packhorses.

We followed a rutted horse trail northward from Tsaile through a juniper-piñon forest. The cliffs of the Chuska and Lukachukai Mountains rose up like a red wall on our right. As the sun warmed the ground, tiny sulfur butterflies appeared, dipping and reeling among the sage plants and Indian paintbrush. On our left the land fell away to the Chinle Valley before rising again to meet Black Mesa some thirty miles distant.

The horses were rested, well fed, and lively. Selene was in a prankish mood. As we rode, she grabbed fistfuls of juniper berries from the trees and pelted us with them, giggling. Acomita raced along, nose to the ground, glad to be back on the trail.

▽ ▽ ▽

We were departing slightly from Monster Slayer's route, crossing the mountains a few miles north of where he had crossed over the backs of the two giant snakes. We were looking for a large Anasazi ruin called the Lost City of the Lukachukais, buried deep in the redrock canyons of the Lukachukai Mountains. From there we would ride down on the New Mexico side of the mountains and end our trip near the sacred pinnacle of Shiprock, what the Navajos call *Tsé bit'a'í*, the Rock with Wings. This was where Monster Slayer killed a pair of enemy gods, and in so doing created all the birds of the world.

As the day wore on a thunderhead seethed above the mountains and expanded, shrouding a peak the Navajos called *Tsé bináayolí*, the Rock in the Whirling Winds. The light ebbed as the clouds lowered over our heads. Ten miles north of Tsaile, we struck the small town of Lukachukai, a motley collection of house trailers, corrals, and hogans scattering alongside Totsoh Wash. We stopped at the Totsoh trading post, a whitewashed cinderblock building standing on a dusty flat. We tied up the horses in the dirt parking lot and went inside.

Just inside the front door was a large freezer with various advertisements for ice cream pasted on it.

Selene let out a shriek of pleasure. "Look!" she cried, "they have *Fat Boys* out here!" She made for the freezer to confirm the miracle and pulled out the largest ice-cream bar I had ever seen.

"Hold on here," I said.

"I want one too," said Christine.

We all broke down and ate Fat Boys.

It was an old-fashioned trading post, a general store that served the Navajo people living in the area rather than tourists. Inside, all manner of goods were stacked up for sale: used saddles, lariats, stovepipes, canned foods, mutton, soda pop and candy, video rentals, muscle-building magazines, ammunition, clothing, livestock drugs, batteries, kerosene, sacks of beans and flour, pots and pans, Pendleton wool blankets.

Curious, I asked for the trader and went upstairs to his office. He was sitting at his desk, an Anglo man with a bull neck and mustaches, hunched over a paper plate of beans. A new cowboy hat sat on his desk, on top of a tottering pile of papers. He looked up as I came in. His name was Hank Blair.

"Howdy," he said, indicating a seat. "What can I do for you?"

I explained myself and told him about our ride.

"I know that trail," he said. "One of John Wetherill's grandkids came out and they was gonna ride that trail. He pulled his horse over on top of himself there where the trail gets real bad, hurt himself pretty good. Had to quit."

"What was it like in the old days?" I asked.

He chewed on his lunch, then swallowed hard, looking suspiciously at the tape recorder I had removed from my pocket. "Well, all right," he finally said, grinning at the machine. "It was a hard life in the old days. I grew up on the rez. When I was a kid, we were up at Red Mesa, in between Teec Nos Pos and Mexican Water, and it was eighty miles of *bad* dirt road to Farmington. One of my earliest memories was herding sheep and seeing little boxes up in the trees, babies that had died. They put 'em up in the trees because the ground was frozen or they were too poor to own a shovel. Back then, people were *poor*. Everyone had TB. My friends' moms, they were all up in the Sanitarium in Denver or Salt Lake. Half the babies died.

"Back then the trading business was all barter, and we got paid twice a year. Lambs in the fall, wool in the spring. No money. Once in a while we'd get someone come back from working on the railroad with a twenty-dollar bill, and my mom and dad would be digging through their pockets and turning the place upside down trying to make change."

He laughed and scooped a forkful of beans into his mouth.

"We bought and sold wagons, we took trade-ins. We had a used-car lot out there, only it was horse-drawn wagons instead of cars. They started fixing up the roads in the sixties and then the Navajos started buying trucks. Before that, it was all wagons."

"So you got paid in lambs? What did you do with them?" I asked.

He smiled with the memory. "We'd herd them every fall over the mountains to Farmington. There we'd load them on the narrow-gauged railroad that went to Silverton. All the traders would get together. It took two, three weeks, because you didn't want to move 'em too hard and cause them to lose weight. It was a lot of fun. I used to sleep in the back of the wagon."

"Have things changed a lot since then?"

"You bet," he said. "Things are a lot better now than they were then. The Navajos have really thrived. They're real adaptable. On the other hand, I'd say the traditional way of life is definitely dying out. My generation—I'm forty-five—was the last traditional generation. Now we've had two generations come along since then grown up in a totally different way. Twenty years ago, eighty or ninety percent of the kids spoke Navajo long before they spoke English. Now there's some kids don't even speak Navajo at all. *I* speak more Navajo than my kids. My wife's Navajo, you see. These friends of mine have five kids, and the first three speak Navajo. Then the last two, no matter how hard they tried to teach it to 'em, they wouldn't learn. You talk to 'em in Navajo and they answer in English. But look, my mother was a first-generation German, but she can only say a couple of prayers in German and that's it. It's hard when the dominant society speaks English. But the Navajo people will definitely survive. *More* than survive."

He leaned back with a vast cracking of the chair and grinned.

"Back east, they all talk about how the Indian is dying out. Well, in the fifties there were fifty thousand Navajos and now there's two hundred thousand. There's Vietnamese Navajos, Chinese Navajos, Japanese Navajos, German Navajos. My kids are Navajo. When you marry a Navajo, like I did, they consider your kids Navajo, not white. Now that's not like many of these Pueblo tribes, like the Hopi. If you got even a drop of white blood you're *white*. You're excluded."

Hank's wife came in, a perky, cheerful, bustling woman. He introduced her and they talked about business and she left with a fistful of papers. Then one of his daughters came in. She had dark skin, beautiful brown Navajo eyes, and Anglo freckles. It was a very attractive combination.

"Yeah," he said, putting his arm around his daughter. "These people that say the Indian is dying out haven't come around here, that's for sure. I think the Navajo people have a great future in this country. I really do." He grinned and squeezed his daughter.

"Oh *Dad*," she said, smiling.

▽ ▽ ▽

As we rode out of Lukachukai a dust storm blew up out of the valley, followed by a light rain. The piñon forest thinned out and we found ourselves in badlands of indescribable colors: blood reds, light greens, yellows, grays. The rain had soaked the striated earth. It was like the wetting of a dull stone to bring out the color: the land glowed with a magnificent intensity, almost a phosphorescence. Petrified tree trunks eroded out of the badland humps, some nearly a hundred feet long and three feet in diameter.

The rain was falling heavily in the Lukachukais. Here and there a waterfall tumbled off the cliffs, the thread of water unraveled by the wind before it reached the ground. The mountains looked dark and impregnable, the clouds moving like smoke among the peaks.

As evening approached we came across a hidden arroyo, with a small stream running through it and thick grass along the bottom. At the head of the arroyo was a small earthen dam to impound and divert rainwater.

We unpacked the horses, covered up the gear, and set up

our tents. Selene crawled inside her sleeping bag and I could hear the electronic sounds of her Gameboy drifting across the evening air.

As I was hobbling the horses, I saw a stout, bowlegged figure standing against the sky, six-gun strapped to his waist, wearing a straw cowboy hat. He slowly picked his way down the hill, stopping about ten feet from me.

"This is your place?" I asked, eyeing the gun a little nervously.

He nodded.

"And here we are, just making ourselves at home and helping ourselves to your grass," I said.

He laughed, exposing a nearly toothless mouth. "You folks welcome to stay as long as you like! Help yourself to the grass! Plenty for everyone!"

He stepped closer and lowered his voice. "We got a pack of wild dogs around here, been killing stock and going after people." He patted the ancient Colt .45 at his hip. "If you got a gun, wear it."

It rained hard all night, and when we awoke in the morning the little earthen dam had washed out.

The old man came back with a shovel. Jim and I helped him lift rocks to repair the dam, while we talked.

"I just come back from Nevada," he said. "Worked forty-four years for the railroad but I ain't getting no pension."

"Why not?" Jim asked.

"Got to prove you're sixty-five to get the money. I don't have no paper."

"Paper?" I asked.

"Them birth papers. I wasn't born in no hospital and I don't know how old I am. But I know I'm over sixty-five. I think I must be seventy by now! So I go over there, bus cost fifty dollars, they don't give me nothing. Say I don't have no paper."

▽ ▽ ▽

The next day we packed up the horses and continued northward along the base of the mountains. The trees vanished and we found ourselves riding in an empty landscape of grassland mesas and broad washes running with muddy red water. In the north, through a yellow curtain of watery light, we could see two massive buttes. They were Los Gigantes, the Giant Ones; the *Diné* call them *Tsé álts'óóz íí'áhí*, Two Slender Rocks Standing Up.

Beyond Los Gigantes, jutting from the plain, stood Round Rock, a fabulous isolated mesa with complicated spires, arches, and windows carved by wind and rain.

The sky darkened ominously and then a hard rain began to fall. We were soon soaked. The horses plodded along glumly, flicking the water off their ears. Redbone's lower lip hung in dejection, water dripping from his chin. The rain just kept pouring down and the world dissolved into layers of gray. The aroma of mud, wet horses, leather, and sagebrush filled the air. The water began to collect in the saddle and trickled between my legs, a most unpleasant sensation.

We rode in miserable silence for about three hours, the only sound the steady hiss of the rain, and then I heard a thin wail going up from Selene.

"What's wrong?" Christine asked.

"Whaddya mean, 'what's wrong'!" she hollered. "I'm totally *soaked!*"

"I know," said Christine. "We're all wet."

"Well what are we going to *do* about it?" she wailed.

"What is there to do?" Christine said. "Just keep going."

"Keep going? Are you nuts?" she sobbed.

"Well," Christine said, "it's a day's ride back to Lukachukai and a day's ride ahead to Round Rock. So how do you propose that we get out of this place?"

"With a *helicopter!*" Selene shouted.

"And where's the telephone to call for the helicopter?" Christine asked.

There was a shocked silence as Selene realized just how far out in the desert we were.

I stopped and waited for them to catch up. Selene was bowed in the saddle, her face squeezed up in a wail of frustration.

"This is *horrible!*" she sobbed. "It's not *supposed* to rain in the desert! If I only had three wishes!"

"What would you wish?" Christine asked.

"Number one," she shouted, "I'd wish this trip were over! Number two: I'd wish I'd never have to be outside in the rain again!"

She choked up.

"What about number three?" Christine asked.

She stopped crying and thought for a moment. "Number three," she said triumphantly, "I'd wish for a *million* dollars!"

Christine and I burst out laughing.

"It's not funny!" she wailed.

▽ ▽ ▽

In the early afternoon we glimpsed through the gray rain an isolated hogan standing on the edge of a wide mesa. Just below the lip of the mesa were some horse corrals, and a broken scarecrow stood against the sky, a shred of cloth flapping in the wind.

"Hey look!" Selene cried. "Let's go there! Let's knock on the door and get out of the rain!"

As if in answer to her shout, we heard the thudding of hooves and a dark form on a buckskin horse materialized out of the rain. The man wore a black hat, a black duster, and a leather vest. He had a huge brown beard and his pigtails flew out from underneath his cowboy hat. He reined up and leaned on the saddle horn. To my great surprise I saw he was a white man, scruffy and hirsute, the rain dripping from his hat. He had a rifle scabbard on his saddle, but I noted with relief it was empty.

He raised his hand from the horn. "How you folks doing?" he said.

"Fine, fine!" we cried out a little nervously.

He nodded. It was impossible to see his face under the dark hat and beard.

"Maybe you'all'd like to come on over for some coffee," he said, "and dry yourselves out."

"Thank you very much!" Selene whooped. "Thank you! Thank you!"

"You're welcome," he said with a grin.

We rode behind him to the hogan. We tied our horses in the corral and crowded into his tiny hogan. It was warm and tight, with a packed dirt floor and a single window. The rain drummed loudly on the tarpaper roof. A worktable on one side was covered with pieces of leather and antler. A braided quirt hung from a Coleman lantern, and a well-oiled .30-.30 leaned against the back wall.

"Make yourselves at home," he said, gesturing to several lard cans and packing crates that served, apparently, as furniture.

The man shoved some pieces of juniper into the barrel stove and put a blackened coffeepot on to boil. Soon we had settled back with mugs full of hot black coffee. The stove glowed with warmth and our clothes steamed. I had never felt quite so comfortable in my life.

"Lewis Foss is the name," he said, and we shook hands all around.

"What are you doing out here?" I asked.

"Herding cattle for a guy named Kee Joe," he said. "Get room and board in return."

He spoke with a strange accent, a mixture of backwoods Maine and Western cowpoke. He had not had white visitors in months.

"Where you folks headed?" Lewis Foss asked.

"Up by Los Gigantes and over the mountains," Jim said.

"You got a place to camp tonight?" he asked.

"We're planning to camp up near Stella Goldtooth's place," Jim said, "where there's a windmill."

"Don't know her," Lewis said. "If you don't object I'd like to ride a ways with you. I know where there's some good drinking water along the way."

"That would be most helpful," Jim said.

The rain finally let up, and we got back in our wet saddles and rode northwest. Snarled mists rose from the ground. Los Gigantes kept emerging and disappearing in the mists, ghostly and insubstantial, two wet, silent stumps of rock. I watched with dismay as another storm gathered over the Carrizo Mountains to the north of us, the sky as black and cold as bottomless water. The storm swirled and eddied above the mountains and started spreading like a great fungus.

"That looks terrible," Lewis said, spitting tobacco juice.

"Maybe Stella Goldtooth will have a place we can spend the night in," Jim suggested.

At this suggestion Selene perked up. "I hope so! I like hogans!"

"Don't get your hopes up too high," Christine said.

We crossed some steep, severe badlands, smoking in the weak light. The horses floundered and skidded through the mud, and I could see they were rapidly becoming exhausted. Great balls of the sticky desert mud had collected around each hoof, and with each misstep clots of mud were flung up all over us.

We topped out on a high benchland, and nestled into the lee of a sand hill was a hogan, made of adzed logs with a dirt roof on which was growing snakeweed. From the stovepipe a trail of smoke whipped back and forth in the changing wind. A dark old lady sat on a stump next to the hogan, hands folded in her lap, in a traditional red velvet dress, wearing turquoise jewelry. She watched us approach with a stony face.

"I think we better stop here and ask directions," Jim said. "I'm not sure where we are and it wouldn't be polite to ride by."

The door to the hogan rattled open and in it stood a man of about thirty. He greeted us with an enthusiastic Hello!

"That's Lorenzo," Lewis said. "He only knows the one word, 'Hello.' Nobody else here speaks any English. That's Lorenzo's mother."

Lewis got off his horse and walked to the old lady while we dismounted and waited at a respectful distance.

"*Yá'át'ééh, shimásáni,*" he said. Hello, grandmother.

The woman looked at him saying nothing, and then looked at us, and her face softened considerably. "*Yá'át'ééh,*" she said.

"Hello!" said Lorenzo. "Hello!"

"*Goldtooth hoogan tó bá'as'á?*" He made a sign for a windmill with his hands. The woman said a few words in Navajo, pointing over some sand dunes that clung to the lip of the mesa above us.

We got back on our horses and rode up a winding trail through the sand dunes and came out on a high plain, with the wind in our faces. Los Gigantes stood about two miles in front of us. In another mile I could see the Goldtooth windmill just poking over the curve of the plain, the blades whipping around. A quarter mile to the side of the windmill sat a hogan, outbuildings, and corrals.

"We've got to hurry," said Jim, looking at the sky. A storm of evil intensity had blackened the earth to the north.

The hogan was locked up tight with a brand-new Master padlock. A log hut stood a hundred yards from the hogan. I tried the door and found it unlocked. I pushed it open. In the dim light of a smokehole, I could see it was an abandoned weaving studio. An exquisite rug, half woven, rotted on a loom. Skeins of decaying wool and decomposing fleeces lay about on the dirt floor. Fast-food trash was piled in a corner, Styrofoam McDonald's containers and crushed cups covered with spiderwebs and dirt.

Lewis looked in behind me.

"This Stella Goldtooth lady," Lewis said, "looks like maybe she died."

To our great relief the bulk of the storm was passing to the north of us, a mammoth column of rain as opaque as blued steel,

with lightning crackling above it. The air around us was heavy
with ozone and moisture. The rolls of thunder came once every
second or two, like an artillery barrage.

We put our gear and saddles in the weaving studio and
pitched our tents in the lee of a roofless log outbuilding.

Lewis decided to stay for dinner. He unsheathed an enormous knife, almost a machete, and hacked up some old pieces of
wood to build a fire. His pigtails flew with each whack of the
blade. We shielded the fire with a discarded lard can. The sparks
swirled out and danced away from us in a cold wind. The rain
started to fall hard again and we huddled around the fire, trying
to keep warm.

"Guess what, everybody!" Selene suddenly said. "It's May
20th. It's Doug's birthday!"

I had completely forgotten. There were murmurs of congrat-
ulations and Christine gave me a nice kiss.

"How old're you?" Lewis asked.

"Thirty-six," I said.

He laughed. "You're *young* still."

"Let's open the presents!" Selene said.

"We'll open them in the morning," I said. "Everything will
get wet."

"No!" Selene protested. "I want to open them now!"

"It's pouring rain," Christine said.

"You're supposed to open them on your *birthday*," Selene
said grumpily. "It's no *good* in the morning. Anyway, it'll probably be raining in the morning."

"All right," I said. "Let's open presents."

"Yay!" Selene cried, and dragged a stump over. "You sit
down here, and I'll hand them to you."

Selene gave me an old Hopalong Cassidy knife, with a picture of the gunslinger in black holding a drawn gun. Christine
gave me a kite and a book, *In the Spirit of Crazy Horse*. They had
both lovingly carried the presents for some three hundred miles
on horseback, keeping them hidden from me.

I tried to cook pizza in the Dutch oven. Whenever I opened
the lid to check on it the rain poured in and it was soggy and
revolting in the end. As soon as I removed the pot from the fire
the rain put it out. Night was falling.

"Well," said Lewis, sheathing his knife. "I gotta get going."

"You better not go," Marci said. "It's pitch-black out there."

"I'll be all right," said Lewis, "the horse knows the way."

Selene began to sing, "*The horse knows the way/To carry the sleigh/Through the bright and drifting snow, hey!*"

I saw a momentary flicker of something cross Lewis's face, and then he collected his horse and we heard hoofbeats fade into the darkness.

"He's going to be in serious trouble," said Marci. "It's too dark out there, even for a horse."

Selene crawled into our tent with us to warm up before going to her own. The blackest of black nights clamped down on the camp. I hung a little flashlight from the peak.

"It's cozy in here," Selene said, curling up in our sleeping bag.

"Yeah," I said.

"Well, happy birthday," Selene said.

"I never thought," I said, "that I'd be spending my thirty-sixth birthday at a God-forsaken place called Los Gigantes with my future wife and daughter in the middle of a storm. Did you?"

"I haven't had a thirty-sixth birthday yet!" said Selene.

"You know what I mean," I said.

"No," she said, "I never thought I'd be in a place like this ever, and I hope I never will again."

"Come on," I said, "this isn't so bad, is it? We're warm and cozy and what's most important, we're together."

"Yeah," said Selene, burrowing deeper, "this isn't so bad."

We listened to the rain and the wind shaking the tent.

Selene giggled. "Well," she said, "I've been thinking about it."

"Thinking about what?" said Christine.

"About you two getting married and Doug being my dad."

There was a moment of silence.

"Well," said Selene, matter-of-factly, "I've made a decision."

We waited.

"I've decided," she continued, "from now on, to call you *Dad*."

"Who, me?" I asked.

"Who else! Geez!"

"Oh," I said. I could hardly get another word out.

"Now listen," Selene said, "I might forget once in a while and still call you *Doug*, but you're allowed to remind me when I do that. Okay, *Dad*?"

"Okay," I said.

She giggled. "Dad. It feels so *funny* saying that! Dad. Dad, Dad, Dad." She dissolved into gales of laughter.

"Selene, that's wonderful," Christine said. "I'm so proud of you."

"Yes," I said. "I hardly know what to say."

"I love you, Dad," she said, and giggled again.

"And I love you, Selene," I said.

"Well," said Selene briskly. "Now *that's* settled."

She crawled out of the tent and into her own, which she had set up connecting to ours so she didn't have to go outside.

"Goodnight, *Dad!*" she called out into the darkness.

▽ ▽ ▽

In the middle of the night Christine and I awoke. We listened in the darkness and heard some faint, desperate shouting.

"Oh my God, it's Lewis," said Christine.

I shouted back, and he answered, and I shouted again. Then all was quiet.

The next morning, when we got up, Lewis's horse was in the corral. When I went to the weaving studio, I found Lewis wrapped in a tarp, snoring heavily.

I turned the horses out of the corral and hobbled them, so they could graze the sparse grass growing close to the foot of the bluffs. As we cooked breakfast Lewis made his appearance, rubbing his eyes and looking disheveled.

"Was that you last night?" I asked.

He shook his head. "That was some journey I had last night."

"What happened?"

"I started back but it got so dark my horse was blind. It was *black*. I couldn't tell where the ground was or where the sky was or anything. It was like floating in ink, I lost all depth perception. There wasn't a star, a light, or anything. I was sure my horse was gonna just walk over one of those cliffs. So I turned around and tried to find my way back, and I rode and rode. I was calling out for you guys. I must've circled all around here yelling for hours."

He shuffled and rubbed his face and stood by the fire.

"I passed a hogan back there," he said, "and I think I scared someone half to death. Probably thought I was a skinwalker."

We settled down to breakfast, warming ourselves by the fire.

Lewis hacked up some more wood and crouched by the fire, balancing the huge knife in his palm, then letting it drop point first into a piece of wood.

"So how did you end up here?" I asked.

He slid the knife back into its scabbard and spat a stream of tobacco off to the side.

"Kinda curious, aren't you?"

"I am," I said.

"All right, why not," he said, chunking another piece of wood on the fire and looking at my tape recorder.

"If you don't mind," I said.

"Here goes, you asked for it." He laughed and spat some more tobacco. "I grew up in Maine. My dad was a gunrunner. Remember when Quebec was trying to secede from Canada? He was running guns into Quebec. That's where he met his demise. Got pulled over and tried to shoot it out with the cops. Took one hundred fifty rounds inside of his old flat-nosed Ford van. According to newspaper clippings he had enough arms and munitions in the back of that van, he could've held 'em off for a good three or four months if he wanted to. But not him. He preferred to use his old single-action Colt peacemaker. Six shots to their one-fifty."

He shook his head. "Stupid guy . . .

"My mom was a total bitch. In plain English. I couldn't tell you if she's alive or dead. I haven't seen her in ten years. They smoked pot, drank beer, whiskey, done all sorts of weird drugs. On a daily basis, I'm not talking once-in-a-while-get-drunk. They would go through a keg of beer a night. I decided if I wanted my head to stay on my shoulders, I'm gonna have to move, get away from it. They didn't like my thinking. In the Bible it says there's a season for everything, but I don't believe there's a season for smoking pot every single *day*.

"I was a long-haul driver. Later, I was driving through Maine, and my truck threw a bearing. While it was out being fixed, I was in the bars. Doing a little drinking. Got into a scuffle with a French guy up there. I'm not sure right now what it was all about. His aim was bad and my knife was closer to the action and . . ."

He paused, looking into the fire, his face utterly expressionless.

"He ended up dying over it. Cops came. It was clearly in self-defense. The thing that helped my case is when they ran the

guy's prints, he'd just escaped from Thompson Federal Peniten-
tiary, he was a convicted cop-killer. And then evidently he
wounded two prison guards in the escape."

Lewis grunted a laugh, and shifted on his haunches.

"In Maine there's two things they don't like. They don't like
faggots and they don't like cop-killers. If the cops'd caught him
no way would he have survived the arrest."

He balanced his knife by its point on a piece of wood and
turned it slowly.

"Anyway," he continued, his voice quiet, "I made an
agreement. Instead of arresting me they said, 'You get out, we
don't want to see you in Maine for a long time. Twenty years,
minimum.' They even paid to fix my truck. So I had to leave.
Maine. I don't miss it. Except once in a while I'd sure like to take
out a johnboat and do a little fishing . . ."

His voice trailed off, and I could see a terrible loneliness in
his face.

"Christine and I are getting married in Maine in July," I
said.

"That so? Well, when you get there, send me something.
Send me some maple sugar candy."

"I sure will."

He looked at the ground. "Anyway, I took off, drove the
truck all over forty-eight states plus Alaska, Canada, and Mexico. Seeing nothing. So I quit in Fort Collins, Colorado, Christ-
mas. Six, seven years ago. Started doing ranching work. Worked
my way south to Tucson, arrived in Tucson January 18th last
year. And it was eighty-seven degrees. In January. I said I *gotta*
get myself back north, hit some high country.

"That's where I came across the rez, coming through this
area, Lukachukai. No longer had a vehicle, didn't have *nothing*,
just the clothes on my back. I was riding with someone. So we
drove up here, went to a peyote ceremony. They start about
dusk and they don't finish till maybe seven, eight o'clock next
morning. Soon as it was finished we hopped back in the car,
went up the Bluegrass Festival in Telluride, which I'd always
wanted to see. And I realized it wasn't it, it wasn't what I was
looking for. So I says turn me around and drop me back off at
Lukachukai. Soon as I got back here, I went to another ceremony
that night.

"Yeah," he said slowly. "I found the people out here are
really *good*, the traditional people. I get along better with the

older people than I do with the younger people out here. The younger people, all they want is change. They're restless. They want what every white man has. They want to be messed up by all the things that messed us white folks up."

He paused. "It's really sad. Because the older people, out here, they're watching their way of life going down the drain. It's dying. They're mournful. For them, it's like the end of the world."

Lewis sighed and stood up, looking around. "When they see someone that's trying to live the old way of life, like me, even though I'm not Navajo, I'm more easily accepted than a young Indian. They've accepted me. Jennifer Joe, the little girl back there at Kee Joe's place, asked me once what I was like when I was a white man."

He laughed.

"The only thing is my beard, it scares some of the old-timers. They never seen a beard before. But my answer to them is, cutting my beard violates one of the laws of nature. Plus it violates a law of God, in my opinion, because in the Bible it says we are made in His image. Who are we to mess with what He made? It's like getting your hair dyed red, or a nose job. It's like you're telling God I ain't satisfied with what you gave me, I think I'm gonna mess with it. Which is typical of the white man, they mess with everything He makes anyway. So I figure, that's gonna be one of the rules I live by. If my hair's supposed to be this long, it'll be this long. If it's supposed to be short, it'll stop growing. I'm just gonna be what God meant me to be, nothing more, nothing less.

"Living here, I've come to realize that out there America's going to hell. It's finished. Look at what they're *doing*, what they're allowing to happen in the name of progress. Civilization. When I go back into civilization, I look around me and I marvel, I wonder, how can they survive all this? All this hustle and bustle and rushing around and noise and greed. And what do they end up accomplishing? Not a thing. Oh they may have a fifteen-thousand-dollar car, a big house, whatever. But is it *really* theirs? It falls apart and then they die.

"Out here, there's a remnant of real spirituality left. I been to quite a few ceremonies. There's something in those ceremonies. In fact I'm getting ready to go to another peyote ceremony. The religion most Navajos believe is a religion that combines the peyote ceremony, that is, the Native American Church, along with their own beliefs, plus Christianity. They're the only group of people I've seen that can take a mix of religions, and take the best things out of all of them and combine them in such a unique way. There's a lot of Christian thinking in those peyote ceremonies, plus they sing a lot of Sioux songs. These Navajo medicine men, the singers, do something for the *whole* person, not like white doctors that only fix the body."

Lewis seemed energized, and he breathed deeply. He started walking toward the corrals.

"I better be pushing off. But to answer your question, I'm out here learning a way of life. A way of life is like a religion. Just like a religion should be a way of life, not just something you do on Sunday. So that's what I'm doing out here. Learning a way of life."

He picked his bridle rope off the corral fence and slung it over his shoulder.

"Now where's my horse gone to?" he said.

"I hobbled him with the others," I said. "He's over there."

"I appreciate that," he said, and walked off and caught the horse and brought him back to the corral and handed me the lead rope I had used as a hobble. He swung the saddle on his back, cinched him, and patted his neck. Then he placed a foot in the stirrup and lofted himself into the seat.

"Well," he said, looking at the horizon.

"Thanks for the story," I said.

"Don't forget that maple sugar candy," he said, and trotted into the rising sun.

Chapter 23

NAVAJO SANDPAINTING OF
BEAR
—BIG STAR CHANT

Lukachukai Mountains
Mexican Cry Mesa
May 21 and 22, 1992

We watered our horses at the windmill and rode past Los
Gigantes and through a narrow opening in the mountains. We
entered a broad, secret valley of sand dunes surrounded by
thousand-foot red bluffs, a place called Splashing Water Canyon, although I could see no sign of water, just a dry arroyo. An
astonishing extravagance of wildflowers grew out of the dunes,
the flowers and grasses switched and turned by the breeze, each
drawing its own little arc in the sand. We passed a hogan where
nobody spoke English, and Marci gave them candy, which
caused a sensation. The valley narrowed to a canyon that finally
boxed up, and we ascended a rocky trail that switchbacked up
through layers of sandstone and gnarled trees. We climbed for
several hours, while massive thunderheads as solid as marble
piled up above the mountains. The trail vanished in a high
meadow. Beyond there was a gap, through which we could see,
thrusting two thousand feet from the desert, Shiprock itself, *Tsé*

bit'a'í, the Rock with Wings. It stood alone on the vast plain, small and insignificant.

The Rock with Wings, according to the Navajo creation story, was once home to a pair of enemy gods and their brood, the *Tsé nináhálééhké*. They were enormous taloned birds that swept down upon people and carried them off to kill and eat on its craggy heights.

When Monster Slayer crossed the mountains just south of us, he came down onto the plain of the San Juan Basin and walked across the desert toward the Winged Rock. He still carried one of his trophies from the killing of *Déélgééd*, the section of bowel filled with blood.

As he approached, he heard a rush of wings and a shadow fell across the plain. The dust rose about him in a whirlwind and one of the great birds made a pass over him, "beating at the sky with its wings until the wind howled as it does during a winter storm and darkened everything the way the heavens are darkened on a moonless winter night."[41]

The bird made several sweeps before seizing Monster Slayer in its talons. He spiraled upward to the highest pinnacle of Shiprock, and there he released him to fall a thousand feet on the jagged rocks, where the monster's foul brood lived, squawking and clamoring to feed on the battered corpses. But Monster Slayer still had a sacred eagle-feather fetish given to him by Spider Woman, and he invoked its power and floated down to a shelf next to the brood. There he lay as if dead and secretly sliced open *Déélgééd*'s bowel, letting the blood run over the rocks. The bird monster flew off, satisfied he had been killed, and the brood flapped toward him with greedy eyes.

Monster Slayer then leapt to his feet and drew his weapons. The fledglings shrank back in fear.

"Tell me at once!" Monster Slayer cried. "When will your father come back? And where will he perch when he returns?"

They told him the male bird would return during a thunderstorm and perch on a crag to the right of the nest. They also revealed when and where their mother would come back.

Monster Slayer hid in a safe position, and soon a great thunderstorm swept down on the rock, with the lightning striking all around. At the height of the storm, the male bird dropped from the sky like a great shadow. Monster Slayer shot an arrow of sheet lightning at it and killed it instantly. Likewise, when the female bird came home to roost, carrying the corpse of a Pueblo woman to feed on, he struck her dead.

When the young birds saw that their parents had been killed, they set up a terrible howling and flapping.

"Stop your wailing," Monster Slayer cried. "I won't kill you . . . There is time for you to become something else: something useful to my people."

He seized the oldest of the birdlets and swung it back and forth four times. "You shall provide feathers to men to use in their ceremonies," he said. "You shall provide bones for whistles. You shall soar overhead peacefully and thereby make men aware of the vast expanse of sky." As he released it, it was transformed into an eagle, and it flew skyward, crying *Suk! Suk!* [42]

Monster Slayer then changed the second bird into an owl, saying: "As for you, you shall provide prophecy for Earth-Surface people who wish to determine their fate. Sometimes you shall speak the truth. And sometimes you shall lie. It will be for men to decide what is true and what is false from what you say. That way they shall learn to tell the difference between wisdom and folly." And the owl flew off, crying *Uwuu! Uwuu!*

Monster Slayer then found himself in a predicament. He was stranded high on the pinnacle, unable to descend. Finally he saw an ugly old lady, Bat Woman, walking slowly along the ground below. He called to her, but she hid behind a rock, ashamed of her ugliness. He pleaded and begged, and finally promised Bat Woman that she could have the beautiful feathers of the two bird monsters to decorate herself with if she would help him down. So she flew up and lowered Monster Slayer in her basket to earth. She then filled up the basket with glossy, iridescent feathers, slung it over her back, and began to shuffle away through a large field of sunflowers.

As she entered the dancing sunflowers, the feathers started turning into birds and flying out of the basket. Monster Slayer called out a warning, but Bat Woman did not heed him.

"And as she walked," the creation story goes, "more birds fluttered out of her basket: birds of all sizes, birds of all varieties of feathers, birds such as she had never seen before: birds emerging in flocks and filling the air around her head; birds flying in all directions; birds chirping and clattering as they flew until the sky was full of the sound of them. . . . She tried to hold them in. She tried to grab them as they came flying out. . . . And she flailed at all of them in an attempt to draw them back in the basket."

But it was to no avail. Thousands of birds had been released into the world, and no feathers were left for Bat Woman to decorate herself with. She sat down in the middle of the sunflower bed and wept, "as ugly as she ever was and as ugly as she always would be."

▽ ▽ ▽

When Monster Slayer returned to his mother, Changing Woman, with the trophies of his killings, she sang a song of joy. It seemed to them that all the alien gods, the devouring ones, had been killed. The Earth had been returned to *hózhó*, to beauty and balance.

But as they celebrated, the Wind stirred and whispered in Monster Slayer's ear. The most subtle and terrible of the alien gods still lived. Her name was *Sá*, Old Age Woman, and she would bring old age, feebleness, and death to all the People. She would bring certain death even to Monster Slayer himself, but in such an elusive way that he would not be aware of her approach. "She devours life so gradually that from one day to the next you cannot feel yourself being consumed," the Wind whispered to Monster Slayer. Lesser monsters also lived, the Wind said, including Poverty, Hunger, and Cold.

Monster Slayer asked his mother, Changing Woman, where he might find these creatures. But Changing Woman was frightened, and told her son that there were some things better left as they were in the world. To meddle with such things, she said, was far too dangerous. But the Wind curled into Monster Slayer's ear again and told him where he could find the remaining alien gods, and Monster Slayer set out to kill them.

▽ ▽ ▽

The high meadow was covered with clumps of grama grass. We turned the horses loose to graze while we ate lunch. The mountains and mesas loomed all around us, and the deserts beyond plummeted away into blue space to the edges of the earth. Here desert and mountain mingled; prickly pear, sagebrush, and yucca grew among ponderosa pines, spruce, and Douglas firs. Columbines and lupines peppered the meadows along with Indian paintbrush and snakeweed. Great red canyons filled with cottonwoods cut through cool mountain slopes leafed in aspen trees.

The storm continued to build over Kinusta Mesa, which rose above us like a long flatiron. There was a sharp roll of thunder and a smell of electricity. A high open field was not a good place to be in a thunderstorm, so we quickly rounded up the horses and rode south through the piñon trees at the base of the mesa. The storm pinned us down in a grove of junipers. We cowered under an ancient tree while the rain poured and lightning walloped the mesa above us.

With each strike, Selene counted out loud the seconds until the crash of thunder arrived.

"That one was only a half a mile away," she said. "Seven seconds equals a mile."

There was another flash. She barely got to one when the thunderclap sounded.

"Eek!" she said, covering her head with her arms, "that one almost hit us!"

There were a half-dozen more strikes and the arroyo near us ran with water as red as blood; and then the storm ended abruptly, and all was silent except for the sound of dripping water.

"Look at this!" Selene cried when she untied her horse. "My saddle is soaked! No way am I going to ride in a wet saddle!"

"Then you plan to walk?" Christine said.

There was a silence. "Daddy," she said, "will you please dry off my saddle for me?" She untied her bandanna and handed it to me like a princess.

"Of course," I said.

I carefully dried off her saddle and then lifted her up into it.

"Thanks Daddy," she said.

As we rode, Christine turned to me with a smile. "With this 'Daddy' business, you're becoming a real pushover, you know that?"

▽ ▽ ▽

After the storm, Marci suggested we ride to an area where she knew water collected in some potholes in the rock. We followed her for several miles across slickrock ledges to a cliff, where there were a series of depressions in the sandstone brimming with fresh, clean rainwater. We drank deeply and filled up our canteens. I was startled to look into one pool of crystal water and see the bottom carpeted with purple flowers growing out of a thin layer of soil.

We camped in another high meadow on the edge of a red-and-yellow canyon. The storm drifted off to the west and the evening was clear and pleasant. The sun sank behind Black Mesa in an orange eddy of cloud. We built a crackling fire and sat around it on horse blankets while the horses grazed in the distance and the birds chirped their twilight songs. The rain had released the fragrance of sagebrush and pine, and we breathed in the cool, sharp air.

We awoke inside a world of gray silence, surrounded by clouds. The rising sun was a faint glow, but it gradually grew brighter and the clouds broke into rivers of mist that poured off the meadow, swirling and flowing over the peaks of the Chuska Mountains in the south. The sun poured across the meadow, ricocheting off the dew, until the whole field sparkled as if it had been sprinkled with crushed diamonds.

During the night, the hobbled horses had traveled across the meadow to a grassy ridge. They were silhouetted against the river of cloud, grazing, Redbone's cowbell tinkling faintly. I walked up to check on them.

The ridge afforded another sweeping view toward the east, where the clouds had parted, bathing the mountains in the orange sunlight of morning. I could see for the first time an odd little butte, sticking out of the shoulder of a mountain a few miles away. The Navajos call this butte *Dził dah neeztíinii*, which translates cryptically as Mountain Went Out on Top, or perhaps more idiomatically, Mountain on Top of Another. It is named Roof Butte on the Anglo maps.

Roof Butte was the home of the *Té'é'í*, the Poverty Creatures, among the last of the alien gods that Monster Slayer finally set out to kill. These two beings destroyed people by gradually using up their possessions, wearing out their clothes and weapons, and leaving them naked and cold. After Monster Slayer left his mother he journeyed into the Lukachukai Mountains and climbed to the top of Roof Butte to battle these monsters.

There he was shocked to find not a pair of savage creatures, but "a tattered old man and a filthy old woman" living in a barren house. They had no food or possessions.

Monster Slayer raised his weapons and said, "Grandmother. Grandfather. It gives me no pleasure to tell you so, but I have come here to kill you."

The two old people looked at him sorrowfully. "Stop and think for a minute before you destroy us," they said. "If we were to be slain, people would have no reason to replace anything, no cause to improve upon the tools they are accustomed to using.

"But if we go on living and continue slowly to wear out what others use, ingenuity will flourish among them. They will think of better ways to sew and carve. Garments will become more beautiful. Tools will become stronger and more useful."

Monster Slayer listened to what they had said. Finally he lowered his weapons, and turned away, deciding to spare the lives of the two people of Poverty. The old man and the old woman live on Roof Butte to this day, wearing out clothing and making tools fall apart, so that people will constantly strive to make things better and more beautiful.

Monster Slayer likewise sought out Cold Woman and Old Man Hunger, and also spared their lives because of their reasonings and pleadings, learning in the process why such things need to exist in the world.

But there was one monster he was determined to kill, and that was *Sá*, the devourer, the Woman of Old Age and Death, the bringer of so much misery and sorrow to the world. She would destroy all people just as surely as the most deadly of the alien gods Monster Slayer had killed. *Sá* lived high on the slopes of *Dibé nitsaa*, the Sacred Mountain of the North.

Coincidentally, from my vantage point on the ridge I also had a splendid view northeastward to Hesperus Peak, which was *Dibé nitsaa*.

Monster Slayer left home before dawn and set off northward to *Dibé nitsaa*, to rid the Earth of this most terrible of beings. He crossed the San Juan Basin in front of us, made his way up Mancos Canyon and past the ruins of Mesa Verde, and climbed the slopes of the Sacred Mountain of the North. He came to a blasted place at the treeline, a place nearly devoid of life, where the cold winds blew. In the distance, he saw an ancient woman walking along slowly with the help of a stick. Her back was bowed and her white hair streamed in the wind. She raised an impossibly wrinkled face and looked at him.

They stood facing each other on the barren slopes, among the rocks and a few twisted trees.

"I have come here to kill you," Monster Slayer said.

She smiled and leaned on her staff. "I do you no harm, grandson," she replied. "So why would you want to kill a feeble old woman like me?"

Monster Slayer became angry. "What you say is untrue," he said. "For you will slowly sap my strength with the passing years. And with the passing of the years you will likewise sap the strength of the five-fingered Earth Surface People when they come to exist in the world. Eventually you will devour everyone just as *Naayée'* the alien monsters would have done."

For a moment *Sá* was silent, looking on Monster Slayer and smiling a gentle smile. Then she began to speak.

"Grandson," she replied. "I hear that you have performed great deeds. I hear that it has been your purpose to make this world a good place for your people."

Monster Slayer listened, saying nothing.

"Very well, then, grandson," she continued. "But think it over before you kill me. For once the people discover that *Sá* will no longer slowly sap their strength with the passing of the years and finally devour them, they will have no incentive to beget offspring. The boys will not become fathers when their bodies are ready for fatherhood. The girls will not become mothers when their bodies shape them for motherhood. When they are all past their prime, worthless old men and wasted old women will live on. So the people will stand still and never increase.

"Is it not better that people die at length and pass their wisdom and their responsibilities to those who are younger?

"Let me live, my grandson. Let me live to inspire people to bring children into the world. Let me live to inspire them to nurture those children. Let me live to inspire them to teach their young and to pass their wisdom on."

Monster Slayer listened to these words and understood them. He realized, with pain and sorrow, why there must be old age and death in the world. He accepted that there were proper limits to human control over their ultimate fate; there were some forces in the universe that human beings could not, and should not, have dominion over. He lowered his head and put away his weapons of war, knowing that by doing so he consigned himself, and all people, to old age and death.

He returned to his mother, Changing Woman, and said, "Some things are better left as they are." His battles were over. The world was finally ready for human life.

He removed the great stone knife, the leggings, his bow and arrow, and all the articles of war that his father the Sun had given him, and laid them aside, never to use them again.

Then he and his brother, Born for Water, set out to see the world at peace.

On this journey, they went back to their birthplace on Navajo Mountain and performed the first Enemy Way ceremony, to cleanse themselves of the taint of death and bring to life all the people killed by the alien gods. When he returned, he spoke to his mother. "I find that this is now a peaceful world," he said. "Everywhere I go I find that I am treated like a kinsman. . . . And now there is order and harmony in this world." And he began to sing:

Now the enemy slayer arrives:
From the house of the dark stone blades he arrives.
From where the stone knives hang he arrives.
And the treasures he has won are yours, oh you gods.

With his work done, Monster Slayer, and his brother Born for Water, withdrew from the world to make room for the five-fingered Earth Surface People who would replace them. They traveled northward and vanished into a place called Where the Waters Join, at the junction of the San Juan and Los Piños Rivers.

Today that place is deeply sacred to the Navajos, where they can pray for harmony and balance in the world, and for victory over their enemies. But Where the Waters Join no longer exists, having been flooded by a dam across the San Juan River. It is said that "there we may see their reflection when, after a summer rain which brings the rainbow, the mist rises from the water as the sky clears. The bright colors shimmer in the moist light and the forms of the monster-slaying twins materialize."

Chapter 24

Navajo defender, Ute
Raid Panel
—Canyon del Muerto

*Lost City of the
Lukachukais
May 22, 1992*

The sun climbed into the sky and I could feel its thin warmth on my face. Seventy-five miles beyond Shiprock, the distant snowcapped peak of *Dibé nitsaa* turned from violet to blue and slowly vanished in the brilliance of the horizon, as if the mountain had evaporated into sky. I thought of the bent old woman with white hair and a gentle smile, who lives on the mountaintop to this day, bringing us death so that we might live.

▽ ▽ ▽

I untied the horses' hobbles and led them back to camp for the day's ride. That afternoon, we hoped to reach the Lost City of the Lukachukais.

I saddled Redbone and swung up, the old slick-seaṭ saddle as comfortable as a rocking chair. While there was no water in our camp, a night of rich, dew-laden grass had left him alert and eager to be off. As I looked about at the mist pouring into the canyons, I thought there was something wonderful about being on a horse, high above the ground, with the wind at my back and the smell of cedar smoke in the air.

We rode along red sandhills at the base of Kinusta Mesa. High above us we could see several old uranium mines, dark holes punched into the rimrock, each with a pyramidal tailings pile below it. They looked like the burrows of some evil insect.

It was in these mountains that much of the uranium for the U.S. weapons program was taken in the 1940s and 1950s. There were abandoned mines throughout the Lukachukai Mountains. These mines produced so much high-grade ore that the Kerr-McGee Corporation built a uranium-processing plant near Shiprock. Almost all the mine workers were Navajo, and later most of them fell sick from cancer and other diseases from working in unventilated shafts breathing radioactive uranium dust. The Navajos, with the untiring help of Stewart Udall and his son Tom, sued the government, but the Justice Department fought the lawsuit and dragged it out for so many years that by the time the Navajos won almost all the miners had died. Enriched Lukachukai Mountain uranium and the plutonium made from it still sit in the cores of many of our nuclear bombs. It was an evil that not even Monster Slayer could have imagined would beset his people and the world.

▽ ▽ ▽

Very few Navajos live in these mountains today, and those who do only come up here in the summer months with their livestock. There was evidence everywhere of occupation in centuries past. We rode past the ruins of several hogans, including one forked male hogan, an ancient type that had not been built since the last century. Only the skeleton remained, leaning into a sand drift.

On the far side of Kinusta Mesa we rode over a pass and came down into a forested plateau cut with great red canyons. Lupines, scarlet gilia, and penstemon grew in profusion, and for a while we followed the fresh tracks of a bear in the damp sand, meandering at the beginning, then more hurried as the bear sensed our approach. The sky was darkening and a wind picked up, bringing with it the distant cries of crows and the smell of wet pine trees. A coyote began yipping and howling, a lonely, frightening cry that seemed to come from several directions at once. A great horned owl dropped down from a tree limb and flew away.

We halted near the edge of a canyon, tied up the horses, and made our way to the edge. The canyon was a fantastic sinuosity cut seven hundred feet deep into the mountains, bursting with cottonwoods and willows, a secret tunnel of life. It was impossible to tell where the canyon began or ended.

Opposite us, wedged into the rock about 150 feet off the canyon floor, stood a shattered Anasazi cliff dwelling: the Lost City of the Lukachukais. We stared into its dead recesses, its rows of squat granaries and room blocks with their keyhole doorways. It had once been a city nearly as big as Mesa Verde, but the roof of the alcove had fallen in, destroying most of it. A faint hand-and-toe trail, pecked into the rock, wound its way up from the canyon bottom, but a section of it had peeled away. The ruin was completely inaccessible from either above or below.

Christine took my hand and stepped closer to the edge of the cliff, peering over. "My God," she breathed, "it makes you *feel* what time really is. In the end, we're so utterly insignificant."

I gently tugged her arm, pulling her back from the brink.

"Time is vast," I said, "and we're awfully small. But I've always thought we make up for that in complexity."

"Life is still horribly short," she said, and wrapped her arm around me and squeezed. "Doug, promise me this. Promise me we won't wake up years from now, all old and creaky, and have to ask ourselves: Where did all the time go? What have we done with it?"

"I promise," I said.

A cold wind rose up from below, shaking the limbs of an old cedar that, even in death, clung savagely to the rimrock. We continued gazing down at the forgotten city in silence, lost in our thoughts. It was so utterly remote that we wondered how long it had been since white people had gazed on it: years, perhaps, even decades?

This ruin was first seen by white people around the turn of the century. The story goes that two missionaries, Fathers Fintan and Anseln, were riding across the Lukachukai Mountains when they happened to glimpse, in the distance, "a beautiful silent ruin half hidden in the deep shadows of an arched recess." To the fathers it appeared more perfect and lovely than the ruins at Mesa Verde. But the ruin was hidden in an inaccessible canyon, and the two were in a hurry, so they continued on.

Later they went back and tried to locate the ruin, but could never find the place again. Word of the "Lost City of the Lukachukais" spread and became a local legend in the San Juan Basin area.

In the 1920s, the archeologist Earl Morris—the same person who excavated Mummy Cave in Canyon del Muerto—made several trips into the Lukachukai Mountains with a Catholic priest looking for the legendary lost city. He finally heard from an old Navajo man that such a city had indeed existed in the mountains, but that the roof of the cave had collapsed, burying it forever. Nevertheless, Morris explored the area and, from a "mountain summit" (probably Kinusta Mesa behind us), saw a canyon with deep alcoves and ruins in it. Two years later he was able to raise the financing to explore the region. In the biggest of the alcoves, he found himself "in a recess two hundred feet long and some thirty feet deep at its widest point whose floor was covered with a large mass of small rock which had fallen from the roof." They explored many other caves in the canyon complex. The ruin became known as the Lost City of the Lukachukais, although whether it was the original one seen by the Catholic fathers is not known.

Morris excavated a few sections of the ruin and made spectacular finds, including more mummies. He also found a series of witchcraft figurines, some stuck with cactus spines and thorns "as if for magical practices wherein one sought to destroy an enemy." When he finished his work, they back-filled their holes and the ruin was forgotten; the artifacts are mostly buried in storage rooms at the Arizona State Museum.

▽ ▽ ▽

The birds stopped singing as the dark clouds spread across the sky.

Selene peered over the edge. "Not much left of that one," she said matter-of-factly and retired to a nearby rock. There was a rustle of cellophane as she unwrapped a candy and popped it into her mouth.

The Lost City was fearfully silent and lonely, and there was only the sound of the wind muttering through the dead branches of the cedars. The horses stood with their heads dropped, drowsing with half-lidded eyes, as if waiting for something to happen.

There was something sorrowful about this wrecked city, which had been so thoroughly humbled by time and the elements. With Chaco or Mesa Verde we can at least marvel at the architectural splendor of the vanished Anasazi. This scatter of rubble had no such dignity; it was a reminder of their mortality and of our own. Gazing into this forgotten canyon, I could feel the unbearable weight of time; I felt a great sadness in the slow succession of worlds that had come and gone in this land, and that had left their marks on the Earth.

▽ ▽ ▽

The ruins reminded me that civilizations rise and fall; it is the way of history. In the Navajo view of history, human beings periodically disrupt *bózhó*, or balance, in the world through disorderly actions; the Earth then cleanses itself and a new cycle starts. The Anasazi, they say, destroyed themselves in just this way. They disrupted *bózhó* in their world and were forced to scatter. This is a very different view from the popular idea that the Anasazi were a gentle, spiritual people living in harmony with their environment. Looking down into this nameless canyon, I thought that the Navajo view was the more logical one: people do not construct a great city only to abandon it for no reason. Something untoward happened here, as it did in Chaco Canyon and countless sites across the Southwest.

▽ ▽ ▽

What does the archeological record show? Does it support the Navajo view of the demise of the Anasazi?

Around A.D. 1050, a great civilization arose in the Southwest, centered at Chaco Canyon. Archeologists today call this sudden florescence of Anasazi culture the "Chaco Phenomenon," because it was so different from what came before and after. Why this civilization centered at Chaco Canyon rose and then fell had been one of the great questions of Southwestern archeology.

It wasn't until 1895 that archeologists began excavating Chaco in an attempt to answer these questions. In that year, Richard Wetherill, rancher and amateur archeologist, arrived in the canyon. He was thirty-eight, stubborn, tough, high-handed, and endlessly curious about the Anasazi. He was later hired by the American Museum of Natural History in New York to excavate the canyon.

"The ruins there are enormous," he later wrote, "the greatest in New Mexico and almost unknown." He spent more than a month digging at Chaco and found "relics in quantity." Wetherill, who knew about the Navajo fear of the dead, kept potential thieves away from his equipment by piling it up and placing an Anasazi jawbone on top.

In hopes that the Navajo living in the area might know something about this vanished civilization, Wetherill often visited Navajo hogans near the ruins, asking questions. He was the first of many such archeologists who have gone among the Navajo, asking questions about the Anasazi ruins—a common practice even today. Almost every archeological report on Anasazi ruins in the *Diné Bikeyah* includes legends and stories about the ruins collected from the local Navajos.

The Navajos of Chaco, however, told this strange white man nothing. They may have been disturbed by his digging into the ruins, which were sacred. As with Earl Morris, some may have thought he was a witch. They began calling Wetherill "Anasazi," a nickname he enjoyed repeating to his friends but perhaps did not fully understand.

The first season's work, when shipped back to the American Museum of Natural History in New York, filled an entire freight car. When the Wetherill/American Museum expedition ended in 1900, the haul was staggering. An incomplete inventory in 1901 listed more than 50,000 pieces of turquoise, 10,000 examples of pottery, and thousands of bone, stone, and wood objects— including some very rare effigies and fetishes, painted ceremonial staffs, wooden tablets, mosaic work encrusted on baskets, trumpets made of conch shells, and turquoise pendants. Wetherill's work was sloppy and destructive, and he tore through walls, sawed through prehistoric roofs, and ripped up floors to get at pretty artifacts, destroying much important information. All these collections are stored away in the vaults of the American Museum in New York City, and almost none of them has ever been exhibited to the public.

After Wetherill, a flood of expeditions to Chaco followed. One archeologist called it "the ruin of ruins, the equal of which in point of magnitude and general interest, is not to be found among the world's collection of discovered prehistoric structures." Almost all these expeditions questioned the local Navajos about the ruins, but still the Navajos would say nothing.

Wetherill stayed on at Chaco, working a trading post and running sheep, and he became embroiled in disputes with the local Indian agent and Navajos who owed him money. On June

22, 1910, a Navajo stopped Wetherill and one of his cowboys in the canyon. What happened next was so confused that we will never know the truth. Shots were fired and Wetherill fell from his horse. The Navajo then walked up to Wetherill, said, "Are you sick, Anasazi?" and blew half of his head away with a point-blank shot. Wetherill's body was buried near Pueblo Bonito.

In the twenties, the National Geographic Society mounted a major excavation of Chaco. Unlike Wetherill's earlier work, this one was carefully planned and executed, and for the first time a complex and quite mysterious picture of Chaco Canyon and its people began to emerge. The Geographic excavation was followed by other digs. In addition to exposing the Great Houses and their kivas, the work discovered Chaco's sophisticated irrigation systems, the now-famous Chacoan road system, a network of far-flung signaling stations and lighthouses, and hundreds of "outlier" sites built in the same style and at the same time as Chaco. Archeoastronomers discovered Chaco's solar and astronomical marking systems, including the Sun Dagger on Fajada Butte. An intensive survey of Chaco and its immediate vicinity uncovered no fewer than 2,220 archeological sites. The mystery of Chaco, far from being solved, only seemed to deepen.

The culmination of work on Chaco Canyon came in 1985, with the completion of the Chaco Project, an exhaustive study of the ruins. The longtime director of the Chaco Center, the brilliant archeologist James W. Judge, proposed a theory about the Chaco Phenomenon that was the first interpretation to make sense of the mysterious and conflicting data from the site. It is today the most widely accepted explanation for the rise and fall of Chaco Canyon.

Judge painted a very different picture of Chaco culture from the popular idea of a people living in spiritual and physical harmony with their environment. His viewpoint was, indeed, almost identical to the Navajo idea of a people seriously out of balance with their environment.

▽ ▽ ▽

According to Judge, Chaco Canyon probably started out as a small series of settlements in the highly marginal area along Chaco Wash. From A.D. 900 to 1050, rainfall in the canyon was highly variable. Had the people of Chaco Canyon been typical Anasazi, their settlements along the wash never would have amounted to much. In this early period, the Anasazi were scattered across the Southwest, living in independent communities, possibly speaking several different languages, but all practicing a similar culture and religion. They built small settlements and moved often, usually when the local game, timber, and other resources had been played out. If they followed the typical pattern, the people of Chaco would eventually have moved on, leaving a few scattered houses. It would have been a minor site.

But the people of Chaco were not typical. They had, Judge theorized, a unique skill: the ability to process and finish a deeply sacred and valuable material: turquoise. The people of Chaco, apparently, traded in raw turquoise and traded out beautifully finished beadwork, inlay, mosaic work, pendants, and carvings. Enormous quantities of polished and inlaid turquoise were found at Chaco—more than at any other place in the Southwest.

Turquoise was probably the most valuable trade item of the Anasazi. It came from the largest prehistoric mine in America, in the Cerrillos Hills south of Santa Fe. Prehistoric Cerrillos Hills turquoise has reportedly been found in places from Canada to California. Some of the treasures Moctezuma gave Cortés had Cerrillos turquoise inlay. The Spanish crown jewels are said to contain Cerrillos turquoise.

During the days of Chaco, the turquoise had to be mined by hand using stone tools and then transported several hundred miles southwest to Chaco. There it was carved, drilled, polished, and inlaid without metal tools, using only stone, bone, wood, and grasses high in silicates for polishing. The Chaco workshops turned out exquisite work, including beads that were almost microscopic in size with holes drilled that would barely fit a human hair. It took immense skill to work the soft, easily breakable turquoise without metal tools or the wheel.

Around 1020, Chaco seems to have developed a monopoly in the processing and distribution of this sacred material—what Judge called "the primary symbol of the ritual." Turquoise was probably an essential aspect of the rain ceremonies. As a result, Chaco started to become an important religious center. An elite priesthood class—something previously unknown among the Anasazi—appears to have developed. At the same time, Chaco seems to have gained cultural and perhaps political ascendancy over communities beyond the canyon boundaries.

Then, from 1050 to about 1085, there came an extraordinary and fortuitous change in the climate. At Chaco Canyon and all across the San Juan Basin the rains began to fall. And they fell, and they fell. Not once did the rainfall dip below the seasonal averages. In an area where a mere inch or two of rain could mean the difference between a bumper crop and a burnt-out field, this steady rainfall made a tremendous difference.

The increased rainfall, Judge theorized, had an enormously strengthening effect on Chaco's power and influence. By controlling the supply and distribution of turquoise, Chaco had gained control over the rain ceremonies and religious system of the Anasazi. And then year after year, like never before, the rains came. What more proof could the Anasazi have needed to affirm this great religious experiment centered at Chaco?

Vast building projects began in Chaco Canyon. Across the San Juan Basin, too, dozens of magnificent Chacoan structures started to be built, linked to Chaco by ceremonial roads dotted with religious complexes, shrines, and lighthouses.

The permanent population of Chaco was never large, probably less than a thousand people. However, studies of the trash mounds indicate that there were large seasonal influxes. Chaco Canyon appears to have become a great religious center, visited regularly by numbers of "pilgrims" traveling in splendid ceremonial processions along the road system.

The timing of these religious gatherings would be determined by the priests at Chaco, who (through their astronomical and solar observatories) could track the movements of the sun, moon, planets, and stars. Announcements of ceremonies could be sent at short notice across the San Juan Basin using the network of lighthouses—towers or hills on which fires were built.

Around this time, immigrant groups seemed to have moved into Chaco Canyon, bringing different and even non-Anasazi influences. At Pueblo Bonito, the evidence is that two different peoples (perhaps even speaking different languages!) lived in the same structure at the same time. On the north side of the canyon, across from the magnificent Great Houses, a different sort of people lived. They were poorer, with cruder pottery and more primitive buildings. Their religious kivas, moreover, were slightly different from kivas elsewhere in the canyon. These people might have been a laboring class, or they might have represented a different cultural tradition. The Chaco Canyon experiment was becoming increasingly diverse.

As long as everything went well—that is, as long as the rains fell—people across the Anasazi world laid aside their cultural, linguistic, and theological differences. Whether this was a voluntary confederation of communities or Chaco gained absolute control over the Anasazi is still a matter of debate among archeologists.

Chaco Canyon had indeed become the Mecca of the Anasazi world.

"As the system expanded," Judge said, "these pilgrimages would be attended by increasingly large numbers of people, involve increasingly complex ritual, and thus would require increasingly larger degrees of control and administration by those in charge, presumably those resident in Chaco Canyon."

The rains, as always, continued to fall.

The entire edifice was built on a single, grotesque illusion: that the priests of Chaco had gained control over nature. As Judge noted dryly: "Embedded in ritual, yet tied intimately to the continuation of a favorable environment, the system would also become increasingly vulnerable to environmental fluctuation."

That "environmental fluctuation" came in 1085 and again in 1095, when the canyon and the entire Anasazi world suffered back-to-back droughts. These droughts, while not unusual for pre-1050 Chaco, appear to have shocked the Chaco system. They caused a breakdown of sorts. The Chacoans started enclosing their open plazas with fortified walls, leaving only a few doors open. In succeeding years, even those doors were walled up until there were no ground-floor openings at all; access to rooftops was through ladders that could be pulled up at the first sign of trouble. This puzzled archeologists, who made a diligent search for possible enemies of the Chacoans. No likely candidates turned up. The archeologists could only conclude that the Anasazi were protecting themselves from . . . themselves.

There were other signs of trouble. Around this time the Chacoans' diet changed—from larger mammals such as deer and antelope to smaller animals such as turkeys, rats, and squirrels. It appears that this was caused by two factors: the trading system had been disrupted and the Chacoans had severely overhunted their area.

Overhunting wasn't the only environmental damage wrought by the Chacoans. The nearby stands of trees had long since been clear-cut, and even those stands thirty or forty miles away appear to have been devastated. Chaco Wash started cutting into its bed, making irrigation impossible. The water table dropped. This sudden erosion may have been natural. More likely it was caused by clear-cutting of trees and brush in the side canyons and along the wash, overfarming the floodplain, and trampling of the canyon bottom's vegetation by large numbers of people.

What was worse, the canyon soil, over-irrigated and over-farmed for years, was becoming exhausted of nutrients and salinized.

All this may come as a surprise to many people who consider the ancient Anasazi to be a people living in harmony with their environment. Quite the contrary. The archeological evidence strongly suggests that the ancient Anasazi, *wherever* they settled, soon caused "resource depletion"—the archeological term for environmental damage. Again and again, Anasazi settlements, towns, and cities were abandoned because the Anasazi exhausted and alkalinized the soil, cut down the trees, and depleted the game. Chaco merely carried this trend to an extreme.

The system might have collapsed, except for one thing: the rains began again in 1095. For another thirty-five years the rains continued without interruption. Building and ritual activity continued.

Nevertheless, the system had suffered a shock. A general cultural malaise showed itself. New construction showed a marked "architectural degeneration." The building was sloppy and the masonry ugly. The painting on the pottery became cruder. The firing of the pots was less carefully controlled. The population seems to have declined. The drought had, perhaps, shown that the priests were fallible. The system had cracks.

And yet, the excessive building in the canyon continued. The system limped along of its own inertia, burdened by its very complexity, while thirty-five more years of steady, above-average rainfall came.

Around 1129, another drought hit the canyon. This was not the vicious drought sometimes described in popular writings: it was certainly nothing Chaco Canyon had not experienced from time to time prior to A.D. 1050. This time, however, the drought had a deadly effect. The system, strained even when the rains fell, began to collapse. As crops failed in the canyon, the outlying communities probably balked at supporting a bloated priestly class at Chaco. After all, they were no longer able to generate the rain. The compact was broken, the illusion revealed.

The vast trading and distribution network centered at Chaco

disintegrated. The degraded Chaco environment could not support even a small resident population, let alone a vast artisan and priesthood class. In three years following the inception of the drought, all building in the canyon came to a halt, and in twenty years Chaco was totally abandoned.

The collapse extended across the Anasazi world. Dozens of Chacoan "outlier" pueblos were abandoned. The roads themselves were ritually closed, lined with burning brush. Over time, most of the San Juan Basin was depopulated.

It was, however, an orderly and gradual departure. Household items such as pots and baskets were carefully stacked in corners, canteens hung on walls, the rooms left clean and orderly. Most ritual items appear to have been taken, and those that were left behind were carefully wrapped and stored. This was not a cataclysmic upheaval in fire and violence, but rather a civilization-wide acknowledgment of failure.

The Chaco Phenomenon was finished. It had lasted less than a century. Never again would the Southwest see the kind of centralized control or cooperation evident at Chaco, or the high degree of achievement in pottery, architecture, trade, engineering, and surveying. For a brief shining moment, the diverse Anasazi peoples had laid aside their differences and had come together in a great religious and political experiment centered on the ceremonial control of nature. That experiment failed.[43]

Christine and I stood at the edge of the canyon, saying nothing, while the world fell into shadow. This ruin, the Lost City of the Lukachukais, was, possibly, one of the casualties of the Chaco collapse. There is even evidence of a Chaco road connecting these remote cliff dwellings to Chaco itself.

But the Chacoans, according to the Navajos we had met, had destroyed themselves through witchcraft. Was there any evidence for that? Witchcraft almost certainly existed among the Anasazi. The evidence is circumstantial but convincing. A number of apparent witchery items have been recovered in archeological digs, including in the Lost City of the Lukachukais and in Chaco Canyon itself. Witchcraft is still considered the most heinous of crimes today among the Pueblo Indian descendants of the Anasazi. Clyde Kluckhohn, the Harvard anthropologist and author of the brilliant work *Navaho Witchcraft*, defined Navajo witchcraft as "malevolent activities which endeavor to control the course of events by supernatural techniques." By this definition, the efforts of the Chacoans to influence nature might just be classifiable as witchcraft, in a metaphorical way.

This doesn't answer the question of whether or not there was a surge in *actual* witchcraft activity at the end of the Chaco Phenomenon. Unfortunately, the question is fundamentally unanswerable. We do not even know the details of Anasazi beliefs, let alone what would constitute a perversion of those beliefs. Witchery objects are usually perishable or so common as to be impossible to identify. Among the Navajos, for example, witchery items include such things as beads, small bones, gall liquids from certain animals, fingernail parings or hairs, wood from a tree struck by lightning, ashes from a ghost hogan, fragments of sweat-bath rock, or powder from a corpse. As for the reversed spiral that is so prominent among Anasazi petroglyphs, the fact is we do not know what most Anasazi petroglyphs mean, let alone whether they were related to witchcraft. It is true that many Anasazi spirals are counterclockwise, including the secondary spiral which is part of the famous Sun Dagger on Fajada Butte. Counterclockwise to the Navajo is the witchcraft direction, as opposed to the clockwise or "sun-wise" direction said to duplicate the sun's motion across the sky. Was the same true for the Anasazi? We do not know. And, of course, the same spiral can be clockwise or counterclockwise depending on whether you trace it from the outside or the center.

The idea that witchcraft might have accelerated the breakdown of the Chaco Phenomenon is not, however, a far-fetched one. According to Clyde Kluckhohn, there is often a surge in witchcraft and accusations of such in societies that are undergoing stress. This happened to the Navajos right after the Long Walk, and also in the years leading up to World War II, when the Navajos came under increasing pressure to become "white."

Kluckhohn also made a fascinating observation: he found that accusations of witchcraft among the Navajo were most often directed by poor people against powerful and rich medicine men. Such accusations were often devastatingly effective and sometimes resulted in the execution of the medicine man in question.

If we look at the declining days of Chaco—the drought deepening, the priests losing control, the ceremonies ineffectual, the crops failing, the trading networks in disarray—what we see is a society undergoing enormous stress. Accusations of witchcraft may very well have been leveled at the priests, the medicine men, and the wealthy of Chaco by the poor who had been oppressed by the system.

Taking this speculation a step further, it is not implausible that the priests may have actually *turned* to witchcraft in a last-ditch attempt to control nature, bring rain, and save their position. Both Navajo and Pueblo medicine men are believed to have witchcraft power, should they choose to use it. Is it possible that the priests of Chaco also had a knowledge of witchcraft? Would they have tried to use this knowledge in the desperate, last days of Chaco? We will probably never know.

What we do know is this: one thousand years ago, the Anasazi embarked on a great religious experiment at Chaco Canyon, an experiment based on the (illusory) control of nature. It was an experiment whose ultimate consequences the Anasazi did not foresee. And it failed.

▽ ▽ ▽

As the twentieth century draws to a close, we find ourselves involved in a similar effort to control nature, only this time on a much larger scale. Our experiment is not based on ritual but on technology. We believe, as the Chacoans did before us, that we have gained a certain mastery over nature. Our God gave us dominion.

The question is: have we really achieved it? Could our mastery of nature be as much an illusion as the rain ceremonies of the Chacoans? Are we, like the Anasazi, headed for an environmental or technological disaster?

This is the parallel that the Navajo legends have drawn: between the last days of the Anasazi at Chaco Canyon and what the Navajos perceive as the last days of *Bilagáana* the White People in America.

When traditional Navajos look on our great works, they see something very different from the triumph of technology and the upward progress of civilization. They see our technology and science as challenging, overturning, and even perverting nature. They see the ascendancy of the values of materialism, invention, and competition, which are not positive values in Navajo society. They see white people coming into the *Diné Bikeyah*, boring into the earth seeking uranium, stripping the land for coal, felling the forests, damming the rivers, drilling for oil, and stringing vast powerlines across the landscape. They see ski resorts and logging roads and toxic waste dumps being placed on or about the four sacred mountains. To them, this kind of progress looks more like an attack on the sacred. They see occurring right now, before their eyes, the ultimate disruption of *hózhó*. They see the white man doing what the Anasazi did. They see witchcraft: the reversing of the spiral.

As Monster Slayer learned in his final confrontation with Old Age Woman, there are some things better left as they are; there are things in this world that we cannot, or should not, attempt to overcome.

This is a lesson our culture could take to heart. There seems to be no limit to the reach of our science and technology. We are still acting out our Genesis, acting out the orders of the God whose image we mirror: commanding, creating, multiplying, enforcing our dominion over nature. There is no brake on our search for better technology, for weapons of mass destruction, for artificial intelligence, even for the re-engineering of the human genome. Our arrogance is breathtaking. If we can do it, we will do it. The time may come when we have the ability to overcome death itself with our medicine. I ask: when we meet death in this final battleground, will we have the wisdom of Monster Slayer? Will we lay down our weapons of technology and proceed no farther?

It is not likely.

▽ ▽ ▽

The Earth was not created for us. We evolved to live on this planet, and everything, down to our very genetic code, is exquisitely tuned to that Earth. In this way the landscape of the Earth *is* sacred; according to E. O. Wilson's biophilia hypothesis, we carry a primitive mirror image of this landscape in our very genes. If we transfigure the Earth, we literally destroy something within ourselves.

▽ ▽ ▽

A year later, I was discussing these things with Edsel Brown, a Navajo spiritual leader. We were sitting in the twilight darkness, at a camp in a forest on the slopes of a remote mountain on Black Mesa which the Navajos call *Dził nitsaa:* Big Mountain, the heart of the Earth.

"This cycle goes back to a long time ago," he said. "It goes back to the first invention that was created. It goes back to when the *Bilagáana* realized they had the *power* to make things. They had the power to *create* things. And they started to look on the land as a *resource*. They didn't look at the land as relatives, as living beings, which it is. And they made these inventions, electricity, dams, cars, bombs, pesticides, everything. They kept thinking that all these inventions would help them. And yet they're still not helping them. And now, today, things are starting not to work for them, and they have no place to go, and they have a hard time realizing what is happening.

"But the Earth has already told us this through stories and ceremonies: 'Have patience. There's no way you can stop this turn, this cycle. The world is already unbalanced. It's already on its way, going full momentum. And in this manner, when this world ends, you will eventually go in a peaceful manner. In a respectful manner. Because you human beings, you may be gone, but the Earth is always here. It will revive itself. If you all die, that doesn't mean the Earth will die too. The Earth is going to become a new, fresh, and beautiful world again. There will be new life, and it will be beautiful. So have patience, and go to the end in a respectful manner.' This is what the Earth has said."

Chapter 25

ONE OF THE ALIEN GODS
DEFEATED BY MONSTER
SLAYER
—*SANDPAINTING FROM THE
BIG STAR CHANT*

*The Diné Bikeyah
May 23, 1992*

The Lost City of the Lukachukais darkens in the shadow of its overhang. A large storm is approaching. As we remount our horses, a glittery light breaks through the clouds, turning the landscape the color of beaten silver.

As we set off, Acomita comes tearing out of somewhere, yelping, her muzzle filled with porcupine quills. We stop to pull them out. She endures the operation in whimpering gratitude.

We ride through the twisty little cedars, following a curve of exposed sandstone, looking for water. Marci knows the location of a small spring hidden along the rimrock somewhere.

The spring lies underneath a rim of sandstone, where erosion has carved a slot through the rock. It is no more than a seep, dripping water drop by drop onto a sandstone ledge. A faint, chiseled channel in the sandstone directs the trickle to a pothole, which holds about two gallons. We tie the horses up and collect all the water in our canteens. When we finish, I watch as the spring drips water into the channel, drop by drop, where it trickles back into the empty pothole with infinite slowness. In five or ten hours there will be another two gallons. I wonder how old the tiny channel in the sandstone is: a hundred years? a thousand? It speaks of the eternal preciousness of water.

Just as we remount to head back to camp, the silvery light is abruptly snuffed out. The cloud has covered the sky and the land begins to blacken, and blacken, until the darkness is like midnight, swallowing trees and mountains alike in the murk.

Then we hear, rising in the east, a tremendous roaring sound, like a great waterfall or an approaching train. The horses prick up their ears and I can feel Redbone tensing with fear along his flank. I instinctively shorten the reins.

"What the *heck* is *that?*" Selene asks.

We are engulfed in an explosion of ice. Fat white hailstones come winging out of the sky and whacking the backs and heads of the horses and ourselves. The horses twitch, rear, and kick, and we quickly dismount and tie them under piñon trees, whose stiff branches and thick bundles of needles break the momentum of the hail. We ourselves retreat under the protection of the piñons.

I have never seen such large hailstones, some close to an inch in diameter. They rattle down through the trees like pinballs and ricochet across the ground, bringing with them a thick shower of twigs and needles. Once in a while a hailstone will strike my hat with a loud whack and go flying off down the mountain. An intoxicating smell of crushed and bruised piñon rises in the air, sharp and icy in the nose. Speech is impossible; we cannot make ourselves heard above the roar.

In ten minutes the hail ceases as suddenly as it began, and the darkness lifts.

"Look at this!" Selene cries, holding two hailstones up, one in each hand. They look like golf balls. "Have you ever seen any so big?"

"No," I say.

"Boy, they *hurt!* How can something as big as this come out of the sky?"

"Powerful updrafts of wind in a thunderhead," I say, "keep them aloft and they just grow bigger and bigger."

"I'd hate to own a greenhouse up here," she says, tossing the hailstones behind her. "This is a *really* weird place."

"I feel the same way," I say. The surreal light and the intense fragrance of resin in the air make me feel as if I have stepped outside reality, as if the world beyond the rising curtains of mist has disappeared. Everything is smoking; the wet black branches of the trees, the dark red clay, the horses' backs, our hats. The mist is an infusion of light, as if we are drowning in liquid silver. Christine wraps her arm around me and we huddle under the dripping trees.

"I can hardly remember what it's like to live a normal life anymore," Selene says. "It seems like years ago that we left. I think about my friends and school, and it doesn't seem real anymore."

"It's like we're starting life over again," Christine said. "On a new planet."

"Let's call it *Selene's* planet," Selene says. "Where everything is magical, and ghosts and witches exist but aren't mean, and there are dark forests and beautiful streams and the animals talk just like people, and where there are no televisions or malls." She shivers at the wonderfulness of the thought.

"And where a slice of strawberry rhubarb pie costs five cents," Christine says.

"Mom! On Selene's planet there *is* no money!"

"How are people supposed to pay for things?"

"People trade everything. Nobody is hungry or poor. And all the mountains and rivers are alive, and you can talk to them too."

"Glug, glug, burble," says Christine.

"That sounds like a great place," I say. "Let's go there."

"We *are* there," Selene says.

I hold out my bare hand. A plume of steam drifts off my skin and rises into the air. "We're being transformed," I say, "into some other life form."

Selene takes off her wet glove and holds out her hand. It is also smoking. "It's happening to me too," she says.

"Maybe we can bring the magic and beauty of Selene's planet back home," I say. "We'll roll it all into a little stone and carry it back in the horse panniers."

Selene picks up a pebble and breathes on it. "Here's a good stone."

"The world will be totally different from now on," I say, rubbing the pebble and putting it into my pocket.

"Yeah," Selene says.

"Do you feel changed by this trip?" I ask.

Selene is silent for a moment. "I guess so . . . but I really don't know how. I feel so *different*. Now I know you're really my *Dad*. You're not like Mom's other boyfriends."

"Other boyfriends?" Christine says, sitting up.

"You know," Selene says, "easy come, easy go."

"*What!*" Christine cries. "You make it sound like I had all these boyfriends!"

"Aha!" I say. "The truth finally comes out."

Christine splutters in embarrassment. "I've only had *two* boyfriends since you were born. You're making me out to be a—!" She doesn't finish the sentence.

"Easy come, easy go," Selene giggles, delighted to have struck a nerve.

"You're just trying to make me mad."

Selene jumps up and starts pelting us with hailstones. "Easy come, easy go!"

Christine chases her around a tree. "You rascal, I'm going to tickle you as a punishment."

She grabs the tail of Selene's duster and reels her in.

"Help!" Selene shrieks. "There's no tickling on Selene's planet! It's against the law! I order you to stop!"

An immense raven, startled by the sound, detaches itself from the shadow of a tree and disappears into the mist, croaking softly. I can hear the sound of its wings, like silk being brushed.

When everything settles down we pull our irritated horses out of the trees and brush the twigs and hailstones off. I help Selene into the saddle and we're off again.

We ride past an ancient Navajo sweat lodge, a skeletonized tent of juniper branches. The light struggles through the clouds. As the hail begins to melt, streamlets start trickling off Kinusta Mesa and running down the arroyos, making a pleasant sound of gurgling water. The mist fills the hollows like pools of smoke, eddying around our horses' feet as we walk down the trail. The world really does look different.

▽ ▽ ▽

We continue to gain altitude, passing across Mexican Cry Mesa and riding up onto Cove Mesa, a sacred mesa known to the Navajos as *Chooh Dínéeshzhee'*, Where Animals Are among the Wild Roses. The fog lifts. At the top of the mesa we come out on a high plateau with endless views in all directions. Virtually the entire *Diné Bikeyah* is spread out before us, the four sacred mountains, the mesas, canyons, and deserts, all vanishing into vast blue distances where earth and space dissolve together. On either side, the mountainsides are riddled with enormous red canyons, a thousand feet deep, penetrating inward from east and west until they almost meet at a bridge of land a mere thirty feet wide. This is a sacred place, a stopping point on the Journey for Knowledge and Power described in the Navajo Wind Way chant. The landscape here is crisscrossed with the tracks of the gods.

I have never in my life seen such a place, the beauty of which, truly, cannot be rendered in words. We have broken through into another world.

At the edge of the trees stands a little Navajo hogan with a red bandanna shading the one window. Past the hogan, high on the side of a grassy hill, an old man is wandering through the sagebrush, peering into the red canyons with a pair of battered army binoculars.

Selene gives a shout and gallops over the crest of the hill, followed by everyone else. I ride up to the old man.

The man lowers the binoculars and watches me approach. He wears two shirts, one on top of the other. The outer shirt, of an indeterminate plaid, only has one button left and it is buttoned crooked, the shirttails hanging down unevenly. His pants were once, it appears, a khaki color, but now they are dark with the dust and soil of the mountains. His K-Mart workboots have acquired the ancient patina of the earth. He wears no hat, only a bandanna with his hair tied in a traditional bun. His back is hunched and he moves with great deliberation, as if every motion were painful. He looks at me with a small, extraordinarily animated face, a face that crinkles and uncrinkles with great rapidity. When I stop and dismount he grins, exposing a single tooth.

"*Yá'át'ééh*," I say.

He says something in Navajo, slowly raising his arm to point off into the canyons. I can only shrug in ignorance.

"Goats," he says. "See goats?"

"You lost some goats?" I say.

He nods. "Lost goats," he repeats. "You see?"

"No," I say, "we haven't seen any lost goats."

He holds up eight fingers.

"Lost," he says again. He pantomimes, putting the binoculars to his eyes, looking around. "Lost." And he holds up eight fingers again.

"You lost eight goats," I say. "What do they look like?"

"White. One blue."

"I'm sorry, but we haven't seen any," I say. "If we see any, we'll come back here and tell you."

His face uncrinkles and he looks stricken. "No see?" he asks.

"No. How long have they been lost?"

"Week," he says. "Maybe coyote kill. Eat."

"I'm very sorry," I say. I can see from his face that the loss of eight goats is a terrible blow.

"You go where?" he asks, gesturing sideways with the flat of his hand.

"We're riding toward Shiprock," I say.

He leans forward, not understanding.

"Tsé bit'a'í," I say, pointing to the great pinnacle rising from the desert, visible to the east.

He scrunches up his face in puzzlement, and then suddenly understands.

"Tsé bit'a'í!" he cries, pointing and nodding. He is delighted.

"We started our journey at *Naatsis'áán,*" I say. "Navajo Mountain."

"Naatsis'áán," he repeats puzzled, and then his face lights up. "Ah! *Naatsis'áán!*" He points to the northwest. I am as delighted as he is that I can be understood.

I point to Roof Butte, one of the sacred mountains created by First Woman, the home of Old Man and Old Woman Poverty. I try to speak its name, *"Dził dah neeztíinii."*

"Heh?" he asks, leaning forward again.

"Roof Butte," I say. *"Dził dah neeztíinii."*

"Dził dah neeztíinii!" he cries out, nodding vigorously.

Then he points to the Carrizo Mountains.

"Dził nahoozilii," he says. He swings around and points to another mountain, a low flat peak, also sacred, called Beautiful Mountain. *"Dziłk'ihózhónii,"* he says.

I point to Black Mesa.

"Dził Yíjiin!" he cries out.

I point to a prominent mesa in the northwest called Waterless Mountain.

"Tó ádin dah'azká!" he says.

I point down to Los Gigantes.

"Tsé álts'óóz íí'áhí!"

I point to the mountains south of us.

"*Łók'aach'égai łeeshch'iihdeesgai!*" he cries.

In the remote distance I can just see Agathla pointing up.

"*Aghaałá*," I say.

He nods again. "*Aghaałá. Aghaałá!* Good!"

I feel a chill going up my spine. We are naming the sacred landscape of creation in the Navajo language, something that is not done lightly or without some purpose.

"*Tsoodził*," I say, pointing at Mount Taylor, the Sacred Mountain of the South.

He stops for a moment, looking intently at me, and then turns to look southeast. "*Tsoodził*," he repeats, slowly, his dark eyes reflecting the blue of the sky.

Then he slowly points west: "*Dook'o'oosłííd*." He points northwest: "*Dibé nitsaa*." He points northeast: "*Sisnaajiní*."

He names the sacred mountains with a simple, quiet reverence that I find unbelievably moving. Then he falls silent. I notice that his rheumy eyes have suddenly filled with tears. His lips are wet, and he smacks them a few times, looking down at the ground. I am embarrassed.

"I guess this place where you live is about the most beautiful on earth," I say.

He looks at me kindly but says nothing, and then turns back toward the horizon. Moisture escapes through one of the creases around his eyes and creeps down his face. He stands at the edge of the hill, above the canyons, an old man weeping silently. Is he weeping for his goats? I wonder. But in my heart I know that is not why he is crying.

▽ ▽ ▽

From the top of the rise, I hear Selene's shrill voice calling down to me. I look up. She is sitting on her horse, silhouetted against the sky, shouting and waving her hat.

"Hey *Dad*, gallop up here! Go as fast as you can! It's fun! There's tons of water over here in the rocks! We can go swimming!"

There is an awkward silence. I tell the old man that I will watch for his goats, and I swing into the saddle. I turn back once and he is still standing there, looking eastward into the distance. I spur Redbone and gallop to the top of the rise and over the crest, reining to a halt. Ahead stretches a slickrock bench ending in an immense double canyon, a thousand feet deep and three miles across, cut into the great wrinkled upthrust of the Carrizo Mountains.

Selene rides alongside me and takes my hand, and we walk our horses together through the wet sagebrush, toward the vast red canyons of eternity.

A Note on Pronunciation

The pronunciation of Navajo words is exceedingly difficult, and until you have actually heard the language spoken it is impossible even to imagine the sounds, let alone imitate them. However, I will describe here a few rules of pronunciation relating to some of the stranger orthographies of the Navajo alphabet.

▽ ▽ ▽

The apostrophe in a word, as in *ch'il*, "plant," indicates a glottal stop.

The slashed l, *ł*, as in *dził*, "mountain," is an unvoiced l. It sounds like "th," only the tip of the tongue is placed not on the teeth but on the upper palate. Air is expelled between the sides of the tongue and the palate, and no voicing comes from the throat.

An accent over a letter, such as á in *Bilagáana*, "white person," indicates a higher tone. The absence of an accent indicates a lower tone. The two together, as here, indicate a higher tone dropping to a lower tone.

Double letters indicate a drawing out of the tone, as in *bááh*, "bread." Single letters indicate a more clipped vowel, as in *tsé*, "rock."

There are many other unusual sounds, but these are the ones indicated most prominently in the Navajo alphabet.

Notes

1. Slim Woman of Kayenta, recorded by Hoffman Birney in 1927, reproduced in Luckert, *Navajo Mountain and Rainbow Bridge Religion*.
2. Zolbrod, *Diné Bahane'*.
3. New York: *The New Columbia Encyclopedia*, 1975. The Navajo word *Bilagáana*, white person, is believed to be a corruption of the Spanish word "Americano."
4. Matthews, *Navajo Legends*.
5. As with all oral history, there is no absolute agreement among Navajo medicine men and singers as to the details of this and the following stories. Some say this is the Fourth World; some say it is the Fifth World. Some say Monster Slayer was born on Navajo Mountain; others say he was born on Huerfano Peak. Unlike Christianity, where differences of dogma are considered extremely serious, among the Navajo these differences are not important. A Navajo medicine man will often explain a difference by saying, "If that is what you were taught, then that is what is true for you." As I mentioned, the Navajo creation story in this book is based on three major sources: Matthews's *Navajo Legends*; Zolbrod's *Diné Bahane'*; and the Blessingway ceremonials transcribed by the missionary Father Berard Haile, published in Wyman, *Blessingway*.
6. This is all corroborated by the archeological evidence. The Navajos learned farming from the Pueblo Indians and received from them the first seeds of corn. Indeed, the Navajo word for corn is *Naadáá'*, which means "the food of strangers."
7. Zolbrod, *Diné Bahane'*.
8. Part of a Protection Way prayer recited by Floyd Laughter to Karl Luckert, published in *Navajo Mountain and Rainbow Bridge Religion*.
9. This song was excerpted from a long Blessing Way chant recorded by Fr. Berard Haile from a person he merely calls Informant X.
10. Zolbrod, *Diné Bahane'*.
11. Zolbrod, *Diné Bahane'*.
12. Another version of the story says that the men also practiced bestiality and impregnated wild animals.
13. Zolbrod, *Diné Bahane'*.

14. "Begay" comes from the Navajo *Biye'* meaning "His Son." Navajos traditionally do not give their ceremonial names or even their common names to strangers, so when young boys were sent to BIA boarding schools and asked their names, they would often reply, "George Begay," meaning "George His Son," usually as a way of avoiding speaking their real name. Others simply gave a description of themselves: *yazzie* (short), *tso* (big), *tsosie* (slim). Those who refused to give any name at all were sometimes listed as BIA (Bureau of Indian Affairs), and there are many Navajos today whose last names are Bia.

15. Zolbrod, *Diné Bahane'*.

16. I've changed the name here.

17. It is perhaps worth mentioning here that in the argot of the reservation, and much of the Southwest, the word "Anglo" refers to any American who is not Indian or Hispanic. It thus includes blacks, Asians, and other ethnic groups not normally thought of as Anglo.

18. Wyman, *Blessingway*.

19. Not his real name.

20. The Carrizo Mountains are the legs of the sacred male being mentioned earlier, which is paired with the sacred female being whose body is Black Mesa. Quoted in Walter Dyk's *A Navaho Autobiography*, p. 116.

21. McPherson, *Sacred Land, Sacred View*, p. 19.

22. Kammer, *The Second Long Walk*, p. 211.

23. Matthews, *Navajo Legends*.

24. Zolbrod, *Diné Bahane'*. *Nináhálééh* and *Bináá' yee agháníí* are the names of alien gods killed by Monster Slayer.

25. Wyman, *Blessingway*.

26. I've changed his name.

27. Sapir and Hoijer, *Navajo Texts*.

28. I use the term "New Mexican" to denote the original Spanish settlers of New Mexico, as opposed to the newer Anglo settlers.

29. The Chuska Mountains.

30. They rectified their error later by decapitating a Navajo killed by Zuni Indians and sending the head back to Philadelphia.

31. To "box a spring" is to build a box around it to impound the water so that large numbers of livestock may be watered at once.

32. Canyon de Chelly actually consists of two great canyons cut like a chevron into the Defiance Plateau. The name Chelly, pronounced "shay," comes to English through a Spanish corruption of the Navajo word *Tséyi'*, meaning, simply, rock canyon. The northern canyon was named Cañon de los Muertos (the Canyon of the Dead) by an American archeologist on account of the Anasazi burials he recovered there. The Spanish name was later corrupted to Canyon del Muerto.

33. Matthews, *Mountain Chant*.

34. Quoted in John Upton Terrell, *The Navajos*, pp. 218–19.

35. The term "Long Walk" is used by the Navajos to refer not only to the forced march to Fort Sumner, but also to the events surrounding the march: the destruction of the *Diné Bikeyah* by Kit Carson's troops, the years of imprisonment, and the return journey.

36. A year later, after almost all the Navajos had surrendered, American troops entered Canyon de Chelly again and, gratuitously, chopped down all the Navajos' ancient, beautiful peach trees, which had provided them with fruit for centuries.

37. This expression refers to the life-giving wind, which enters our feet and hands and is expelled from our mouths when we talk; that the hope is carried on this sacred wind itself gives the statement the profoundest emphasis.

38. Matthews, *Navaho Legends*.

39. *Diné bizaad*—Language of the People, that is, the Navajo language.

40. Kluckhohn and Leighton, *The Navaho*.

41. Zolbrod, *Diné Bahane'*.

42. This is somewhat typical of the internal contradictions in the Navajo creation story; eagles were created after Spider Woman gave Monster Slayer an eagle-feather fetish—and indeed long after First Man and First Woman were created from corn and eagle feathers. Unlike Christianity (particularly the many sects of Protestantism), Navajo religion is not overly concerned with dogma, and thus such contradictions are not considered important. There are many aspects of the Navajo creation story, and many versions, that are different, but this is not a source of concern or argument with traditional Navajos.

43. Contrary to popular belief, there has never been a mystery as to where the Anasazi went. The Pueblo Indians of today are the direct descendants of the Anasazi. When the Anasazi left Chaco, they broke up into numerous groups, families, or clans, and went in all different directions. Some went eastward to the slopes of Mount Taylor, southward past the lava flows, some northward into southern Colorado and Mesa Verde, and others still farther east to the Jemez Mountains and the Rio Grande. Some groups journeyed westward to the isolated mesas of Hopi or Zuni. The Zunis and Hopis, among other Pueblo groups, have legends of people from Chaco joining their tribes. A few isolated groups may have returned to Chaco for brief sojourns, perhaps seeking a revival of past glory, but those settlements never lasted long. The next real inhabitants of the canyon were Navajo Indians, who moved in (according to the best information we have) in the 1700s.

Acknowledgments

I would like to thank many people for their help with this book, starting with my agent, Thomas Wallace, and my editor, Michael Korda. I would also like to express my very great appreciation to Paul Zolbrod for his invaluable help, as well as to Bruce Bernstein, who has given me excellent advice and suggestions from the beginning. I am also grateful to David Brugge, archeologist, anthropologist, and historian for the Navajo tribe, for reading the manuscript and making excellent suggestions. I would also like to thank Harry Walters, Mike Marshall, Tim Maxwell, John Adair, Marcia Keegan, Martha and Tom Bennett, Marci and Jim Matlock, Laurence Yazzie, Bruce Hucko, and Betty McElvain and her son Mack, who made the exploration of the Chaco roads possible.

I will not thank separately most of the people already present in this book. I would, however, like to express my very deepest thanks to Norman Tulley and Edsel Brown, who taught me so very much and who shared their friendship with me. And I am also very grateful to Nevy Jensen, James Fatt, Victor Begay, Stanley Mitchell, Eugene and Emerson Hasgood, Katherine Smith, Thomas Banyacya, Andy Chee, Terrill Spencer, Kee Benally, and the many other kind and generous people who shared with me their knowledge. I am deeply indebted to the Brown family of Red Valley, in particular David Tsosie, for their kindness. I would like to thank Ed Black for a most beautiful saddle blanket. I thank the Navajo Nation and the Navajo Parks and Recreation Department for their help.

And finally I would like to thank Stuart Woods for that first memorable airplane ride over Monument Valley and the Lukachukai Mountains.

Bibliography

Austin, Martha, and Regina Lynch, eds. *Saad Ahaah Sinil: Dual Language Dictionary*. Chinle, Arizona: Rough Rock Press, 1983.

Bailey, Garrick, and Roberta Glenn Bailey. *A History of the Navajos: The Reservation Years*. Santa Fe: School of American Research Press, 1986.

Bailey, L. R. *The Long Walk*. Tucson: Westernlore Press, 1988.

Brugge, David. "A History of the Chaco Navajos." Unpublished manuscript at the Laboratory of Anthropology, Santa Fe, 1977.

Brugge, David. "Historic Sites in the San Juan Basin," in *The San Juan Tomorrow: Planning for the Conservation of Cultural Resources in the San Juan Basin*. 1982.

Clark, H. Jackson. *The Owl in Monument Canyon*. Salt Lake City: University of Utah Press, 1993.

Condie, Carol J., and Ruthann Knidson, eds. *The Cultural Resources of the Proposed New Mexico Generating Station Study Area, San Juan Basin, New Mexico*. Albuquerque: Quivira Center Publications 39, 1982.

Cordell, Linda. *Prehistory of the Southwest*. San Diego: Academic Press, 1984.

Correll, J. Lee. *Through White Man's Eyes*. Window Rock, Arizona: Navajo Heritage Center, 1979.

Dyk, Walter, ed. *Son of Old Man Hat: A Navaho Autobiography*. Lincoln: University of Nebraska Press, 1938.

Faris, James C. *Nightway*. Albuquerque: University of New Mexico Press, 1970.

Folsom, Franklin. *The Life and Legend of George McJunkin*. Nashville: Thomas Nelson, 1973.

Fransted, Dennis. "An Introduction to the Navajo Oral History of Anasazi Sites in the San Juan Basin Area." Research conducted under a purchase order from the National Park Service, Chaco Center (PX 486-8-0224). Unpublished manuscript.

Frazier, Kendrick. *People of Chaco: A Canyon and Its Culture*. New York: W. W. Norton, 1986.

Frisbie, Charlotte. *Navajo Medicine Bundles or Jish: Acquisition, Transmis-*

sion, and Disposition in the Past and Present. Albuquerque: University of New Mexico Press, 1987.

Gabriel, Kathryn. *Roads to Center Place: A Cultural Atlas of Chaco Canyon and the Anasazi.* Boulder: Johnson Books, 1991.

Goodman, James. *A Navajo Atlas: Environments, Resources, People, and History of the Diné Bikeyah.* Norman: University of Oklahoma Press, 1982.

Grant, Campbell. *Canyon de Chelly.* Tucson: University of Arizona Press, 1978.

Greenberg, Joseph H., and Merritt Ruhlen. "Linguistic Origins of Native Americans." *Scientific American,* November 1992.

Haile, Berard. *Beautyway: A Navaho Ceremonial.* Edited with commentaries by Leland C. Wyman. New York: Pantheon Books, 1957.

Haile, Berard. *Women Versus Men: A Conflict of Navajo Emergence; the Curly To Aheedliinii Version.* Lincoln: University of Nebraska Press, 1984.

Hammerschlag, Carl. *The Dancing Healers.* New York: Harper & Row, 1988.

Hoffman, Virginia. *Navajo Biographies,* Vol. 1. Rough Rock, Arizona: Navajo Curriculum Center Press, 1974.

Horgan, Paul. *Great River: The Rio Grande in North American History.* Austin: Texas Monthly Press, 1984.

Johnson, Broderick, ed. *Navajo Stories of the Long Walk Period.* Tsaile, Arizona: Navajo Community College Press, 1973.

Judge, James. *New Light on Chaco Canyon.* Santa Fe: School of American Research, 1984.

Kammer, Jerry. *The Second Long Walk: The Navajo-Hopi Land Dispute.* Albuquerque: University of New Mexico Press, 1980.

Kincaid, Chris, ed. *Chaco Roads Project, Phase I: A Reappraisal of Prehistoric Roads in the San Juan Basin.* Albuquerque: Bureau of Land Management, 1983.

Klah, Hasteen. *Navajo Creation Myth: The Story of the Emergence.* Santa Fe: Museum of Navajo Ceremonial Art, 1942.

Kluckhohn, Clyde. *Navaho Witchcraft.* Boston: Beacon Press, 1989.

Kluckhohn, Clyde. *To the Foot of the Rainbow.* Albuquerque: University of New Mexico Press, 1992.

Kluckhohn, Clyde, and Dorothea Leighton. *The Navaho.* Cambridge: Harvard University Press, 1974.

Lekson, Stephen, et al. "The Chaco Canyon Community." *Scientific American,* July 1988.

Lister, Robert H., and Florence C. Lister. *Earl Morris and Southwestern Archaeology.* Albuquerque: University of New Mexico Press, 1968.

Lister, Robert H., and Florence C. Lister. *Chaco Canyon.* Albuquerque: University of New Mexico Press, 1981.

Locke, Raymond Friday. *The Book of the Navajo*. Los Angeles: Mankind Publishing Company, 1976.

Luckert, Karl. *The Navajo Hunter Tradition*. Tucson: University of Arizona Press, 1975.

Luckert, Karl. *Navajo Mountain and Rainbow Bridge Religion*. Flagstaff: Museum of Northern Arizona Press, 1977.

Matthews, Washington. *The Mountain Chant: A Navajo Ceremony*. Fifth Annual Report of the Bureau of Ethnology, 1883–84. Washington: Smithsonian Institution.

Matthews, Washington, trans. *Navajo Legends*. Salt Lake City: University of Utah Press, 1994. (Facsimile of 1897 edition.)

Matthews, Washington. *The Night Chant: A Navajo Ceremony*. New York: American Museum of Natural History, 1902.

McNeley, James K. *Holy Wind in Navajo Philosophy*. Tucson: University of Arizona Press, 1981.

McNitt, Frank. *Richard Wetherill: Anasazi*. Albuquerque: University of New Mexico Press, 1957.

McNitt, Frank. *Indian Traders*. Norman: University of Oklahoma Press, 1962.

McNitt, Frank. *Navajo Wars: Military Campaigns, Slave Raids, and Reprisals*. Albuquerque: University of New Mexico Press, 1972.

McPherson, Robert. *Sacred Land, Sacred View*. Salt Lake City: Brigham Young University, 1992.

Newcomb, Franc Johnson. *Navajo Folk Tales*. Albuquerque: University of New Mexico Press, 1967.

Nials, Fred, et al. *Chacoan Roads in the Southern Periphery: Results of Phase II of the BLM Chaco Roads Project*. Cultural Resources Series No. 1. Albuquerque: Bureau of Land Management, 1987.

Quaife, Milo, ed. *Kit Carson's Autobiography*. Lincoln: University of Nebraska Press, 1966.

Reichard, Gladys. *Navajo Religion: A Study of Symbolism*. Princeton: Princeton University Press, Bollingen Series XVIII, 1950.

Richardson, Gladwell. *Navajo Trader*. Tucson: University of Arizona Press, 1986.

Roessel, Robert. *Dinetah: Navajo History*, Vol. II. Rough Rock, Arizona: Rough Rock Demonstration School Press, 1983.

Sapir, Edward, and Harry Hoijer. *Navajo Texts*. Iowa City: Linguistic Society of America, 1942.

Simpson, James H. Frank McNitt, ed. *Navaho Expedition: A Journal of Military Reconnaissance from Santa Fe, New Mexico to the Navaho Country Made in 1849 by Lieutenant James H. Simpson*. Norman: University of Oklahoma Press, 1964.

Spicer, Edward. *Cycles of Conquest: The Impact of Spain, Mexico, and the United States on the Indians of the Southwest, 1533–1960*. Tucson: University of Arizona Press, 1962.

Terrell, John Upton. *The Navajos*. New York: Harper & Row, 1972.

Underhill, Ruth M. *The Navajos.* Norman: University of Oklahoma Press, 1956.

Vanderwerth, W. C. *Indian Oratory.* Norman: University of Oklahoma Press, 1971.

Van Valkenburgh, Richard. "Diné Bike Yah." Window Rock, Arizona: Department of the Interior, photocopy of manuscript, no date.

Walters, Harry. "A New Perspective on Navajo Prehistory." Unpublished manuscript, no date, given to the author.

Waters, Frank. *Book of the Hopi.* New York: Ballantine, 1963.

Wheelwright, Mary C. *Emergence Myth According to the Hanelthnayhe or Upward-Reaching Rite: Recorded by Berard Haile.* Santa Fe: Museum of Navajo Ceremonial Art, 1946.

Wheelwright, Mary C. *Hail Chant and Water Chant.* Santa Fe: Museum of Navajo Ceremonial Art, 1946.

Wheelwright, Mary C. *The Myth and Prayers of the Great Star Chant and the Myth of the Coyote Chant.* Santa Fe: Museum of Navajo Ceremonial Art, 1956.

Williams, Jerry L. *New Mexico in Maps.* Albuquerque: University of New Mexico Press, 1986.

Wormington, H. M. *Prehistoric Indians of the Southwest.* Denver: Denver Museum of Natural History, 1947.

Wyman, Leland C. *Blessingway.* Tucson: University of Arizona Press, 1970.

Yazzie, Ethelou, ed. *Navajo History,* Vol. 1. Many Farms, Arizona: Navajo Community College Press, 1971.

Zolbrod, Paul. *Diné Bahane': The Navajo Creation Story.* Albuquerque: University of New Mexico Press, 1984.

Epilogue

▽ ▽ ▽

THE GREAT TERROR

In the twenty-four years since Talking to the Ground
*was published, there have been many changes in our lives.
I married Christine and adopted Selene. She is now thirty-
six, with a successful career as a television DP and camera
operator. Christine and I had two other children, Aletheia
and Isaac, both now adults. Time marches on. But that is not
what this epilogue is about. . . .*

One of the greatest mysteries in American archaeology, and a
major subject of my book, is what caused the collapse of Chaco
Canyon and the dispersal of the Anasazi.* In the years since *Talking to the Ground* was first published, that mystery has, at least in
part, been solved.

During the Chaco period and afterwards, many Ancestral
Puebloans moved into remote canyons, building their dwellings in
vertiginous cliffs or on mesa tops behind fortified walls—dramatic
evidence that they felt fearful of some enemy. But who was this
elusive and terrifying enemy?

Several decades ago, a physical anthropologist named Christy
Turner II made a series of discoveries that threw a startling new
light on Chaco Canyon, its collapse, and the social breakdown
that followed. It started when he was examining Puebloan teeth

---

* I should mention that the term "Anasazi" is no longer acceptable in describing
the prehistoric Pueblo people of the Southwest, because the name carries a
pejorative meaning. The term "Ancestral Puebloans" is now preferred, and I will
adopt that convention here.

in the Museum of Northern Arizona, in Flagstaff, attempting to trace a peculiar trait known as the three-rooted first molar. On the last day of his research, he asked the curator to bring down a large, coffin-shaped cardboard box from a top shelf. The accession record said that the box contained remains from a remote area along Polacca Wash, an arroyo situated below First Mesa, on the Hopi Indian Reservation. The remains had been excavated in 1964 by an archaeologist named Alan P. Olson. Turner removed the lid and found himself gazing at a bizarre collection of more than a thousand human bone shards. Thirty years later, his memory of the experience was still vivid. "Holy smokes!" he recalled having exclaimed to himself. "What happened here? This looks exactly like *food* trash." The fragments reminded him of broken and burned animal bones that he had found in prehistoric garbage mounds. As he looked more closely, another thought struck him. Like many physical anthropologists, he had sometimes done forensic work for police departments. Once, in California, the police had asked him to examine some remains that had been found in the Oakland Hills—a skeleton still wearing a pair of boots. Turner had informed the police that the person had been savagely beaten to death. "Now," he said, "I could see the same violence done to the Polacca Wash bones."

Turner presented his findings in a paper he read at an archaeological meeting in Santa Fe. Word of what the paper would say had gotten around, and the room was packed. Co-written with a colleague, the paper was entitled "A Massacre at Hopi." Turner informed the audience that the bones belonged to a group of thirty people—mostly women and children—who had been "killed, crudely dismembered, violently mutilated." The skulls, in particular, showed extreme trauma: "Every skull is smashed, chiefly from the front, and massively so. . . . The faces were crushed while still covered with flesh." Most of the skulls had received a number of "blunt, heavy, club-like fracturing blows." The bone material had still been "vital" at the time the blows were struck, meaning the beatings had happened at the time of death. He wrote, "The many small pieces of unweathered teeth and skulls and postcranial scrap suggest, but do not prove, that the death of these people occurred at the burial site." Moreover, "every skull, regardless of age or sex, had the brain exposed." Heads had been placed on flat rocks and smashed open, apparently so that the brain could be removed.

He went on to say that most of the bones also showed marks of cutting, chopping, dismemberment, butchering, defleshing—and cooking. The larger bones had been broken apart and the marrow scraped out, or, in the case of spongy bone, reamed or pounded off. The skulls had been roasted in a way that would cook the brain. Turner concluded that the Polacca Wash bones represented "the most convincing evidence of cannibalism in all Southwest archaeology."

The bones were not prehistoric, as Olson had assumed. Turner had had the bones radiocarbon dated, and the results had come back as 1580 CE plus or minus ninety-five years. Given the date, Turner wondered whether some historical record or legend might still exist telling what happened—perhaps an oral tradition at Hopi about a number of fellow tribespeople being massacred and eaten at this date, of this age and sex composition. When he looked into the stories early anthropologists had collected at Hopi, he made a chilling discovery: the Polacca Wash site was probably a place known in Hopi legend as the Death Mound. Hopi informants had first described the legend to an anthropologist at the end of the nineteenth century. According to the story, sometime in the late 1600s a Hopi village called Awatovi had been largely converted to Christianity under the influence of Spanish friars, who had later been expelled (or killed) by the Hopi. But even after the friars were gone, Awatovi clung to the Christian religion, which created much anger among the other Hopi. They also suspected the village of practicing witchcraft. Eventually, five other Hopi villages decided to purge the tribe of this spiritual stain. An attack was organized by the chief of Awatovi himself, who had become disgusted with his own people. Warriors from the other villages secretly gathered and attacked the apostate village at dawn, surprising most of the men inside the kivas—sunken ceremonial chambers of the Pueblo Indians—and burning them alive. After killing the men, the warriors captured groups of women and children. As one of these groups was being marched away, a dispute broke out over which village would get to keep the captives. The argument got out of hand. In a rage, the warriors settled it by torturing, killing, and dismembering all the captives. Their bodies were left at a place called Mas-teo'-mo, or Death Mound. "If the stories are correct," the anthropologist who first collected these legends wrote, "the final butchery at Mas-teo'-mo must have been horrible."

When Turner finished reading his paper, arguing that the bones were the remains of a cannibal feast, the lecture room became very quiet. "You could *smell* the disbelief," Turner recalled. Most of his colleagues felt that there simply had to be another explanation for the strange bone assemblage. To suggest that the Hopi could have deliberately tortured, murdered, mutilated—and then cooked and eaten—a defenseless group of women and children from their own tribe seemed to make a mockery of a hundred years of cautious, diligent scholarship. The paper was looked upon with deep skepticism by many of Turner's peers, and the Hopi objected to what they considered a vicious slur on their ancestors.

Over the next thirty years, Turner looked deeper into the archaeological record for signs of cannibalism—going all the way back to the Hopi's Puebloan forebears. To his surprise, he discovered that a number of claims of Ancestral Puebloan violence and cannibalism had been published by archaeologists, but the profession, perhaps blinded by the conventional wisdom, had ignored the reports, the notes, the evidence, even the very bones. The idea of cannibalism among ancient Puebloans never took root among archaeologists, let alone percolating into popular culture, even though a surprisingly strong record of it already existed.

Turner went on to identify and reinvestigate a number of Puebloan sites that he believed represent "charnel deposits"—heaps of cannibalized remains. His results were published by the University of Utah Press in a book entitled *Man Corn: Cannibalism and Violence in the Prehistoric American Southwest*. (The term "man corn" is the literal translation of the Nahuatl [Aztec] word *tlacatlaolli*, which refers to a "sacred meal of sacrificed human meat, cooked with corn.")

Man Corn scrutinized seventy-two ancient Puebloan sites at which violence or cannibalism seem to have occurred. Turner claimed that cannibalism probably took place at thirty-eight of these sites, and that extreme violence and mutilation occurred at most of the others. He calculated that at least two hundred and eighty-six individuals were butchered, cooked, and eaten, with a mean of between seven and eight individuals per site. As a control to see how widespread cannibalism might have been, Turner also examined a collection of eight hundred and seventy skeletons in the Museum of Northern Arizona. He found that overall 8 percent—one skeleton in twelve—showed clear evidence of having been cannibalized. And when he mapped and dated the cannibal sites, almost all seemed to be associated with Chaco Canyon and its outlying Great Houses.

Turner carefully compiled a list of what physical characteristics had to be present on bones to conclude that they were indicative of cannibalism. The list consisted of:

- Bones that were broken open and the marrow scraped out
- Bones that showed cutting and saw marks from butchery and defleshing
- Skulls with "anvil abrasions," indicating they had been broken open using rocks
- Spongy bone (rich in fat) scraped or pounded off
- Tips of broken bones that showed microscopic "pot polish" from being boiled in rough ceramic pots, turning around and around in the water.

When Turner published his work, his theory was met with disbelief and outrage from Pueblo Indians and many archaeologists. They argued that he had misinterpreted the sites. While the bones may have been butchered, scraped, broken, boiled, and cooked, there was simply no proof that the meat was *actually eaten*. They said that Turner hadn't considered other alternatives, such as bizarre mortuary practices or the execution of accused witches, which sometimes involved the complete destruction and burning of the body. The Hopis pointed out that Navajos, Apaches, and Utes all raided the Hopis, killing men and stealing women and children—they could have been responsible for the charnel heap in Polacca Wash. Others accused Turner of insensitivity in presenting such inflammatory findings. The insensitivity accusation was certainly grounded in truth. Turner had not involved Native Americans in his research, and he had a reputation among many of his colleagues for being a jerk. "He's not nice," one colleague complained. "He's a pain in the ass." Another called him "loud" and "a bully." His critics pointed out that Turner had no *proof* of cannibalism; it was all extrapolation. One critic was quoted in *National Geographic* saying that Puebloan cannibalism would not be proved until "you actually find human remains in prehistoric human excrement."

Not long after Turner made his controversial claims, an archaeological team won a contract to excavate a group of sites at the base of Sleeping Ute Mountain, in Colorado, on the Ute Indian Reservation. The Ute planned to irrigate and farm seventy-six hundred acres of land, and the law required them to excavate any archaeological sites that would be disturbed.

At a site called Cowboy Wash, at a small site, the archaeological team made a grotesque discovery. There were three ceremonial kivas at the small village. In the first kiva they found a pile of chopped-up, boiled, and burned human bones at the base of a vent shaft leading up and out of the kiva. It looked as though the bones had been chopped up and cooked outside, on the surface, and then dumped down the shaft. There were cut marks on the bones made by stone tools, and the long bones had been systematically broken up for marrow extraction.

In the second kiva, they found the remains of five individuals. In this case, it appeared that the people had been butchered and roasted inside the kiva itself. The skulls of at least two of the individuals had been placed upside down on the fire, cooked, and broken open, the brains scooped out. In that same kiva, the team found a stone tool kit, such as was typically used in butchering a midsized mammal. The kit contained an axe, hammerstones, and two large flakes with razor-thin cutting edges. The flakes tested positive for human blood—they had been used to cut human flesh.

The third kiva contained only two small pieces of bone, which had apparently been washed down from the surface. In the dead ashes of the central hearth, however, the team made an "extremely unusual" find. It was a desiccated human turd, or coprolite. After the fire had gone cold, someone had squatted over the hearth and defecated into it. The archaeologists sent off the coprolite to a lab at the University of Nebraska for analysis. A biochemical analysis indicated the presence of human myoglobin protein (from human muscle) in the coprolite. More human protein was found on the interior walls of a cooking pot found at the site.

In three nearby sites, another group of excavators also found chopped-up, boiled, and burned bones scattered about. The four sites, which seemed to constitute a small community, contained a total of twenty-eight butchered individuals. Mysteriously, all four sites were filled with extremely valuable, portable items, such as baskets, a rabbit blanket, pots, and beautifully made stone tools. Little, if anything, appeared to have been taken.

It was clear what had happened. The year was approximately

1150. The area was in the grip of a drought. Pollen samples showed that it was late spring, and a crop failure had probably occurred the previous year. The community was attacked and the people were killed, cooked, and eaten. Then, in an ultimate act of contempt, one of the killers defecated in the hearth of a sacred kiva. Instead of looting the site, the invaders left the buildings and their many valuables untouched for all to see. And the site remained unlooted forever.

These discoveries confirmed that Turner was correct, and that a vast outbreak of cannibalism had occurred in the prehistoric Southwest around the time of Chaco Canyon. Was this starvation cannibalism, driven by drought, famine, and desperation, like what happened with the Donner party in California? Or was it something else?

It is easy to rule out starvation cannibalism. Starving people driven to cannibalism do not engage in torture and mutilation of an individual before consumption. Nor does it explain the enormous size of the charnel deposits, consisting of as many as thirty-five people, all cooked and eaten at the same time, in one giant feast. (That's almost a ton of edible human meat.) Nor does it explain the bones discarded as trash or the contemptuous treatment of sacred kivas. Furthermore, there was no evidence of starvation cannibalism (or any other kind of cannibalism) among the Ancestral Puebloans' immediate neighbors, the Hohokam and the Mogollon, who lived in equally harsh environments and endured the same droughts.

All this pointed to something far more sinister than starvation cannibalism. Turner proposed that this was cannibalism used as a weapon of terror. A powerful elite, he hypothesized, used cannibalism in the Southwest as a form of social control—to frighten, intimidate, and subjugate people. He wrote, "What better way to amplify opponents' fear than to reduce victims to the subhuman level of cooked meat, especially when they include infants and children . . . whose consumption would surely further terrorize, demean, and insult their helpless parents or community?" This elite appears to have been established at Chaco Canyon. The maps showed that the cannibal deposits were often situated near Chaco Great Houses, which were impressive stone structures connected to Chaco Canyon by a sophisticated road system and signaling system that used lighthouses placed on high points and pinnacles of rock. The eating of human flesh seems to have begun as building started at Chaco Canyon around 900, peaked at the time of the Chaco collapse and abandonment around 1150, and then gradually disappeared in the chaotic centuries following. (Polacca Wash was a notable exception.)

The terrorism aspect would explain why the community at Cowboy Wash was left untouched after the attack: the killers left everything as a public warning of their power, ruthlessness, and implacability. Passersby also avoided it and its abandoned wealth as an accursed place. The motivation was similar to the placing of the heads of executed people on pikes at city gates or the videos of ISIS beheadings posted on the Internet. It was an announcement of "This is who we are, and this is what we can do."

So who were these cannibals? Were they homegrown or did they come from elsewhere? One does not have to look very far to find a likely source. One culture not so far away from the Southwest practiced cannibalism on a dramatic scale: the Toltec Empire in Mexico. The Toltecs—the precursors of the Aztecs—dominated central Mexico from about 800 to 1100 CE. Cannibalism was central to Toltec religion and ceremony, and they used it to subjugate conquered tribes by demanding tribute in the form of human beings to be sacrificed to the gods and eaten. The Toltecs also are believed to have spread the practice of cannibalism to their Maya and Chichimec neighbors.

Turner hypothesized that around 900 CE, a heavily armed group of Toltec warriors or, as he called them, "thugs" headed north and entered the Four Corners area. There they found a "pliant population" of Puebloans living a peaceful existence among their farms and villages. The Toltecs seized control and imposed on the Puebloan people "the theocratic lifestyle they had previously known in Mesoamerica." Under Toltec dominance and coercion, the Puebloans built Chaco Canyon, the network of roads and lighthouses, and the far-flung Great Houses. Those Great Houses might have been fortified bastions for warriors to project their power over the conquered Puebloan people.

In other words, the flowering of Chaco society that we have so long admired—in engineering, astronomy, architecture, art, and culture—was the product of a small, heavily armed gang from Mexico who marched into the Southwest to conquer and brutalize.

This is not such an improbable idea as it may seem at first. Archaeologists have long documented a strong Mesoamerican influence on the prehistoric Southwest. There was extensive trade between Mexico and the Southwest going back thousands of years, long before Chaco Canyon. Turquoise from the Southwest has been found throughout Mesoamerica, and parrots and macaws were brought live from Mexico. Corn, pottery, and cotton came into the Southwest from Mexico.

Cannibalism seems to have peaked in the Southwest at the time of the Chaco collapse. Turner believed this was because the system of terror, like many such, could not be sustained; the terror and oppression at Chaco, combined with other factors like drought and environmental degradation, eventually begat social chaos. Cannibalism may have been a factor—perhaps *the* missing factor—not only in the rise of Chaco but in its collapse. The retreat of the Puebloans into fortresslike cliff dwellings and mesas now makes sense. It takes a long time for terror this extreme to subside. It wasn't until the late 1300s that the Puebloans finally emerged from their redoubts and moved down into the river valleys of the Southwest, where the Spanish conquistadors found them in the 1500s, living once again in peaceful coexistence with each other. What happened to the Toltec ruling class after the collapse of Chaco is unknown.

These new theories throw an interesting light on the subject of *Talking to the Ground*, the Navajo creation story. The Navajos were probably arriving in the Southwest around the collapse of Chaco. The Navajos mingled with the ancient Puebloan people, sometimes fought with them, and ended up adopting many of their beliefs, gods, ceremonies, and farming practices. The "mythological" stories the Navajos tell about Chaco Canyon, recorded in this book, appear to be based on what actually happened there, according to Turner's theories of coercion, cannibalism, and collapse. According to the Navajo stories, Chaco was a place of evil, dominated by a tyrant, where the people abused sacred ceremonies, practiced witchcraft and cannibalism, and made a dreaded substance called corpse powder by cooking and grinding up the flesh and bones of the dead. Like many "myths," these now appear to be grounded in the truth. According to the Navajo creation story, the evil at Chaco threw the world out of balance and the Chacoans were destroyed. It was not a mythical story but a description of what the Navajo people actually witnessed.

This destruction, told in the creation story, became a warning of how not to be, how not to live. The story contained lessons for all Navajos, and it embodied the Navajo rejection of hubris, inequality, greed, and the manipulation of nature.

The collapse of Chaco as described in the creation story also gave the Navajo people a vision of what the end of the world would look like.

And that vision, described in this book, is what many traditional Navajos see happening in the world today.

About the Author

Douglas Preston is the author of more than thirty books, both fiction and nonfiction, twenty-four of which have been *New York Times* bestsellers. Before becoming a writer, he worked as an editor at the American Museum of Natural History in New York and taught nonfiction writing at Princeton University. His first novel, *Relic*, coauthored with Lincoln Child, launched the famed Pendergast series of novels. His latest #1 *New York Times* bestselling nonfiction book, *The Lost /City of the Monkey God*, tells the story of the extraordinary discovery of an ancient city in the unexplored jungles of Honduras. In addition to books, Preston writes about archaeology and paleontology for the *New Yorker*, *National Geographic*, and *Smithsonian Magazine*.